Best Wishes and Bright Futures!

Bob Jamarkin

The New Gatsbys

Also by Bob Tamarkin

The Young Executive Today

The New Gatsbys

Fortunes and Misfortunes of Commodity Traders

Bob Tamarkin

William Morrow and Company, Inc.
New York

Library of Congress Cataloging in Publication Data

Tamarkin, Bob.
   The new Gatsbys.

   1. Commodity exchanges—United States.   2. Chicago
Board of Trade.   I. Title.   II. Title: Commodity
traders.
HG6049.T36   1985   332.64′4′0977311   84-29573
ISBN 0-688-02878-0

Printed in the United States of America

   3 4 5 6 7 8 9 10

BOOK DESIGN BY JAMES UDELL

For Mom and Civia

Acknowledgments

A book of this nature needs the cooperation of many people. I want to thank the nearly two hundred traders who over the years allowed me into their personal and professional lives, down to standing within earshot of a number of them while they worked the pits. I also want to thank those traders who slammed the door in my face, because it made me dig all the harder. To protect the privacy of some of the traders and their families, I have changed some names or used nicknames.

I'm grateful to Everette B. Harris, former president of the Chicago Mercantile Exchange for twenty-five years, for permitting me access to his records and personal papers. I'm also indebted to Owen Gregory, the Chicago Board of Trade archivist, who took time away from his book to work with me. And Warren Moulds for the use of his files. A special thanks to psychologist Ira Levin and Dr. William Friedman for their observations on risk psychology.

There are those who were kind enough to share their insights, impressions, and sources with me: Asa Baber, Robert Brody, John Coleman, Arlene Drucker, Pamela Futterman, Ronald L. Futterman, Larry Green, Anita Howard Greenberg, Fred Greenberg, Murray Greenberg, Aram A. Hartunian, Jean Howard, Michael Laurence, Fern Netzky, Alan Rosenthal, Faye Schwimmer, Joy Wellington, Ronald Wild, and Donald Zochert.

I also want to applaud the support and encouragement of Edwin Black, Elizabeth Black, Mort Edelstein, Beverly Frankel, Richard Frankel, Judith Shapiro, Howard Stone, Susan Stone, along with a warm embrace for Esther Levin.

My deep appreciation goes to Victoria Pasternack and my initial editor at William Morrow, Elizabeth Knappman, both of whom had faith in the concept of this book. For his counsel, patience, and editorial input, I am indebted to my current editor, Barry Schwabsky, who moved the book into high gear whenever it began to sputter.

A final note of gratitude goes to my children, Michael, Michele, Meridith, and Elisa, for their good-natured willingness to endure, and to my wife, Civia, whose idea it was to write this book. Without her love, support, and editorial advice I could never have done it.

Contents

10

The New Gatsbys

PART I

Limit Up, Limit Down

Bargain and shout your way to fun in this card trading free-for-all. At the sound of the bell, everyone tries to corner the market on hay, barley, corn, rye, flax, oats or wheat—just like a trader in a real grain exchange.

> —From the directions of *Pit*,
> a Parker Brothers game

1

So You Want to Play the Market?

They are obsessed. They are the new wave of commodity traders in hot pursuit of the Big Money, the new generation of Jay Gatsbys and George Babbitts, men in their twenties and thirties, mostly, for whom materialism is an ideal, an ecstasy, a romantic faith. For them, the timetable of success has moved forward in a quantum leap. The days of working from Chevy to Buick to Cadillac are over. . . .

I am not a new Gatsby, or an old one either. But from time to time I have dabbled in the murky waters of the commodities market strictly as an amateur. Those occasions left me hemorrhaging emotionally and financially. The first plunge was back in the late 1950s, when I was a college student. My cousin Maurry, a lovable math whiz of sorts, began speculating in corn futures and invited me to join him. Each of us put up $200 and borrowed the balance of the $1,000 we needed to buy two contracts of corn. The $600 came from friends we enticed with an offer they couldn't refuse: a 10 percent return on their money, a rate three times above the going rate that banks and savings and loan associations were then offering.

It all seemed simple enough at the time. In commodity trading you either bought or sold a contract for goods to be delivered in the future. If you thought the price of the commodity was going up, you bought. If you thought the price was going down, you sold. Money could be made either way. A futures contract is like an option to buy a parcel of land at a specified future date. If the value of the land increases, the value of the option rises proportionately. It was sheer speculation since no more than 5 percent of all contracts traded are ever fulfilled—that is, discharged with a commodity's actually being delivered to a user. A speculator has no interest in the underlying commodity. Yet the speculative market performs an essential function: to offer producers and users of various commodities a means of protecting themselves against the potential risk of adverse price fluctuations. That enables everyone from the Illinois soybean farmer to the giant Minneapolis grain trading company to the Boston baker to the Texas cattle rancher to make educated forecasts. Each can determine just how much he will have to spend to buy the raw commodities for his product or, in the case of the farmer, how much he can count on receiving for selling his crops and livestock as much as twelve months in advance.

In essence, a futures contract is an insurance policy of a kind, permitting people to lock in a guaranteed future price for a commodity. If, for example, Coca-Cola fears that sugar prices will rise sharply over the next several months, it can buy futures contracts now that guarantee delivery of sugar next spring at today's price level. There's risk, of course, in this strategy; the price of sugar may fall even as the company locks itself into contracts at the current price. Or take Farmer Old McDonald who, say, expects to harvest 50,000 bushels of corn. He finds that the six-month future price of corn is $2.75 per bushel, a fair price, he figures, for his crops. So he guarantees he will get that price by hedging, or agreeing in advance to sell a contract for 50,000 bushels at that price in the futures market. Sly Old Mac has protected himself against a drop in grain prices.

What if corn jumps to $3 a bushel in six months' time? Old McDonald would have to shrug it off and forgo that extra 25-cent-a-bushel profit. But he is more than willing to do that in order to guarantee in advance what he considers a fair return. Farmers, Coca-Cola, and other companies like General Mills, Pillsbury, ITT Continental Baking that buy and sell commodities they need are called hedgers in the jargon of the trade. These hedgers could not play the game were it not for the thousands of speculators like Maurry and me who are willing to bet against them.

For me the lure of this paper-shuffling game was pure and simple: to turn a profit with a relatively small up front investment. That was the sweet thing about commodity trading. You didn't need a huge bankroll to get started. In fact, compared with stocks, it was practically penny ante. A trader need put up only a fraction (usually less than 10 percent) of a contract's face value as margin or earnest money. It's a bargain compared with stocks. (Unlike a securities margin, however, a commodity margin is not an extension of credit toward the purchase price of the commodity; it is a guarantee to the broker or clearinghouse against a loss on the futures contract.) A down payment of $1,000 can secure a futures contract for $1 million worth of treasury bills, whereas a similar investment in stocks, with a 50 percent margin requirement, would take a down payment of $500,000. If you're right, profits can be quick and stunning. An interest movement of less than 1 percent, for example, could triple a speculator's investment in a treasury bill contract. But if you are wrong, prepare to lose big. Anyone who had bet in the autumn of 1979 that January 1980 wheat prices would be headed up ended up in numbing despair in the wake of President Jimmy Carter's grain embargo against the Soviet Union. If a speculator had bought the permissible number of 600 wheat futures contracts, he could have lost $600,000 in a single day during the first week of January. There were some who did. There were others who had bet that the prices would decline in January and ended up reaping huge profits.

Had I bothered to look at the odds of the commodities game, perhaps I would have approached it with less bravura and more logic. Forget about understanding the mechanics of the market. The fact is that the odds have always favored the professional traders, just as they favor the dealer at a blackjack table in Las Vegas. Does that mean that amateurs can afford to lose? Of does it mean, as the Wall Street maxim goes, that the public is always wrong? It doesn't take the deductive reasoning of a Sherlock Holmes to come up with an answer. Crafty Daniel Drew, a master stock market manipulator in the early 1900s, gave it an ol' country boy perspective when he said, "Anybody who plays the stock market not as an insider is like a man buying cows in the moonlight."

The same is true of the commodities market. Against the insiders—those who make their living buying and selling futures contracts on the floors of the nation's commodity exchanges—the public is a school of guppies among sharks. One grim statistic says it all: Nine out of every ten trades made by the public result in a loss. Some think the rate is higher. Hell, the odds are far better in the green-felt jungles of Las Vegas, where there is a 97 percent payout on the $1 "one-arm bandit," a 15 percent and 25 percent payout for the nickel and quarter machines, a 30 percent house edge in some games like keno, and only a chip-thin 1.4 percent on craps.

None of this, of course, entered my thoughts when in June 1959 Maurry and I bought our two contracts (10,000 bushels) of corn due for December delivery. Corn was selling at around $1.15 per bushel, just 1¾ cents from where it had reached its highest point for the year in April. For every penny corn moved higher from where we bought it, we would be $100 richer. Along with the corn we bought nearly six months of time, until the contracts expired and were taken off the trading board of the Chicago Board of Trade. The corn would be delivered to us a week before the end of December unless we canceled our agreement by selling 10,000 bushels of December corn. (If, instead, we had initially sold the 10,000 bushels of December corn, we would have had to deliver the actual grain by the end of that month unless we canceled out the contract by buying before the expiration date.)

We could have bought May, July, September, or March corn. But the December contract, we thought, gave us ample time. And since it was one of the distant month contracts, it tended not to be very volatile. Each commodity is broken down by futures months. And there is marketing logic to the various months, based on the supply of the commodity and the demand by commercial interests and by big grain exporters. December, for example, is an early winter futures month, the time when newly harvested crops are first delivered to markets. March and May are early spring months, when the thaw begins and deliveries can be made via the Great Lakes. July reflects the supply conditions of the new crop harvest from the previous autumn. September is the last contract traded against the old crop year.

Whatever the shortcomings, it beat the way it was done in preexchange days. In the 1800s Chicago's grain markets were wholly chaotic. After each harvest, terminals were awash with grain. Farmers hauled their crops from one merchant to another, hoping to find a buyer. If none could be found, the grain was often towed into Lake Michigan and dumped. By spring, grain supplies were tight and prices soared. In late 1841 wheat trading was hailed as the "harbinger of better times." Six years later, under the pressure of severe shortages, buyers were cursing it as the scourge of the prairie. In 1847 prices rose from 70 cents a bushel in late March to $1.30 in early June. Along with these speculative flurries came a bag of tricks among competitors bent on undercutting each other. When buyers weren't forming minicartels to fix prices, they were sending runners speeding to the rim of the prairie to meet incoming wagons and bargain for the contents. Out of this orderless frenzy, the necessity for a central market, where buyers and sellers could meet, became clear, and the Chicago Board of Trade was organized by eighty-two businessmen on the first Monday of April 1848. It was the beginning of organized commodity trading and the roots of the world's oldest futures exchange. Ever since then the activity of the Board of Trade has virtually become a compendium of history, reflecting war and peace, famine and plenty, panic and prosperity. Whenever the world sneezes, the traders blow their noses.

I knew nothing of the origins of commodity exchanges when I turned speculator. I didn't have to. Besides, how could I think of history with my mind focused on the future? We bought corn from an obliging broker, and that was all there was to it. In doing so, we became bona fide commodity speculators with the willingness to assume price risks which the hedgers wanted to avoid, hedgers that included such giant grain exporters, millers, and food processors as Cargill, Central Soya, Continental Grain, General Mills, Kraft, Nabisco, Pillsbury, Ralston Purina, and Swift. We were the little players. They were the big ones. And though we weren't rubbing elbows in the same game, we were playing in the same league. My guess was as good as theirs. But I lost sight of the fact that I was the amateur and they were the pros.

Perhaps I was merely speculating on beginner's luck. So what? Everyone, it seems, speculates at one time or another. Housewives loading up on sale items speculate that the prices of groceries are going higher. Insurance companies speculate on cars and lives. A child who doesn't do his homework speculates on the anger of his teacher. Speculation, in fact, arrived with the dawn of mankind.

And for a while it looked as if gods, not odds, determined the fortunes of speculators. Adam and Eve speculated on the wrath of God, taking lousy odds from some four-flushing snake only to gamble away paradise. Then came Joseph, who may have been both the first successful commodity speculator and commodity adviser on record. When the seven fat years ended and seven lean years began in Egypt, thanks to Joseph's sage advice, the pharaohs had plenty of grain stashed in their silos. Joseph certainly benefited in the future from production in the present.

That same speculative streak was the foundation of the commodities markets that probably had their roots in seasonal festivals in medieval Europe. Eventually these festivals became year-round markets in areas associated with particular commodities. By the seventeenth century the shoguns of Japan were actually selling receipts for their unharvested rice crops. From that point in history, as fast-growing nations were at the mercy of the ebbs and lows of scarcity and plenty, it was only a matter of time before futures markets as we know them today evolved.

As I mentioned, my mind was a clean slate when it came to the market. While the speculative blood flowed through my veins, marinating in my brain was the notion that naïveté would help me. I mean, hadn't Michael Faraday, with only grade-school mathematics, become one of the founders of modern physics? His greatest tool may have been ignorance. Faraday developed simple, nonmathematical concepts to explain his electrical and magnetic phenomena. In doing so, he broke ground rules of which he was unaware, rules that would have stopped the professional mathematician in his tracks. In a sense I was like Faraday. Although I wasn't out to create a new science or devise a unique trading strategy, I, too, was ignorant. In fact, I possessed a great deal of ignorance about commodities, a trait certainly not in short supply. For a St. Louis kid whose father owned a grocery store, the only thing I knew for certain about corn was that it came from a can. Maurry, it turned out, didn't know much more. We didn't have to.

Maurry was a devotee of what the textbooks call technical analysis. He believed that all the facts affecting the price of a commodity are already reflected in the price. Therefore, the best way to locate a price trend was laboriously to plot the daily price moves on a chart. By analyzing the chart correctly, we would learn what to do from the market. Maurry, in the parlance of the trade, was a chartist.

At the other extreme were the fundamentalists, those unconcerned with the day-to-day price moves, who studied the relationship between a commodity and the myriad catalysts that affect its supply and demand. They spend hours sifting through weather reports, crop forecasts, economic indicators, trade journals, long-term price trends, anything and everything that could have an impact on how much or how little there is of a commodity. Some knew no bounds, pushing to incredible lengths to piece information together. One such fellow was known as Gary the Bug, a cocoa speculator who turned himself into a virtual authority on the mealybug, a devilish insect, it seemed, with a voracious yen for unripened cocoa beans. Gary could tell by the amount of rainfall in Ghana just how well the mealy was doing. As long as it was raining, the farmers couldn't spray the trees to destroy the pesty beetles. Thus he could judge the damage to the cocoa crop by the amount of rain falling in that country, a gem of information he coddled like a flawless diamond.

Using the charting method, we really didn't have to know anything about corn or what was going on in the world that might be affecting it. It could have been jelly beans or Mongolian rabbits just as long as the price was active enough to chart. After all, what is a commodity anyway? Just something people want. The less of it there is, the more valuable it becomes as long as it continues to be in demand. That doesn't mean it has to be something useful; it only has to be something that's wanted and not necessarily needed, for that matter. A hot item on the old St. Louis Merchants Exchange back in 1911 was cat pelts. Why else would "tulipomania" have flourished in seventeenth-century Holland or gold have soared to $800 an ounce in 1980?

A commodity's value at times may be pegged to nothing more than desire. At other times value may be correlated to fear. It is a salable commodity, a market unto itself, with plenty of supply and demand. And there are a host of economic Cassandras, preaching Armageddon, ready to sell it. People, it seems, are always willing to pay $10, $20, $100, or more for a copy of a book or a subscription to a newsletter in order to shudder in horror. Just glance at the best sellers on the *New York Times* list in recent years, and you get the idea: *How to Prosper During the Coming Bad Years, New Profits from the Monetary Crisis, Crisis Investing* ("Opportunity for investing in the coming Great Depression"), *The Coming Currency Collapse* ("Investment survival manual for an age of hyperinflation"). I don't know how much these supersellers helped the finances of their readers, but they made big dollars for their authors. In one way or another such books arouse our insecurities, our innermost fears, our primal instincts for survival. How else are the doomsayers able to create the kind of metals mania that turns the gold market into a perpetual state of twenty-four-karat chaos when this asset represents such a small part of the world's total monetary system?

There is method to turning gold into a refuge for worried money. First, undermine a person's confidence in money itself, convincing him it's smarter to spend the currency on almost anything rather than to save it. Next, as inflation goes up and the dollar slides, persuade him that gold is the hedge against the inflation-weary world. (Maybe throw in the threat of World War III or some other catastrophic possibility.) Then remind him that the more gold he buys, the higher the price goes, and the dollar further slips lower against foreign currencies. The experts have a name for all this: inflationary psychology. I still like the way economist and Nobel laureate Paul A. Samuelson explains it: "Why does gold go up? Because it goes up! Why does gold go down? Because it does."

But make no mistake, commodities are far more than whimsy. They are serious business. The global trade in basic food commodities alone totals more than $60 billion a year. Karl Marx, one who certainly didn't take economics lightly, believed that the circulation of commodities was the headwater of capital. Throughout history commodities have been pursued by man to the limits of his endurance, turning him into a true *Homo economicus,* a creature moved solely by economic motives. Most of the world has been explored in search of commodities. Nations have waged wars over commodities and have toppled from within because of them. They have been used by weaker nations as political weapons to bring mighty nations to their knees. (Think about it the next time you fill your tank at the gasoline station and remember with nostalgia early 1973, when a gallon was thirty cents—shortly before the oil embargo and the long lines of cars.) Nations clashing over cocoa? Don't laugh. During the Renaissance, Venice waged salt wars to control the market, noting that people can live without gold and silver but not without salt. Napoleon Bonaparte once commented that the futures of entire empires hung on the rise and fall of sugar—a bittersweet remark that still rings true in world commerce. It may be not sugar or salt but grain or oil or something else. The importance of commodities hasn't changed.

Cousin Maurry and I, of course, weren't looking at the market with such Napoleonic visions. We didn't for a moment ponder the historical, political, or psychological aspects of corn. Our minds and eyes were focused only on a graph as we laboriously charted the fate of corn with each price change. We had bought our contracts after the chart had given us a clear signal that corn prices were destined to go higher. And we waited: one week; two weeks; three weeks. Then corn began teetering, uncertain whether it was going higher or lower. A day later the chart turned fickle as prices plummeted to the point where it signaled they were going lower. By then it was too late to reverse our position. The situation had changed so fast we were wiped out. So much for mixing tabula rasa and corn.

Thus my first encounter with the commodities market ended in a very painful (aren't they all?) loss of some $500, particularly painful because it was money partly borrowed from my father for a "sure" deal. My father, normally a calm man, wasn't as patient with me as I was sure the great economist Adam Smith would have been had he been around at the time. For I was only following Smith's sensible advice by trying to accumulate capital, enough of it, at least, to pay off my father and friends, who got their 10 percent return. From then on I swore off charts, Ouija boards, horoscopes, beginner's luck, and cousin Maurry when it came to the market. Maurry and I licked our wounds and went separate ways never to team up financially again. I told Maurry the next time to include me among the lenders rather than the speculators.

Had I learned anything from the fiasco? Doesn't a child stop playing with matches once he feels the burn? Not necessarily, I was to discover, when it comes to the heat of the commodities market. There was a fascination to it. When you speculated in commodities, you were always on the brink, like climbing a mountain for the sheer adventure and forgetting the danger though it was ever-present. Uncertainty was precisely why commodity futures markets existed in the first place, feeding on an insatiable diet of interlocking economic and political woes the world over. A famine here, a civil war there moved commodity prices up or down.

And even if a futures contract didn't offer dividends as stocks did, commodities were anything but boring. A stock buyer could put his shares in a safety-deposit box for years before he sold them again. A commodities trader didn't have that luxury. The life of a futures contract usually lasts twelve months or less. The markets were geared for speed and reaction, a lifetime measured in nano-seconds and megabucks. It was a nerve-racking business at best, no place for queasy stomachs or safe bets. In that first plunge I had gone in way over my head. Even the trading argot had me baffled. Arcane terms like *spreading, hedging, straddles, butterflies, shorts, longs* seemed like a new kind of jive talk, a lingo with a porno-graphic ring.

The commodities market had unfolded before me like some great tragicomedy, a blend of high drama and low slapstick. While I hadn't known much about this shadowy world before entering it, I knew that things like wheat, corn, soybeans, oats, rye, eggs, cotton, coffee, cocoa were the stuff of fast fortunes—and faster losses. I had read about the speculative exploits, in wheat and cotton, of the legendary Jesse Livermore, a millionaire one minute, a pauper the next; about the old bucket shops, where people made book, betting on the price swings of a stock or commodity; about manipulation of the wheat market on the Chicago Board of Trade in the Frank Norris classic *The Pit;* about the septuagenarian oil tycoon Armand Hammer, who had cornered the ginger market in his youth. It all was bathed in a veneer of romanticism, but there was something to be learned from it: Luck was a matter of shrewdness and timing. Obviously I had neither in my intitial run at the market.

I took my loss as a personal affront, vowing never to let the market beat me again. If anything, that vow proved I was an amateur. The real pros, I eventually learned, put ego aside every time they entered the trading pit. Those who didn't paid dearly. A smart trader knew when to get out of a position, to admit when he was wrong, to let go of his mistakes. No one was bigger than the market. "You can win a horse race," someone once said, "but you can't beat the races."

Anyway, my lack of capital left me no choice but to wait for another opportunity and to ponder the lessons I had learned. Learning, one of the great philosophers said, came from suffering. In the meantime, my emotions could cool off and my bruised ego heal. Time was my ointment.

2

A Summer of Discontent

Seven years passed before my next encounter with Ceres, goddess of agriculture. I was then a financial writer, covering the Chicago-commodities markets for the late *Chicago Daily News* when I dared the fates once more in the summer of 1966. Surely, I reckoned, enough time had passed for another spin at the wheel. Besides, I was smarter, more seasoned, and understood the mechanics of the market better. Like stocks, the prices of commodities rose and fell with people's hopes and fears, and speculators merely traded guesses. I had also learned something about traders I had interviewed on the exchanges. Many traded by feel rather than by fundamentals, forgetting about things like leading economic indicators, government policies, and even supplies of commodities. They simply tried to catch the market on the way up and ditch it on the way down. In the trading pits they could do it faster and better than any outside speculators because they were squarely in the heart of the action. Their edge over the public was razor-sharp, and never did they hesitate to use it. Despite knowing the pitfalls, I again went ahead. Thus began my reign as an unwilling soybean king.

I'm still uncertain exactly what went wrong. Perhaps somewhere in the fissures of my mind I've deliberately chosen to bury the facts. Nevertheless, they are somewhat hazy, and the records irretrievable. This time, long before they became the manna of the health food gurus, it was soybeans, something I knew even less about than corn. At the time I was living with my wife in a one-bedroom apartment. It was a Friday afternoon when I burst through the door with the news. The exchange went something like this:

"By the way," I opened bravely, "we took delivery today on ten thousand bushels of real soybeans."

"Why?" she asked, biting hard on her lip to keep back a cry of despair.

"I don't know exactly myself. But they were worth twenty-seven thousand five hundred dollars, and I owe only twenty-seven thousand two hundred dollars." By now my mouth was cotton. I was the owner of enough beans to fill 15½ average bedrooms—if the doors opened outward.

"This is only a one-bedroom apartment," she reminded me. "We'll have to move."

"No need to panic. We won't have to keep them here. They can go in a terminal elevator out at Calumet Harbor. It costs only eight dollars a day storage." (I never saw my vast bean holdings; I merely received a warehouse receipt to confirm ownership.) Now that's the trouble with clear, logical explanations like that one. People understand them. I knew my wife did. Why else would she have stood there looking like a hanging judge?

"It was just an oversight," I continued, groping for an answer that made sense to adults and speaking up so I could be heard above the rumbling in my stomach. "My broker was supposed to notify me at least a day in advance of delivery so I could sell my two soybean contracts before they became beans. I guess he forgot."

The temperature in the apartment soared to where a person could have been boiled in soybean oil. It was certainly no time to drop to my knees with the promise of a bright *future*, although I considered doing just that. It wouldn't have been the first time a pun provided comic relief in a tense situation. But given my limited bankroll, I wasn't in much of a jovial mood. Nor was my wife.

Fortunately I hadn't blown my life savings. I had put just $500 into the two contracts, and that grew to $2,000 in a month. I thought for sure that I was on my way and that this time Lady Luck owed me one. Just when I was feeling a bit cocky and confident, it happened again like some cruel joke. The market abruptly turned on me. Without pausing for so much as a hiccup, prices fell ten cents per bushel, the maximum daily limit permitted under the exchange rules at that time. Suddenly there were more sellers than buyers. I was trapped and could only wait and hope. That dime's worth of movement cost me a $1,000 loss on my two contracts. Ironically, I had become the victim of a safety valve in the market. That was exactly what the limit rule was all about. It was there to protect traders like me, to prevent total panic in the market, to keep future prices in line with the going cash market price of a commodity. Soybean prices were allowed to move ten cents above (limit up) or below (limit down) the previous day's closing price before the exchange slapped an arbitrary halt in trading. The limit indeed gave the market and its players a chance to cool down, to sit back and survey the situation with the expectation of some counterbalancing news that might encourage buyers and turn the market around. But in the meantime, I was helplessly locked into my position, praying that the market wouldn't open limit down the next day.

I still don't know what sent the market into a tailspin, but the very next day prices began slowly to move back up. Unfortunately they didn't move fast enough. When I took delivery, prices were still below the point at which I had bought my beans. Waiting for them to rebound to where I had originally bought would have been like waiting for Godot. Within two weeks of delivery I sold my beans to some big commercial interests (I believe it was either Pillsbury or General Mills) and took a loss of $2,268, which included storage fees, carrying charges, and interest.

3

Who's Crying Now?

I wasn't the first amateur speculator to take delivery, nor would I be the last. And there were others before me even more ignorant of the market. One who comes to mind is Dr. Ralph Hershman. They still talk about the Doc down on Chicago's Water Market, the produce center that feeds the city. Hershman, a somber middle-aged man, was a successful dentist with a penchant for trading onions on the Chicago Mercantile Exchange during the 1950s. A stickler for detail, he thought he knew everything about the markets. He knew, for instance, that an onion was the edible bulb of an herb of the lily family and that speculating in onions was as good as any gambling junket he had ever taken to Las Vegas. Even his broker tried to slow him down in those rough-and-tumble days of onion trading on the Mercantile Exchange, which was called the whorehouse on the west side of the downtown Loop by the snooty members of the Board of Trade, located on the east side.

The boys on the Merc traded onions the way I used to trade baseball cards, buying them, selling them, hoarding them. Hardly a day passed, it seemed, without somebody trying to corner the onion market or squeeze prices higher or push them lower. The law of supply and demand became so distorted under all the manipulation that the bags the onions were shipped in became more valuable than the onions themselves. And—you guessed it—some speculators began selling the bags once the onions had turned rotten. At one point so many onions had been dumped on the Chicago market that they were selling for less than a penny a pound. There were more onions than Carter had liver pills, was the way one produceman put it.

It was a classic case of hedgers becoming speculators. A kind of "I'm getting mine" mentality prevailed on the exchange. Onion trading turned into the highest rolling game around. Consider what happened to the March contract.

Trading in the contract opened on August 1, 1955, at $2.40 for a 50-pound bag of golden globe onions. (Each contract called for 600 bags, or 30,000 pounds of onions.) Shortly thereafter onions traded at a high of $2.75, a premium price, considering that golden globes were generally grown and marketed for less than $1. Then, like the steady beat of a jungle telegraph, word spread among the traders on the exchange floor that a bumper crop was coming. Whether it was or wasn't no one knew for sure. But to the ears of the speculators it was the sound of attack. Prices over the next six months were driven up and down their daily 50-cent limits. Subsequently prices drifted lower, and on March 15, 1956—the last trading day in the contract—they broke sharply downward, sinking to their all-time lows. March onions, after touching 10 cents at one point, closed out at an incredible 15 cents per 50-pound bag. This meant that at a wholesale price of three-tenths of a cent a pound, March onions were worth more in the ground than out.

The farmers cried foul. Led by the National Onion Association, onion growers across the country demanded the scalps of the scalpers, those professional day traders who slice off small, quick profits with the slightest spasm in market price, helping to give the market its volatility. The farmers wanted to abolish onion trading. In the wake of the March madness Merc officials found themselves doing some fast talking before congressional committees in Washington that were giving serious thought to a ban on onion trading. The price of onions had drastically fallen below the cost of production because of oversupply, the Merc officials argued. The exchange, they insisted, did not set prices but merely mirrored them like a thermometer registering temperatures; to ban trading would be like breaking the thermometer because it showed the patient had a fever. The analogy fell on deaf ears. In 1958 Congress banned onion trading forever.

Unfortunately the ban hadn't come in time to save Dr. Hershman from himself. Against the advice of his broker, he took delivery on fifty contracts or so-called cars of yellow globe onions at a time when the Chicago produce market wallowed under a sea of onions. It was bad enough to be the owner of rotting onions, but to own so much of something no one wanted was the height of indignity. To find out just how much he did own, Hershman made a trip to South Water Market, where he was in for a big shock. Naïvely Hershman had believed a car to mean just that—an automobile trunk full of onions. His face turned white, his mouth dropped open when he realized a *carload* meant boxcar. Hershman was now the owner of some thirty railroad boxcars of onions, 1.5 million pounds, he couldn't give away. They say he sobbed for a good fifteen minutes. It may have been the first time in history someone cried just from *looking* at onions. In any case, Dr. Hershman's debacle cost him $95,000. Fortunately he could eat the financial loss. It was the embarrassment that was hard to swallow. Who wanted the distinction of being remembered in trading folklore as one of the biggest jokes of the roaring onion era?

"The market is a microcosm of the world," Everette B. Harris, former president of the Chicago Mercantile Exchange, once told me. "It's there to harness human greed for the good of all. It's the good and the bad, the yin and yang," he said. My fling with soybeans was more yin than yang, though thankfully I didn't lose everything. I could have blown my entire yearly salary instead of 20 percent of it. My managing editor, in fact, wondered how I could continue to speculate on a newspaperman's salary. I assured him that I couldn't and that, at last, I had learned my lesson.

The commodities market, I realized, was enough to drive a sober man to drink—or, much worse, to embezzle. That's exactly what a high school classmate of mine had been driven to in order to cover his losses in the market. The story had filtered up to Chicago from St. Louis that he had lost a fortune and had skimmed $20,000 or $30,000 from the company he worked for. He ended up in the state penitentiary. Not long ago a thirty-seven-year-old senior vice-president at the Chicago-based Sears Bank and Trust Company was caught with his hand in the till. This young mover-and-shaker, it seems, needed a fast $13,000 to cover part of the $117,000 he had lost in commodity trading.

Over the years it was these kinds of stories I would see all too frequently in the daily newspapers. They were stories of desperate people who took chances and lost. As far as I was concerned, there were only two types of commodity speculator: the risk takers and the big risk takers. They use "systems," hunches, bluffs, calculated chances and the power of quick intuition. More than a few resort to prayer. No one has come up with a foolproof way to beat the odds. No one ever will.

4

Buck-buck and Potluck

Paul Rosen sat, stoop-shouldered, on the edge of the bed. The fatigue scrawled across his pale, drawn face made his look like a cruel caricature, the way an expressionist painter would distort the look of fear. His eyes, glassy and distant, were fixed on the black sky outside. He greeted me with a yawn of boredom, extending a limp hand.

"I'm glad you could make it," he mumbled in an unconvincing monotone.

It was the first day Paul was fully conscious after four days of lying in a near-comatose state from gulping a fistful of Valium. The tranquil, antiseptic atmosphere of Weiss Memorial Hospital was a marked contrast with the world of the trading pit on the floor of the Chicago Board of Trade, a hellish nightmare of bodies and emotions entangled in capitalistic struggle where Paul's life came unglued. It was a world as hostile to the outsider as the heart of the Amazon jungle. Yet, in the blink of an eye, it could become just as cruel to the insider. Paul was evidence of that. Once an affable, articulate, and seemingly savvy grain trader, now he sat in a daze, mute one moment, muttering impassioned gibberish the next. Paul teetered on the abyss of misfortune, a broken man six years past twenty and more than a quarter of a million dollars in debt. He was a man trying to tiptoe through the quicksand of insanity.

Among the bushels of horror stories about the commodities market and its players and promoters, none affected me as profoundly as Paul's. Paul Rosen is not his real name, but this is a real story, one that bated my curiosity and finally led me to examine a strange breed of capitalists: the young professional commodity traders, those so-called locals who work the trading pits daily on the floors of the mighty Chicago exchanges, where more than 85 percent of the nation's futures contracts are traded. What are their motivations? Their aspirations? Their expectations? How do they take their losses? Why does the game make some of them desperate and others frivolous, almost giddy when it comes to handling the success of the market? Who are the new Gatsbys?

Paul was one of them. At one time he thought he had it all. There was the six-figure income and the creature comforts that went with it: a posh high-rise co-op apartment on Chicago's lakefront Gold Coast; a silver Corniche Rolls-Royce; a forty-two-foot two-masted ketch rig docked at Belmont Harbor; the weekend jaunts aboard a pal's plane to the Bahamas. I never got the feeling, though, that he really enjoyed all these things. Perhaps he had in the beginning, but in the years that I had known him I sensed these things were more like objects of worship than pleasure, trophies from his forays into the pits.

There in the hospital room it really made no difference how he lost it all: That was history. He had been a Lord of the Pit, a Don Quixote tilting at the windmills of the American Dream. Now he was one of the walking wounded, whose future looked as bleak as the autumn sky outside.

"I'd-I'd, uh, like you to meet Janice," Paul stammered, waving his hand toward the corner of the room, where an attractive young woman sat, busily engaged in needlepoint work of some kind. She acknowledged the introduction with a quick and tacit nod, returning to her assault on the needlepoint, her fingers moving furiously as if she were playing "Flight of the Bumblebee" on a piano.

"You want to talk about it, Paul?" I asked, looking for some change in his face that might give me a clue to the sincerity of his answer. The storm clouds darkened the room, turning the atmosphere even more somnolent. Then came his faint murmur.

"They-got-me-the-bastards. This-time-they-really-stuck-it-to-me," he said, his mouth seeming to move independently of the words like one of those eerie Animatronic Disney robots. His dark brown eyes marked by deep, fleshy pockets continued to focus on the clouds.

It was always the ubiquitous *they,* those indefinable conspirators who would inevitably force the market to go the opposite way you were playing it. *They* were the rumormongers who forced stock and commodity prices to fluctuate wildly regardless of the economic climate. *They* were the ones who toyed with the military-industrial complex of the fifties and sixties and then with the oil powers of the seventies. *They* profited from those long lines of gas-hungry cars and the shortages of everything from aluminum to wheat. *They* were the brains, the *real* insiders with all the money to manipulate the markets to make more. *They* were the immovable forces that gave you that lonely feeling that you were up against it, the ones that always profited by your mistakes. *They* were the ones who used pit gossip to create doubts about your stature as a shrewd trader. *They* were the enemy: heartless; calculating; always on the offensive; forever elusive. *They* were everything you weren't. Paul had become obsessed with the *they* factor to the point where he would rationalize away his own trading blunders. *They,* of course, were always around to take the blame for his poor judgment. Damn, were *they* cunning. Sometimes *they* would suck you into the market by letting you win first; then, like a shifty hustler, *they* would wipe you out. *They* would always see you as just a small-time Charlie Potatoes, a Fast Eddie Felson squeezed between Minnesota Fats and Willie Mosconi in a game of cutthroat nine ball. It always worked. You could never learn your lesson. *They* knew just how greedy you were and that small profits would never satisfy you. And just when you were raking it in, inevitably *they* would lower the boom.

Paul was flat broke—belly up or tap city, as those in the trade say. It was one thing to lose all your money, another to turn up emotionally bankrupt, your self-esteem demolished before you were brought to your knees with the sobering fact that *they* could never be beaten. Truth? Fantasy? The line is hard to draw with any man under severe stress. So who the hell were *they?* No one, of course, knew for sure, least of all Paul. But to him, *they* were as real as the guy standing next to him in the trading pit day in day out. To Paul *they* were the real pros.

I had met Paul in late 1970, about a year before he bought a membership on the Board of Trade. At the time he was a stockbroker for a small La Salle Street firm, but he had a better knack for trading commodities than for picking stocks. He was an ideal source for a journalist because he always had an opinion. Quick to poke fun of himself with a sardonic wit, Paul never hedged a remark. Once, for the record in a story I was writing, he described the trading pits to me as "an arena of low brows and low blows," a quote that got me a pat on the back from my editor but got Paul in trouble with his fellow traders. For a while, he joked, his colleagues had him feeling like a West Point cadet undergoing the silent treatment. But that didn't last long. Traders don't like to hold grudges. That's not to say they didn't play hardball. They could alienate, they could menace, they could bluster at the psychic expense of a fellow trader, and they could become street fighters in a capitalistic ghetto slashing at one another just to see the blood flow. But in the end they'd back off because *you* were one of them, one of the elite members of a club as closed and inbred as the New York intellectuals during the thirties. The pit was too small a world to make enemies and keep them. The ranks were too thin to be divided.

More than anything, it was Paul's uncanny ability to see a situation in a matter-of-fact manner that I most admired about him.

"Look," he'd say out of the corner of his mouth, mocking a tough guy, "you ask for the truth, and I give it to you. Then you turn it against me. What kind of business is journalism anyway?" Darn if he didn't have a point.

Paul had street smarts and the rough edge to go with them, projecting a kind of macho image. Maybe that's why he was a James Bond freak and read only cheap paperback detective thrillers. There always seemed to be one sticking out of the pocket of his trading jacket. And there was that flair for the dramatic. I suppose he was more bluff than anything, like one of those wildly hissing snakes that are nonpoisonous. He would lower his voice, puff his nostrils, and raise a sinister eyebrow whenever he'd argue. I'm sure he had picked up the histrionics in the pits, where among the forest of upraised arms, jabbing fingers, and deafening outcries, a facial expression becomes the instant printout of a trader's position. "Even the way a man sweats," Paul often said, "could tell what he was up to."

He liked his image; he was comfortable with it. It caught you off guard. You'd swear he was a product of Hell's Kitchen, a regular Dead End Kid. But he wasn't. Paul was strictly middle-class vintage, reared in the predominantly Jewish neighborhood of Chicago's West Rogers Park, an area of doctors, lawyers, and other professionals. Paul was a "boomer," one of the 76 million members of the baby boom generation. His father was an attorney, his mother a housewife and part-time secretary for a rabbi, and there was an older sister, too. Paul grew up in the sixties, cutting corners and classes and somehow avoiding the long hair, the protests, the flower children, and the draft. Issues were never important to him. And when the rest of the seventies generation was getting its head together—with everything from EST to erroneous zones—Paul was into capitalism.

During his high school years he had been one of the Morse Avenue Beach crowd, a collection of characters out of a junior edition of Damon Runyon. They were jocks, greasers, straights, mostly students from nearby Sullivan High School held loosely together by a common thread: a passion for gambling. Some of them were lousy students; others made straight As. A few, like Paul, played it "cool," embarrassed to admit they did well in their classwork. Not every Morse Beach almunus, of course, went on to make a career of gambling or commodity trading, although a good number did. Others became doctors, lawyers, architects, businessmen, teachers, entertainers—the gamut of occupations. There were the dropouts and even gangsters, too. But in those few years they hung out at the beach, everyone was on an equal footing, brains and brawn alike. You rose to the level expected of you by the crowd, no higher, no lower. You were a hero if you won, a bum if you lost.

Among those winners and losers there was Paul's good friend with the sobriquet of Dopey, a droopy-eyed kid with buck teeth and a mane of blond hair. Another was One-eyed Jimmy, a sneaky cheat who would deal the cards, catching their reflection as they passed over the cigarette lighter that lay in front of him. Hands Seldon was the fastest shuffler on any of the North Side beaches. There were some real veterans, too, such as Ray the Fruit, a cherubic fat man in his thirties. No one knew for sure, and fear kept anyone from asking, but rumor had it that he had syndicate connections. Ray's gofer was Fast Willie, who also doubled as a lookout, keeping an eye open for the cops who regularly patrolled the beaches.

Morse Avenue Beach was the largest of a connecting stretch of beaches along Chicago's Far North Side lakefront. It wasn't the beach of the "beautiful people." Oak Street Beach, across from the Drake Hotel, claimed that crowd, the Near North Side swinging singles, young professionals, stewardesses, sun worshipers. Nor was it the Foster Avenue Beach, where you could always find a pickup game of basketball among the Latinos and blacks from the uptown crowd. Morse Beach with its refreshment stand, washrooms, and grassy knoll dotted with trees and shrubs was a mecca for all ages. Young mothers set up playpens under the trees, old men and women sat on the park benches that flanked a concrete walkway just beyond the shabby courtyard apartment buildings, and teenage girls flocked to the sand to catch some sun but mostly boys. Most of the time, however, the boys were too busy to pay much attention. The game came first, always first.

The game was blackjack or potluck. Everyone played against the dealer. A bettor could match part of the pot or all of the pot, and there were side bets as well. The Morse Beach crowd took potluck seriously—too seriously. But there was, after all, a tradition to uphold. Morse Avenue Beach had been the bush leagues for aspiring gamblers going back to the thirties, a place where you took your first taste of risk and either spit it out or savored it. Here friendships were forged for life, and no one lusted after fame, rank, or prestige—only money.

By no means was it penny ante stuff. In the heat of one game Manny Greene flung the keys to his beloved '57 Chevy into the pot. He won. Others weren't as fortunate, and each summer several car titles changed hands in the games. Riding a streak that was part luck and part bluff, once Paul and Dopey teamed up and bet the entire pot. They ended up winning $230, a heck of a killing for a couple of fifteen-year-olds. That night they took their winnings and headed straight for Sportmen's Park to bet the harness races. A lot of the crowd did that: marathon card games during the day; the horses at night. It sure beat stickball and those other summer games teenagers played.

One day Paul's luck ran out. Three plainclothesmen swooped

down on the game. Everyone scattered, racing along the rocks toward the other beaches, scaling cyclone fences, scurrying through gangways. Everyone except Paul. Before he knew it, he found himself handcuffed to another player on the way to the Summerdale station. His father got him out of it easily enough, just as he was to buy Paul's way out of the Vietnam War years later. Both agreed not to whisper a word of the incident to Paul's mother. Why take a chance on her heart palpitations? Of course, there was the fatherly reprimand, followed by the son's promise to reform. But a week later Paul was at it again. Only this time there were four lookouts.

Sometimes, when the card game slowed down, the crowd turned to buck-buck. This was an adolescent version of red rover. But it was brutal. The crowd played it as if it were some ancient masculine rite, a ritual to prove manhood. It amounted to organized battle between two teams of players, like the rumble scene in *West Side Story*, a kind of choreographed chaos. Here's how it was played: One person anchored himself to a tree by hugging the trunk, and a human chain would form with arms linked around waists. One by one each member of the opposing team would charge headfirst, hurling himself on top of the chain in an effort to break it. As the bodies piled up, so did the broken arms, dislocated shoulders, and pinched nerves. The last person to jump on the chain screamed, "Buck-buck," and held up either one or two fingers. If the captain of the other team guessed the correct number of fingers, the sides changed positions. Looking back on it, you could say that potluck and buck-buck were pretty good training for Paul's eventual life in the pits.

Paul left the crowd behind when he entered the University of Illinois in the fall of 1965. But he never let go of the wise guy notion that school was all right as long as it didn't interfere with his education. So it wasn't surprising that he dropped out after two years and began to drift. For a while he sold soap powder to chain stores for some big midwestern outfit. Then it was retail clothing. After that came selling advertising space for a fledgling business magazine out of Chicago. When the magazine folded, he headed west, dropping out altogether. He skied the slopes at Jackson Hole, Wyoming, until his money ran out. Broke and dejected, he returned to Chicago in the spring of 1970.

A few weeks after his return, as a favor to his father, a family friend gave Paul a back-office job in a small LaSalle Street brokerage house less than half a block from the Board of Trade. The very first time he stepped into the visitors' gallery, soaking up the ambience in the pits below, he knew he wanted to get into the game, to become a trader. Within six months he had both a stockbroker's license and an exchange membership, borrowing $25,000 from his father to pay for the seat.

5

You're a Natural, Kid

Paul's timing couldn't have been better. It was more than a year before the Russian wheat deal, when commodities markets were still pretty much sleeping whales. They were active but not wild. You could make a good living with relatively few mistakes as you learned the fine points of trading. And Paul learned them, along with some things about himself, trading wheat. It could have been any commodity. The lessons in each pit were the same, even though each commodity, and in turn each pit, had their own personalities, their own moods, their own energies, their own legends, their own gossip, their own histories, their own lives. A few years ago, in a *New York Times* article, author Douglas Bauer compared the commodities to ethnic types:

> Corn is slow and predictable, rising and falling with reassuring sanity, the least mystery. Traders say that the corn market is like a dependable brown-bagger, coming to work every day, on time, doing a job free of temperamental extremes. A Swede, perhaps. The [soy] bean market suffers the exchange's most mercurial outbursts, neurotic flights and dips. The bean market is Mediterranean: Italian or Greek. Wheat is schizophrenic, capable of miming corn or beans, one day tracing

safe historic movements up and down, the next day throwing an elusive fit. Wheat is American.

Even the bell that opened and closed trading each day with a resonant baritone "Bong!" had an ethnic ring. It was Oriental. Actually the bell was the successor to a Chinese gong once pounded at the close of each session back in the early days of the exchange. It was the only way to stop trading in the tumult of the pit. An exchange employee would carry a huge gong into the heart of each pit and beat it long and hard until the decibels rose above those of the traders so they could no longer hear one another. Only then would they disperse and call it a day.

From the very first day Paul realized that the traders themselves often took on the qualities of the commodities they traded. The fellows in the wheat pit, for example, were certainly schizophrenic, calm one moment, frenetic the next—American, if you will. Paul saw it. Only minutes before the opening trading bell, he had been casually chatting with a trader standing next to him. It was small talk, but to a nervous Paul it was soothing, like a jockey whispering in the ear of his horse to settle it down in the gate. The entire trading floor, in fact, was reminiscent of the grandstand of a racetrack. Some traders huddled in groups, speculating on where the markets would open, eyeing the prices of each commodity like a string of thoroughbreds parading by before the race on the way to the starting gate. Others penciled their charts as if they were scratch sheets or leafed through the daily newspapers, trying to catch a headline that could possibly have an impact on a particular commodity or on the market itself. There were even touts— traders and brokers talking up various commodities they saw as potential winners because of their commercial interests.

At 9:30 A.M. the bell sounded, and they were off. Suddenly that friendly trader standing next to Paul was a terror. His elbow thrust into Paul's chest, pushing him back and forcing his spectacles to slide down his nose. A mistake but no time to apologize. They all were terrors, reminding Paul of a bunch of small rascals squabbling over a crystal shooter in a game of marbles. The pit had erupted into a pulsating roar of screaming sellers and buyers, their fingers wagging the code of the floor. Paul refused to be intimidated by the sound and fury. He knew he had to establish a pit presence, to fight off the glut of emotions closing in on him. Though that first bid got caught in his throat momentarily, he forced it out with a tumultuous yell that surprised him, but no one else.

"Five for a half! Five for a half!" bellowed a trader a few steps from Paul, offering any buyer 5,000 bushels of wheat, one contract, at $1.42½ per bushel.

"So-so-Sold!" Paul screamed, taking the contract at the price offered, while turning his palm in toward his chest, the hand signal signifying he wanted the grain.

The seller, who knew it was Paul's first day, winked at him and said with a chortle, "Now you're on your way." He had practically handed Paul his first trade, a gift from one of the veterans, a sort of unofficial welcome to the new kid on the block. It was short-lived, like everything else in the pit. From that point on Paul was on his own. He didn't have time to think about the benevolent gesture. The market that day was moving. Less than a minute later he became a seller of wheat.

"Five at three! Sell five at three!" Paul yelled. Wheat had moved up a half cent, and now he wanted to sell his contract. This time he furiously pushed his palm outward away from his chest to show he wanted another trader to take the grain from him. "Sold!" He had found a buyer; he had scalped his first trade for a half cent—$25 for a minute's work.

Beads of sweat popped across Paul's forehead, and his armpits were wet. He felt his throat becoming raspy from yelling, but he loved it. The adrenaline was flowing, and the heart was pounding the way it had when he ran the hurdles in high school. It was an exhilarating feeling, like a runner's high.

There was nothing clinical about Paul's approach to the market. It was a barnstorming, fly-by-the-seat-of-your-pants approach, as it is with most of the apprentice traders. No one, he realized, knew what was going on. Each trader had a theory about what was happening in the next five minutes. If everyone thought the market was going to open higher, but it opened lower, the psychology in the pit changed immediately. It was a herd mentality fed on raw emotion. It was the easy way. Get the trading feel of the crowd in the pit; then jump on board for the move. By the time the public got in, the market ticked that quarter or half cent, and Paul had his profit. The ultimate price of a commodity may have been determined by supply and demand, Paul thought, but in the interim, emotional factors reigned supreme.

Even as he gained confidence, he traded scared, careful not to buck a trend. He would never think of fading, going the opposite way of the majority of traders in the pit. That strategy was for the experienced traders, the big gunners, the princes of the pit who were gifted enough to get the edge, to anticipate the twinges in price and then jump on them to grab a profit before anyone else. It would be a good six months, maybe a year, before he really got going, before he could trade by a gut impulse against the prevailing wisdom of the pit. In the meantime, he would learn the tricks of trading and, perhaps more important, the psychology of survival, the kind that keeps solo ocean voyagers from jumping overboard during the long hours of solitude or during the fiercest storms.

At best it was trial and error, massaging the market to get the right feel, knowing when to back off or charge head-on, understanding the changes in his own personality. With each day in the pit Paul became more aggressive, more hostile, more physical in his body language. Even his jaw became hyperactive, and at the end of the day he'd go home hoarse from shrieking above the din in the wheat pit. But all that was to be expected. Whatever was buried in your psyche could emerge in the pit: You were allowed to put on an act, to cut loose a fantasy every so often. The pit was an ideal stage for such theatrics. It resembled an open-air Greek theater with the central acting area overlooked by a semicircle of tiered seats. The trading pit is an octagon with wooden tiers of narrow steps descending to the lowest spot in the middle. It is trading in the round. But during the heat of some trading sessions you'd swear the pit was a miniature version of the Roman Colosseum, where the gladiators fought it out.

Paul was content with the small victories. As a scalper he moved in and out of the market every twenty or thirty seconds, trying to make a quarter of a cent on each trade. Wheat, corn, soybeans moved in quarter-cent ticks, and each tick was $12.50 per contract. It didn't sound like much, but those fractional cents could add up to megabucks if you traded huge volume, similar to the way grocery chains operate on small markups. If, for example, in a year a trader averaged a quarter-cent profit on 20,000 contracts of wheat (100 million bushels), his annual income would be a quarter of a million dollars. Paul wasn't in that class yet. Scalping was the apprenticeship of trading, and you earned your profits on one contract, or two at a time, winning on some, losing on some, breaking even on some. The idea was that if you traded enough, eventually you'd come out ahead. That's why many traders scalped anywhere from 200 to 400 trades in a day. Timing had a lot to do with it. A scalper was all reaction; a position trader, all digestion. Position traders held their contracts overnight or for much longer periods, looking for the big price moves. It made for a lot of nervous stomachs and restless nights, which you spent thinking about the myriad forces in the world that could affect your position. Some position traders have been known to go to sleep one night and wake up millionaires the next morning. Others awaken to the nightmare of having lost everything. It really made no difference what type of trader you were; the market was an enigma to practically everyone who played it. You could be riding it on one tick and chasing it on the next.

"It's like playing with a trained tiger; any moment it can turn on you and bite your head off," Paul said during one of the rare breaks he took whenever there was a lull in trading. He'd pace the thirty-five steps from the wheat pit to the long cash tables holding grain samples, that ran beneath the five-story windows at the east end of the trading floor. It was usually the only exercise his legs got in a trading day. Most of the time he stood in the same spot for nearly four hours, from the 9:30 A.M. opening to the 1:15 P.M. closing, his business office—10C—defined by the width of his shoe, the length of his sole. He wouldn't have it any other way. Where else could you make $50, $100, $500, $1,000 on one lungful of air? No wonder Paul ate, drank, slept, and dreamed wheat.

6

The Golden Age of Commodities

Then came the "great grain robbery." That was what the critics called it when the Russians secretly bought a quarter of the U.S. wheat crop at bargain prices in 1972. The massive purchases depleted U.S. grain reserves, sending prices to their highest levels since 1917 and eventually wreaking havoc on American food costs. For Paul, who had then been trading for some eighteen months, and the other traders, it was a dream come true. As it turned out, the USSR's disastrous 1972 grain crop unleashed the greatest bull market in the history of grain trading.

Commodities took on a new dimension in the summer of 1972. They became denationalized; food became a global market. In the pre–World War II years world grain trade amounted to some 30 million tons a year. By 1975 it had risen to more than 150 million tons. For nearly forty years before the early 1970s the government subsidized the American farmer to produce surpluses in order to keep farming economically viable. During the late forties some of the surpluses helped in the recovery of war-ravaged Europe and Japan. Under the bountiful bins, however, the lid remained tight on domestic prices. Through the 1950s and well into the 1960s the United States simply did not know what to do with its surplus grain and stored it at a cost of billions. In the sixties we used our surpluses to win friends abroad. American farm products were sold mainly to Britain and to the Netherlands or were given away to India, Pakistan, Egypt, and other developing nations.

All the while the world food situation had its peaks and valleys. There were the mid-1960 droughts in India and Pakistan that caused a food crisis, followed by the Green Revolution— the development of more durable short-stemmed varieties of wheat and rice fertilized with heavy doses of nitrogen—which led to self-sufficiency for such countries as India. In 1970 a corn blight destroyed a sizable portion of the U.S. corn crop. But there was always enough, so much so that during the late 1960s and early 1970s, the grain-exporting countries cut back grain production to reduce surplus stocks. Demand for grain, in fact, exceeded production in those years.

Almost overnight the situation drastically changed through a combination of circumstances brought on partly by nature, partly by man. The Soviet Union experienced severe drought in 1972 and entered the world grain market. It did so again in 1973 in order to prevent a decline in livestock production. Ultimately Russia purchased 20 million metric tons (1 million metric tons is equivalent to 36.7 million bushels of wheat) of wheat and 10 million tons of corn, soybeans, oats, and other coarse grains, boosting its total grain imports three times the previous season's. On top of that, American wheat was sold to Red China for the first time in twenty years.

There was equally stiff demand from other countries. Drought had hit Africa that year, and Korea had a failing rice crop. The European Common Market was a big buyer, as were Japan and Canada, which was normally a grain exporter. As if all that weren't enough, Mother Nature began playing tricks with water. While nearly one-fifth of the world suffered from drought, America's Farm Belt was under a prolonged wet and cold spell during the 1972 harvest that upset forecasts of record yields. At the same time, in South America, there was a shift in the Humboldt Current, a cold Antarctic current flowing north along the coasts of Chile and Peru. The result led to the virtual disappearance of the normally plentiful supply of Peruvian anchovies, a major source of world fish meal supplies. This loss of a key protein source for animal feed sent buyers scrambling for a substitute—soybean meal— and prices soared.

It became a vicious cycle, the summer when demand exceeded supply. As supplies of feed grains tightened and prices rose, cattle, hog, and poultry growers cut back production. In turn, it set off pricing pyrotechnics that had traders reading the U.S. Department of Agriculture's monthly *Hogs and Pigs Report* as if it were *Valley of the Dolls.* The easing of controls on retail food prices by the Nixon administration did the rest. Between 1972 and 1973 the price of a sirloin steak jumped from $1.53 a pound to $1.75, and pork chops from $1.25 to $1.56. All told, in 1973, Americans paid some $2 billion more for food than they had in the previous year. By 1975 the food bill had grown at a record pace by a startling $50 billion.

The years of the bin-busting crops were clearly over. U.S. wheat stocks, for example, dropped from nearly 24 million tons in June 1972 to 7 million tons a year later. Of the Soviet grain sales, then Secretary of Agriculture Earl Butz summed it up with a Muhammad Ali flair: "This is by all odds the greatest grain transaction in the history of the world. And it certainly is the greatest for us." (The mechanics of the Russian wheat deal and its impact on the American economy, farmer, consumer, and giant companies that sold the grain are well documented in such accounts as *Amber Waves of Grain* and *The Great Grain Robbery,* both by James Trager; Dan Morgan's *Merchants of Grain,* and *Sale of Wheat to Russia,* a report of hearings before the House Agriculture Committee in September 1972.)

The Butz comment was made in July 1972, shortly after the news of the grain sales had been made public. Weeks before that, however, the boys in the pits knew something big was happening. They could feel it in their bones; they could see it on the big electronic boards that sprawl along the east and west ends of the room, allowing a trader to see the price of any commodity from any point on the floor. Prices seemed to be moving higher and faster than ever before.

Paul and the other locals, of course, couldn't have an inkling of who was doing the buying or the size of the purchases. Even the giant grain merchants themselves, who were doing the buying, didn't know other giants were buying, too. The Russians had cut deals for wheat with half a dozen grain traders, though none of the firms knew how much wheat the Russians bought from the others. The commitments were huge, led by Continental Grain with 5.5 million tons, Louis Dreyfus Corporation with 2.25 million tons, and Cargill, Inc., with 2 million tons.

Grain prices moved steadily higher, and some days even the traders couldn't believe what was happening. The ticks rattled off like blazing machine guns instead of the usual methodical rifle shots. The market was a runaway. FAST . . . FAST . . . FAST . . . FAST . . . FAST . . . FAST. The blatant alarm that all hell was breaking loose flashed across the tapes in brokerage houses throughout the country. In the pit you didn't have to read the tape; you could feel the explosion coming on, the rumbling of a gusher about to break through the surface. The pit became a scalper's paradise, like someone with a sweet tooth being locked up in a candy store overnight. Traders scalped one-cent and two-cent moves because it was impossible to catch the eighth-cent ticks. (About six months later the days of the eighth-cent ticks were ended. The Board of Trade set the minimum tick for the grains at a quarter cent, or $12.50 per contract.) But there were dog days, too, periods when the drama turned into a torturous wait as prices were bid limit up for three and four days at a stretch. Then no one could make a play. But when prices did break slightly, the buyers would rush in, bidding them up again. The great bull market of 1972–73 was well under way. By August 1973 corn had risen from $1.25 to $4 a bushel, and wheat, which had sold at $1.45 a bushel, hit $5.27, the highest price it had traded in 125 years in Chicago.

As for soybeans, the world simply went crazy to buy them. On January 2, 1973, the first trading day of the year, July soybeans on the Board of Trade closed at $4.10 a bushel. One June 5, July soybeans closed at a historic high of $12.90. This meant that a trader who had bought just one 5,000-bushel contract of July soybeans at the close of trading on January 2 and sold it on the close of trading on June 5 would have made a profit of $44,000 on an investment of $1,500. Even those traders who had jumped into the market late made a bundle; in the twelve trading days prior to June 5 the value of a single July soybean contract rose $24,250. Soybean meal turned in a stellar performance, too, rising from $138.50 a ton on January 2 to an all-time high of $451 a ton on June 5. Every $1,000 invested in soybean meal brought back $31,250. And "beeflation" had its run as the price of a live cattle contract on the Chicago Mercantile Exchange, between January 2 and August 1, surged to $7,480 on just a $400 investment.

By now it had dawned upon everyone that this was no dress rehearsal but a full-scale superproduction of the real thing, the world of commodities playing to a packed house, bowing to supply and demand economics, a compelling performance that had them screaming in the pits for more. The Russians and Chinese, on a shopping spree for U.S. food, added one billion new mouths for American agriculture to feed, wiping out the surpluses and giving farmers their best net incomes in history. It was happening at a time when living standards the world over were rising, and populations expanding, at a time when every American man, woman, and child, on the average, was eating 116 pounds of beef a year—up from only 56 pounds twenty years earlier. It took a lot of grain—seven tons of it—to produce one ton of beef. No one, of course, knew then that in the eighties the surpluses would return, driving prices down, as world markets became critical to American agriculture, which would be exporting a third of what it was growing. For that matter, back in 1973, no one was contemplating the seventies either. It was one-day-at-a-time prospecting, and no one knew when the mother lode would give out. The visionaries were too busy cashing in.

There was no time to pause and examine the good and evil coming from the vagaries of a free-market economy that seemed to have gone awry. The run-up in the grains had triggered the rat-a-tat-tat in virtually every other commodity traded on the nation's commodity exchanges. In the month of July 1973 alone, record high prices were reached in copper, coffee, live hogs, frozen pork bellies, iced broilers, shell eggs, and Maine potatoes. Speculators began prospecting for ways to hype any commodity. And when one was found, it rallied unabatedly. Platinum, for example, roared to new price levels when someone discovered it would be a necessary part of a government-decreed automobile emission control system. For many commodities, it was too much speculation running after too few facts. It was not so much a reflection of supply-demand forces or even inflationary psychology, which had not yet taken hold, as a plain old-fashioned numbers game.

Commodity fever, it seemed, had gripped everyone from the Des Moines dentist to the New York psychoanalyst, from the Miami construction worker to the Los Angeles barber, the same bunch that in the late 1960s had its favorite high-flying stock, one that sold at a multiple of 100 to 200 times earnings projected years in the future.

Many of them were people who just a year before had thought of bellies in terms of exotic dancing. Now they were calling their brokers to buy pork bellies, slabs of uncured bacon. As the price of bellies rose, so did the price of bacon and scores of other items on supermarket shelves. That, in turn, sent the tempers of housewives soaring. In protest some picketed the Chicago Mercantile Exchange, where pork bellies traded. Others—(with logic and a canny knowledge of the markets)—took their complaints straight to the stores; one housewife told her grocer she would not pay $1.40 a pound for bacon because "pork bellies were down the limit and bacon had to follow." Eventually it did.

Clearly public interest in commodities had grown as never before, spurred by the profit potential of the futures markets and the rapid rise in food costs. Commodities were a story the media were anxious to report. It had drama—the intrigue of international wheat deals, explosive price increases, angry housewives, skeptical farmers, profiteering. And it was visual.

Television crews roamed the trading floors of the major exchanges, bringing the drama of the pits into the homes of America in living color. It was a picture of capitalism most Americans had never seen—a noise that shamed Times Square on New Year's Eve, a frenzy that matched the disorderly running of the bulls at Pamplona: capitalism in a turbulent, ferocious form, all in an autumnal palette of red, gold, blue, orange, green, brown trading jackets. To the casual observer it was both confusing and exciting.

"To the outsider this is bedlam, an auction gone mad," bellowed a television reporter above the pandemonium as the camera panned the trading floor around him, "a world where leather lungs and sharp elbows help, but trade secrets and good weather help even more."

To the eye of the camera it was the National Football League of Finance, an event like the Super Bowl, but without slow motion, stop action, or instant replay. The cameras could capture the trading action but not the human subtleties or frailties or the manner in which the pits stole away a man's identity, dictating his mood, his feelings about himself, his passions, his immediate response to things he had no control over.

7

The Rise of
the New Gatsbys

The Golden Age of Commodities had arrived.

Although Chicago was no longer the hog butcher of the world or the stacker of wheat, it was still the stormy, husky, brawling commodity trader of the world. The Board of Trade had been around for 125 years, the Mercantile Exchange for 54, and fully 85 percent of all U.S. commodity trading was done on the two exchanges, where economic theory blended with reality sometimes in sweet harmony, sometimes like the roar of the cannons in the *1812 Overture.*

Attention to the exchanges also meant attention to Chicago itself, a prospect the city's shrewd politicians were quick to parlay. In commodities Chicago was no Second City. Mayor Richard Daley proclaimed the week of November 12–16, 1973, as Commodity Week with all the pride and glory of a Shakespeare festival in Stratford. There were luncheons and speeches and more speeches. And more stories, the kind that fascinated financial writers, stories about boy millionaires and old-timers down-and-out on their luck who suddenly struck it rich after years of prospecting the pits. Every winner, of course, meant there was a loser, a fact often overlooked. The exchange was the only place on earth that could be the Irish Sweepstakes and snake eyes at an exact moment, the place that epitomized the notion that man is an economic animal calculating the value of everything, including human beings, in dollars and cents. Money is the sole means of keeping score on the exchanges.

It was always that way. The exchanges long since had been haunted by the legendary ghosts of crafty and sometimes sinister market plungers, ruthless manipulators, and just plain shrewd traders who made fortunes. But now the present paralyzed the past. There were instant legends, heroes of the hour, more success stories than at any time in the history of the exchanges. At the Board of Trade word had it that Eugene Cashman, an ex-cop and the brother of an ex-cop who was also a trader, made millions in soybean meal and soybean oil. Was it $10 million? Or $20 million? Or $30 million? No one knew exactly how much, and Cashman wasn't about to set the record straight, but the Irish cop who used to pound the beat around the Board of Trade Building had become a multimillionaire. And there were the O'Connor brothers—Eddie and Billy—a pair of quiet boys who shunned the social limelight but grabbed it in the soybean pit. They were gutsy as all hell, limit players trading the maximum number of contracts allowed by exchange rules. By one estimate, they ended up winning more than $25 million. Traders like Cashman and the O'Connors had taken positions that would have had those turn-of-the-century plungers swooning with envy.

There were scores of others emerging who in subsequent years would dominate the exchanges as either traders, politicians, or both. In the soybean and cattle pits, then thirty-year-old Thomas Dittmer was mastering trading power on the way to becoming one of the Big Rich. Along with his stepfather, cattle broker Ray Friedman, he formed Refco Inc. (for Ray E. Freidman & Co.), eventually building it into one of the nation's most powerful brokerage houses and boasting a client list that today includes Texas oil millionaires, pension funds, and the Federal Reserve Bank of New York. A decade later the federal government's watchdog agency, the Commodity Futures Trading Commission (CFTC), would slap a record $525,000 fine against Refco and Dittmer (who by then owned more than 80 percent of the firm) for allegedly exceeding speculative trading limits in cotton, soybeans, corn, and wheat. Neither admitting nor denying the allegations, Dittmer accepted the fine in a consent decree. Refco's trading forays sent tremors through the markets and gained Dittmer a reputation as a fearless trader among his peers.

Another trader leading the pack was Leslie Rosenthal, a hard-charging pit fighter who became chairman of the Board of Trade in 1980 and a millionaire along the way. He too had his legal squabbles with the government and was, as he put it in 1981, "punished financially" by shelling out $500,000 in legal fees during a five-year battle in the federal court with the CFTC, which charged him with fraud in the selling of commodity options traded in London. The charge was dropped when Rosenthal, without admitting any wrongdoing, agreed to stop trading those options.

At the Mercantile Exchange the fast-rising political star was immigrant-trader-attorney Leo Melamed, who became the exchange's youngest chairman and whose impact was taking hold in a new and controversial area known as financial futures.

Henry (Hank) Shatkin's rags-to-riches saga became the dream mill for hundreds of aspiring traders. Busting out early in his trading career, Shatkin hit the Chicago streets as a taxicab driver before recouping his confidence and self-esteem and heading back to the pits to make his fortune—and to become mentor to numerous up-and-comer traders.

Clearly, a new breed of trader was in the making—one with a single-minded penchant for the big play. They were long-ball hitters who were becoming folk heroes of the pits.

Louie the slugger was another heavy hitter if ever there was one. A gravel-voiced, roly-poly man with buffalo eyes and a malicious smirk, Louie started each trading day with his tie loosened and shirttail hanging out. He would load up on soybeans, corn, and wheat, holding contracts beyond the 3-million-bushel limit imposed by the exchange. He bought contracts for himself and more through relatives, friends, and other brokers. At one point he was fined by the exchange and forced to sell off part of his holdings in compliance. The fine was no more than a slap on the wrist, for no sooner had he reduced his positions than he was back buying again. The fines, as Louie the Slugger saw them, were merely part of the cost of doing business, additional overhead. Louie also had gone to the banks, borrowing nearly $3 million. The bankers were getting nervous. There were days when, like investors of a newly released film checking box-office receipts, three loan officers impatiently waited in the room off the trading floor to see how their investment was doing. Louie was on a big winning streak, and no one wanted to close him down. At the end of 1973 he had paid off the bankers and had more than $8 million in his trading account.

Everyone, it seemed, had a story about a commodity trader and told it like an ethnic joke with a derogatory tone and biting punch line. There were stories about the twenty-five-year-old ex-high school gym teacher who had struggled on $12,000 a year in the late sixties and now was a millionaire; about the ex-taxi driver who would have taken thirty years of hacking to earn what he did in six months; about the high school dropout who in 1970 drove a beer truck and three years later could buy a fleet of them; about the Orthodox Jew who made a half million dollars trading pork bellies; about the veteran trader who bellied up twice only to bounce back to make $15 million; about the trader in the egg pit who accidentally bought ten times the volume intended because of a mistaken hand signal and ended up $200,000 richer and with a stake to start a business that today includes cattle feedlots, oil wells, and a printing company; about the trader who could pull down $125,000 in a couple of months just by looking over the shoulders of the traders standing next to him; about the trader who had such a big day he stopped on the way home to buy a Mercedes for cash. . . .

They were stories of too much, too fast, too easy—the kind of publicity that had sent the forty-niners scurrying across a vast country to Sutter's mill. Now the promise of striking it rich on the exchanges lured modern-day prospectors, who descended on the pits like battalions of boll weevils on a gourmet tour of a cotton plantation. They came from the city and suburbs, from New York and California, from Texas and North Dakota, from wealth and poverty, from highbrow, lowbrow, and middlebrow, from former jobs, professions, and from mid-life crisis, all with a single-minded purpose: to make money.

8

Prince of the Pit

You could tell Paul Rosen had made big money by the way he eased into the good life as if he were stepping into a well-worn pair of slippers. He gave up Sears for Gucci and switched from Big Macs to veal Orloff. From a studio apartment in Sandburg Village, a predominantly singles complex on the Near North Side, he moved to a skin-and-bones Miës van der Rohe high-rise on the Gold Coast along Lake Michigan. He bought a Rolls-Royce and paid back the seed money he had borrowed from his father to buy the membership. Just as the Great Gatsby counted his shirts like rosaries, Paul—a new Gatsby—counted his gold chains. He was well on his way to becoming a member of the leisure class, those who live by the industrial and service communities rather than in them. "Admission to the class is gained by exercise of the pecuniary aptitudes—for acquisition rather than for serviceability," wrote economist Thorstein Veblen in his droll and satiric turn-of-the-century diatribe, *The Theory of the Leisure Class.*

While the new Gatsbys were into making money, not all of them were into spending it. A few such as twenty-four-year-old Richard Dennis, one of the most successful traders at the time, dwelt in a kind of pecuniary purgatory, preferring a more ascetic life. The son of an engineer employed for thirty years by the city of Chicago, Dennis felt work was the curse of the masses. He began trading on Chicago's third and smallest exchange, the Mid-

America Commodity Exchange, in 1971, a year following his graduation from DePaul University with a bachelor's degree in philosophy.

Dennis's piercing dark eyes were framed in thick, black-rimmed glasses, and his frizzy hair fell around his face and ended in muttonchops. He looked as if he belonged in the trading pits of the 1890s, but he was firmly planted in the 1970s at a time when the counterculture had not yet become the over-the-counterculture. He was the liberal heart, the Vietnam dove, the environmentalist, the George McGovern supporter, the man who wished Richard Nixon could have changed his birthday so he didn't have to share it with him. Above all, he was the consummate trader, the kid with the knack, who knew from the start it was wrong to invest his ego in his opinions. It was more important to know himself, he believed, than the factors affecting the market.

Like numerous traders, Dennis had his baptism in commodities as a runner on the Chicago Mercantile Exchange. Like bat boys on baseball teams, copyboys on newspapers, and pages in Congress, runners are the gofers, the worker bees, who flit about at the beck and call of brokers, bringing them everything from lunch to orders for execution in the pits. Dennis worked as a runner for $1.75 an hour during college, shuttling between classes and the exchange twice a day. It surely wasn't the money that made him stand in the sub-zero Chicago winters for the bus to work. What kept him coming back, he said, "was the same force that makes people turn on the same soap opera day after day." He wanted to see what was happening next. It was the constant change in the market that fascinated him and the sobering fact that indeed, there was order in this demolition derby.

The MidAmerica membership cost $1,400, and with a $400 stake he began trading in the summer of '71. He had planned to trade through the summer and then head south in the fall to New Orleans to attend Tulane University graduate school. His initial approach to the market was typical of most novices. He traded on hearsay. So it wasn't surprising that he promptly lost like most novices, blowing half his stake. But after a few weeks he settled down, and over the summer his market sense improved. By the time he left for Tulane, he had a $3,000 bankroll. He also had a classic case of commodities fever. After just one day at Tulane,

Dennis knew that he'd had it and that he belonged in Chicago on the exchange instead of in New Orleans in school. He awoke at 9:00 A.M. and a half hour later was on the phone to a New Orleans brokerage firm to find out how the market opened. He quit school that day and flew back to Chicago. Richard Dennis wanted to be a commodities trader, to return to the exchange day after day, to find out what was happening next.

A year later, averaging some 200 trades a day, swinging in and out of soybeans and corn during a hectic twenty-five-hour week, Dennis earned $102,000. By 1973 he had closed in on his first million, earning more than $750,000. He had made it bigger—and faster—than he had ever dreamed. Yet his newfound wealth had little effect on his life-style. A bachelor, Dennis continued to live with his parents on the South Side of the city, dressed in blue jeans and inexpensive knits, and drove a small imported car to work. He enjoyed visiting friends and talking philosophy rather than feeding his stomach at fancy restaurants. His friends said he didn't know how to spend his money, and it tended to pile up unused. He wasn't a Scrooge or a Shylock, and it wasn't the money that drove him—it was the *idea* of wealth. It was the way people perceived you when you had money, the way they deferred to you, the way they listened. Money gave you something more than status, it was a license to take potshots at the moneyed class, to declare open season on the system.

"It's really not for the money," Dennis explained to a reporter back in 1973, "but it gave me a kick to make six figures. Now I could make $5,000 a year for the rest of my life. Here's the thing. You can be critical of the capitalistic system and say: 'Bah, humbug! The system perverts people so they don't enjoy life. They should be chewing their food more instead of worrying about business.' But then someone can come back to you and say, 'You may say that now, but if you were making $50,000, you'd be living it up, too, and you wouldn't be talking like that!'

"There are so many people like this, who make big money and think it means something, think it gives them the right to speak as an authority on any subject. And, in general, I couldn't agree less with their opinions. I just wanted to be able to get up and say, 'I once made $100,000 a year and I still think you are an ass.' That may not be wholesome motivation, but I do think it's part of what drives me."

On one of his best days in 1973, Dennis earned slightly more than $30,000—a little better than $6,000 an hour. But there was a day, too, when he dropped $15,000. Fortunately there were more winning days than losing. By 1976 Dennis had moved from the MidAmerica to play in a bigger game at the Chicago Board of Trade. Already he was worth several million dollars. Dubbed Prince of the Pit by the press, he traded huge volume—300,000 bushels of soybeans at a crack—with unnerving ease. His life-style had hardly changed from the previous years. Today he wears glasses framed in gold wire, and his hair has grown a bit thinner— but not his net worth, estimated at $50 million. He is now in the business of trading other people's money through his own commodities firm.

9

Bellies, Bills, and Clout

Richard Dennis and the MidAmerica Exchange were proof that you didn't have to be a big shooter on a big exchange to make it big. The tiny MidAmerica, tucked away on the second floor of 343 South Dearborn, a few blocks from the Board of Trade, was a place for a person to learn trading skills while playing penny ante instead of table stakes. It was the exchange for the small millers, the small grain elevator operators, the small farmers, the small speculators, where contracts were one-fifth to one-half the size of those traded on the Board of Trade, Mercantile Exchange, and New York's Commodity Exchange, Inc. A wheat speculator on the Board of Trade, for example, had to trade in a minimum 5,000-bushel contract, but on the MidAmerica he could trade in a 1,000-bushel contract. And the MidAmerica could handle a 7,000-bushel hedge, whereas a hedger had to buy at least 10,000 bushels on the Board of Trade.

The MidAmerica had come a long way from its literally shaky start. Originally called Pudd's Exchange, the exchange was founded in 1868. It changed its name in 1880 to the Open Board of Trade because its members traded outdoors, shivering in the bitter cold at the corner of Washington and La Salle streets. In the twentieth century it had a new name—MidAmerica Commodity Exchange—and the new Dearborn Street location, across the Chicago River from the Mercantile Exchange in cramped second-floor quarters above an African art shop, a porno shop, a pawnshop, and a restaurant whose greasy odors of onions and french fries wafted over the trading floor where soybeans, wheat, corn, oats, silver, and silver coins were traded. There was also a washroom for members—upstairs on the eighth floor. In the 1960s the exchange had only 164 members and a net worth of only $164,000, including eight $25-a-piece cemetery lots that someone had bought for aging members who might need them. Like the other futures exchanges in 1973, the MidAmerica was flush with success, tripling its trading volume and more than doubling its membership to 600. In 1974 the exchange moved to more spacious quarters at 175 West Jackson Street, a few doors from the Board of Trade. Two years later membership had risen to 850 and a trading seat cost $7,000, up eightfold from the price in 1966. (Like a little brother wearing oversize hand-me-downs, the MidAmerica took over the trading facilities vacated by the Mercantile Exchange when the latter moved into its new building in 1983.)

Yet despite its growth and feistiness and the fact it could boast traders like Richard Dennis, the big boys on the Board of Trade looked down on the MidAmerica as a mere parasite, feeding off the droppings of the major exchanges. Its prices were keyed to the prices of the Board of Trade and Mercantile Exchange. As traders crowded around one huge pit facing a sprawling blackboard, platoons of clerks furiously scrawled figures from a flashing display tape that carried Mercantile Exchange and Board of Trade prices. A battery of direct-line telephones linked its trading floor to the Mercantile's and Board of Trade's, enabling members to deal directly. If a trade couldn't be executed on the MidAmerica, it could on the other exchanges. It also permitted arbitrage—a trader buying or selling the same quantity of the same commodity at the same time on two different exchanges. He can buy, say, for a quarter cent cheaper on one exchange and sell for a profit on another. Any way you looked at it in 1973, Chicago had a third futures exchange that the public was becoming aware of.

For a time the exchanges and their members reveled in their newfound celebrity. They had become a powerful economic force, one both the city fathers and the bankers courted and coddled. Whenever the City Council threatened to slap a business tax on the exchanges, they threatened to move to the suburbs and the

Council backed down. The big Chicago banks were eager to help novice traders get started and to keep the veterans going. The three biggest—Continental Illinois National Bank, First National Bank of Chicago, and Harris Trust & Savings Bank—usually financed a seat purchased with a loan carrying a floating interest rate typically 1.5 percent above the prime rate.

It was good business as well as goodwill on the part of the bankers. Among the city's three commodity exchanges and their members, they employed 6,000 people, with a payroll of more than $150 million a year, occupying some 2 million square feet of downtown office space. They kept $1 billion in operating funds and a minimum of $500 million in margin money in the downtown Loop banks.

If the exchanges were an economic force to be reckoned with, so were the traders. Now they were being looked at as a group of high-net individuals targeted for all kinds of bank services from personal loans to mortgages. The professional traders, the locals, had come a long way since the 1950s, when the grain markets generally fluctuated a penny a day and a three-cent move sent shock waves across the trading floor. Then a trader got the edge by buying at the bid price and trying to sell at the asked price, content to make an eighth of a cent, or $6.25, on a trade. With the bull markets of the sixties, scalpers looked for half-cent and one-cent moves. But that changed in the golden seventies. The dramatic price moves and dynamics of a world market were beyond anyone's comprehension. Commodity exchanges where you could once expect only to make a steady living, and sometimes just eke one out, were now the stuff of fast fortunes. A number of traders who had been living five-figure life-styles were suddenly flush with six-figure incomes.

They were the nouveaux riches. Their fate had been similar to the junk dealers in the early 1940s whose rusted scrapyards turned into pots of gold during World War II or the real estate dabblers who became tycoons in the severe housing shortage that followed the war. In spite of themselves, they had profited by a change in circumstances and were swept along by something huge. Many of the commodity traders in the early 1970s were also at the right place at the right time and were swept along.

Even those who hadn't made a killing found their net worths

considerably enhanced by the increases in the price of exchange memberships, which reflected the frenetic trading pace. On March 21, 1973, a seat on the Chicago Mercantile Exchange set a record when it changed hands at $125,000, then the highest price paid for membership on any commodity exchange. Just two years before, the same membership—ironically called a seat though traders stand all day—fetched $85,000; in 1964 it had been only $3,000. A membership on the New York Stock Exchange, in March 1973, sold for $80,000, down from the record $515,000 in 1969. At the Board of Trade the seat Paul Rosen paid $25,000 for in 1970 was now worth $65,000—and climbing. A decade later a Board of Trade membership reached $330,000, and on November 25, 1980, a seat on the Chicago Mercantile Exchange sold at an all-time high of $380,000. At the end of World War II, a time when markets were dead and wartime price controls still in effect, Board of Trade memberships cost a paltry $25. Some of the postwar memberships were given away—if you could find somebody willing to take one. Meat-packing magnate Oscar Mayer, Sr., had trouble finding a taker, recalled a former Board of Trade official. Mayer wanted to reward William Edgar, a veteran board of Trade staff member, for the good job he had done over the years. Edgar was offered the membership but politely turned it down because he didn't want to pay the quarterly dues of $100.

Like any other commodity, seat prices depended on supply and demand. The supply was fixed: 1,402 seats on the Board of Trade and 500 on the Mercantile Exchange. The price of a seat moved in direct proportion to the heat of a market. The best membership bargain in recent years turned out to be a seat on the Chicago Mercantile Exchange's International Monetary Market (IMM), which was launched in 1972 for the purpose of speculating in currencies foreign such as Swiss francs, Mexican pesos, and Japanese yen. All Mercantile Exchange members were offered IMM memberships for a nominal $100, and exchange officials had to twist arms to sell them. Two years later, when the federal government permitted private ownership of gold in the United States, the IMM started trading gold contracts along with the currencies. It was a great deal for the exchange members right off the bat. One hundred and fifty IMM memberships were offered to the public at $10,000. That meant an immediate profit of $9,900 to

Mercantile traders who had bought the $100 memberships. Regardless if you paid the public price or the insider price, you were a winner. Six years later on November 24, 1980, as gold was on its way to one of the most dazzling run-ups in history, an IMM membership sold for $280,000.

A membership was nothing more than a license to do business. The price of a seat bought you a badge with the initials of your choice and the right to buy or sell futures contracts on the floor of the exchange for a nominal commission fee of a few dollars instead of relying on a brokerage firm that charged as much as a $60 commission on some contracts. The more the trading volume and price volatility in the pits, the more the demand for seats. If the markets were active enough, a trader easily could make 80 percent of his seat in gross profits in the course of a year. In 1973 it was possible for the experienced trader to do it in a matter of weeks. Some did it in days; a few, in hours. The seat was like an investment in a gas station. If you could pump enough gas to pay for it, then it was a darn good investment. Once the overhead had been taken care of, everything you pumped was pure profit.

What the price of a membership really bought you, though, was a place in an exclusive club for aspiring capitalists, a haven for risk takers that was neither casino nor church but a bit of both. The exchange was a place where buyers and sellers struggled against the odds, totally consumed like slot machine zealots in Vegas, and an economic sanctuary, set apart from the harsh realities of the outside world, where money was held in reverent awe by a growing legion of younger, aggressive traders.

10

Prospecting for Players

Wall Street did its share to fire up the public's interest in commodities. It did so in order to survive. The stock market had turned sour. During the first six months of 1973 the price of an average share of stock traded on the New York Stock Exchange fell 25 percent, and on the American Stock Exchange an average share lost 31 percent. The popular stock market index, the Dow Jones Industrial Average, had hit an all-time high of 1067.20 on January 11, 1973. By July 9 the average had sunk to 863.94, a drop of more than 200 points. The number of shares traded on the exchanges had also dropped sharply, indicating a lack of trading interest. People were looking for other places to invest their money.

They first began eyeing commodities in the wake of the 1969–70 recession, when the stock market also fizzled. As commissions from stocks dried up, brokerage houses that traditionally shied away from commodities saw this untapped source of commission income as an oasis in the desert. Stockbrokers, who had always shunned commodities either because they were too volatile or because of the market's crapshoot image, gave wheat, soybeans, cattle, hogs as much status as stocks lost.

Since commodities involved less paper work than stocks, some brokers were able to net 30 to 40 percent before taxes. Commodity transactions involved no costly transfers and custodianships of stock certificates, the bookkeeping was simple and relatively cheap, and the turnover was fast and furious. One brokerage economist figured that ten good commodity accounts yielded more profit than 1,000 average stockbrokerage accounts.

The Bull of Wall Street, Merrill Lynch, Pierce, Fenner & Smith Inc., which had promoted stocks harder and more successfully than anyone, set up one of the most modern and complete commodity brokerage operations to be found anywhere. The firm's commodity department included a specialist as well as an analyst for each of the then twenty-five actively traded commodities, a separate technical analysis department, and a private commodity news wire service to Merrill Lynch branch offices worldwide. And plenty of promotion. During 1972 the brokerage house sent out more than 75,000 pieces of direct mail a month soliciting new business. The result: more than 42,000 active new leads for its rapidly growing ranks of commodity brokers. Other brokerage houses followed Merrill Lynch's lead, but none with the same vigor.

As the brokerage houses geared up for more business so did the exchanges. They spent millions of dollars on literature and advertising to alert the public. And just like any new business in which demand was booming, they served up new products, which, in turn, lured new players. From 1951 through 1967 the Board of Trade had produced only one new contract, choice steers. (By 1973 they were no longer actively traded.) In the next five years it brought out four contracts: silver, iced broilers, plywood, and stud lumber. Then, in 1973, the Board of Trade opened an entire new market for an entire new set of traders, the Chicago Board Options Exchange (CBOE), to trade call options on stocks (calls are rights to buy 100 shares of a stock at a pre-fixed price within a specified time period).

The Board of Trade had been registered with the Securities and Exchange Commission (SEC) since 1935 but had never exercised the power to trade in securities. It embarked on its options venture only after the SEC had pressured it to exercise the power in its charter or to relinquish it. The timing was right. In the late 1960s commodity prices were depressed and trading volume was sagging. (Dollar volume had topped $80 billion in 1966 and drifted to $34 billion in 1968.) The architect of the CBOE was a then thirty-two-year-old boyish-looking Joseph Sullivan who came to

Chicago from Washington, where he had spent seven years covering Congress for the *Wall Street Journal.* In Washington he met an administrative aide to President Lyndon Johnson, Henry Hall Wilson, who was named president of the Board of Trade in 1967. Wilson hired Sullivan as an assistant with the task of finding new markets. After five years and $2.5 million spent on research, the CBOE opened for business on April 26, 1973, in the old smoking room next to the Board of Trade trading floor. Three years later there were 1,300 CBOE members (about 300 traders were members of both exchanges) in a new $3 million space half the size of a football field. A membership was worth $75,000—a 650 percent increase in three years.

A year before the CBOE opened for business, the Mercantile Exchange started its International Monetary Market. If anyone knew the importance of diversification to keep the exchanges alive, it was the boys at the Merc. The Chicago Mercantile Exchange was an outgrowth of the Chicago Butter and Egg Board, formed in 1898, which initially had evolved from the Chicago Produce Exchange established in 1874 to provide a market in eggs, butter, and poultry. The Butter and Egg Board became a futures market in 1919 and changed its name to the Chicago Mercantile Exchange, with the first trade taking place December 1. Shortly after World War II the Mercantile Exchange's butter-and-egg business dwindled because of changes in the production and marketing of these commodities. Trading was so slow that at times two cantors, who were members of the exchange, would stand at either end of the cavernous trading floor, projecting their voices in deep baritone chants in preparation for the Jewish High Holidays. Obviously the Merc traders could not live on eggs alone.

From the fifties on, exchange officials began serving up a smorgasbord of futures contracts that eventually touched all of us, from the food we ate to the shelter over our heads to the worth of our money. If one commodity failed, they never hesitated to move on to another. For the traders at the Merc necessity did indeed become the mother of invention. Almost overnight the "butter-and-egg exchange" turned into a speculative merry-go-round for onions, scrap iron, frozen shrimp, frozen broilers, hides, and apples—all of which failed to succeed for one reason or another. But for every loser there was a winner that included frozen pork bellies (1961), live cattle (1964), live hogs (1966), lumber (1969), yellow grain sorghum (1971). The list grew longer in the seventies and into the eighties to include contracts on foreign currencies, Eurodollars, and financial instruments such as government bonds, treasury bills, and even something as intangible as a stock-market index. All the prospecting has paid off as trading volume in 1971 on the eleven U.S. futures exchanges grew from 14 million contracts to a record 149 million in 1984. And with every new futures contract you can almost hear the numbers clicking in the minds of exchange officials and brokers who hope that it will create a kind of domino effect of speculation among the public.

11

The Ultimate Commodity

American humorist Will Rogers understood what made the exchanges run back on April 26, 1928, when he was the keynote speaker at the dedication of the then new Chicago Mercantile Exchange building, built by the butter-and-egg men. "You can buy eggs on this market the same as you can buy General Motors stock," he wryly observed. "So, get you some eggs and hold 'em. Somebody will eat 'em. If you can't pay your cold storage bill, hardboil 'em and sell 'em for picnics."

The commodity exchanges have always operated on the Machiavellian rationale that anything goes if it works. The one cardinal rule for survival: Does it work? If trading in a commodity is too thin to furnish a market, it simply dies of its own volition. But it lives if the market is there. Just ask one of those Mercantile onion traders who used to buy and sell the sacks when they became worth more than the onions in them. Learning the rule took longer for some exchanges than for others. After a century of dealing mainly in contracts for hard red winter wheat, the Kansas City Board of Trade started trading stock index futures in 1982, as did the Mercantile Exchange and the New York Futures Exchange, a spin-off of the New York Stock Exchange.

However, it was the Mercantile Exchange—a decade earlier—that had opened the Pandora's box of so-called financial futures with its International Monetary Market. A key figure in the IMM was Leo Melamed, a wiry, chain-smoking dynamo of a man who had joined the Merc in the early 1950s as a $25-a-week runner for Merrill Lynch.

Swarthy, with coal black hair and the intensity of a tight-coiled spring, Melamed bore a slight resemblance to Edward G. Robinson. He was a mover, a man on the go, described by a close associate as the only person he knew who could pass you in a re-volving door after you had stepped in first. Melamed was the leader of a group of dissidents known as the Young Turks who consolidated their control over the Mercantile Exchange board of directors in 1969, when he became chairman. It was an insurrec-tion that took planning and time, and it was carried out covertly through an organization known as the Broker's Club, a band of twenty young traders.

The Broker's Club was all cloak and no dagger. Twice a month the group would meet at a room in the Bismarck Hotel, a few blocks from the exchange, to plan strategy. The exchange was still suffering from the stigma of its shoddy onion-trading image; the Old Guard had to be overthrown. Melamed explained: "The repu-tation of the Mercantile Exchange was almost beyond help. But the worst crime of all was the lack of a mechanism for the ex-change members to be heard. No ideas could filter to the board. As traders we felt we had a stake in the future direction of the ex-change. We still couldn't believe that Congress had actually legis-lated the end of a free market with the ban on onion trading."

The board of twelve men, whose average age was in the sixties, mainly consisted of the sons or grandsons of the Merc's founders. The exchange had always been controlled by a small group of powerful, successful traders. In the early onion-trading days, it was the Highland Park Six, a clique of traders who lived in the posh and secluded northern lakeshore suburb of Highland Park. But the Broker's Club was different. It was out not to grab power but to change the power structure that seemed to be strangling the exchange. The first change had to be in the quorum requirements for the exchange annual meeting. The Young Turks wanted to re-duce the quorum from 300 members to 100 members. Since a quo-rum was never present at the annual meeting, the board could act at will with no opposition from the members. With the help of Ken Birks, a respected Merrill Lynch broker and Melamed's former boss, enough proxies from the out-of-town membership were gathered to change the quorum rule. The second victory came with the election in 1967 of a new chairman, Robert J. O'Brien. Although O'Brien was not one of the Young Turks, he was closely allied with them. It was during his administration that the exchange committees were restructured and given power. If a committee's recommendation to the board was turned down, it could now call for a referendum among the exchange members. There was now a democratic forum at the exchange. And among the traders Melamed was elevated to a kind of folk hero status. In the very next election he was elected chairman.

Melamed's rebels had broken the hold of the butter-and-egg crowd, the older members who were reluctant to trade in such unstorable items as live cattle and live hogs. Diversification was the key to growth, and Melamed knew it. In the coming years he was relentless in pursuing this end.

At thirty-seven Melamed was one of the youngest chairmen in the Merc's history. His rise reflected the new Horatio Algerism that was beginning to take hold on the exchanges. Melamed was exactly what the Mercantile Exchange needed. He knew something about both commodities and survival. In 1939, when he was seven, Leo and his parents fled the Russian pogroms and German blitzkrieg. They were one step ahead of the Nazis, who had gathered up Bialystok's Jewry, including Leo's grandmother and aunts, and burned them alive in the synagogue. After a Dr. Zhivago type of train ride across Siberia the Melameds ended up in Vladivostok and from there went to Japan. In 1941, just before Pearl Harbor, they fled again, heading for the United States. The family settled on Chicago's Northwest Side, where Leo's father taught Hebrew and Yiddish (*melamed* means "Hebrew teacher") at a parochial school.

Those early years left Leo skeptical, wary, and somewhat superstitious. He calls it the Bialystok Syndrome: Disaster is always around the next corner, and you invite it when you begin bragging about your success. That was why one time early in his career he sent out hundreds of letters to friends and colleagues around Chicago, excusing himself for sounding bombastic in a local newspaper feature about his trading exploits. His superstitious nature—common among many traders—continues despite his

71

background in human behavior. Fascinated by the psyche, Leo was graduated from the University of Illinois with a degree in psychology and, at twenty, returned to Chicago to enter John Marshall Law School. To help finance his legal education, he drove a taxicab and worked in the catalog warehouse of Montgomery Ward & Company. But it was the job as a runner on the Mercantile Exchange that set his course. While still at law school, he borrowed $3,000 from his father and bought a seat. He formed a law partnership in 1959, and for the next six years he was attorney and trader. In 1966 he gave up law to become a full-time trader and was elected to the board a year later. Melamed's quick rise to exchange leadership was due, in good part, to the fact that as a lawyer he could articulate ideas with convincing ease. That, coupled with a thick-skinned aggressiveness, meant it wasn't long before Melamed had sold the boys at the Merc on the idea of trading the ultimate commodity—money.

12

Us Against Them

Selling the idea of the International Monetary Market to the rest of the world proved to be more difficult. The stodgy and aloof banking community in the United States and abroad wasn't about to let the pork belly men become the Gnomes of Chicago. Desegregate one of the world's most exclusive financial clubs? Sorry, old boy, said the bankers with sniffs.

Prior to the IMM there was only one way for importers, exporters, multinational companies, banks, and others engaged in international business to hedge foreign exchange risks. This was in the forward market, a small, secretive, and well-organized group of large banks and foreign-exchange dealers in the world's major money centers of New York, London, Paris, Frankfurt, Zurich, and Tokyo who dealt with each other through an elaborate, worldwide telephone-teletype network, exchanging hundreds of billions of dollars annually. Individuals who wanted to speculate in currencies were generally barred from the forward market, although there were no laws prohibiting private speculation. The Federal Reserve Board and the overseas banks they dealt with exerted informal pressure to prevent private speculation because of its potentially disruptive impact on exchange rates.

Renowned University of Chicago economist Dr. Milton Friedman found out about that pressure one autumn day in 1967, when he telephoned a Chicago bank with a moneymaking scheme in mind: to sell short $300,000 worth of British pounds sterling with the idea that Great Britain was about to devalue its currency. To his dismay the bank refused to accept his order even though he was prepared to pledge $30,000 in cash as a security deposit for the transaction. Undaunted, Friedman contacted two other banks with the same proposal. Undaunted, the two banks also politely but firmly refused. For Friedman it was a bitter and frustrating refusal because three weeks later, just as he had predicted, Britain devalued the pound by a hefty 14.3 percent to $2.40. Had the banks allowed Friedman to sell short, he would have more than doubled his money. Subsequently that experience would gain the IMM a much-needed friend in Milton Friedman, the quintessential champion of free enterprise destined for a Nobel Prize in economics a decade later.

It was around this time Merc president Everette B. Harris began scouting for an economist who could help promote the exchange and create new contracts. A strapping, slightly citified country boy from Norris City, Illinois, fond of banker's pinstripes, Harris could chortle a homespun "naw" in one breath and whisper a patrician "indubitably" in the next. At ease slapping the back of a trader or pressing the flesh of a politician, he was a smooth-talking raconteur who could churn out the charm like honey—thick and sweet—with an instant quip, a sturdy handshake, and a meandering homily on economics. His friends saw him as the last *gentle* man in a cutthroat age, the ideal front man willing to work efficiently behind the scenes without grabbing the limelight for himself. At fifty-three he was a hardened veteran of the commodity wars. In the fifties he had fought tooth and nail with the men on Capitol Hill in a valiant—but losing—battle to save the doomed onion futures market. But in 1965 he scored a big victory, pushing through his idea of trading futures on live cattle. Like any trader, he had his winners and losers.

Harris was a scrambler by nature. During the Depression he worked at a number of odd jobs to get through the University of Illinois in 1935 with a degree in economics. Then with a political assist from one of his father's friends he got a job with the U.S. Agriculture Department shortly after leaving school and rose during the World War II years to become the Chicago region administrator of the U.S. Labor Department. After the war he earned an M.B.A. from the University of Chicago, and in 1946 he left government service for an executive's desk at the now-defunct Mandel Brothers' department store chain in Chicago. But Harris and retailing didn't get along, so he began nosing around the Board of Trade, which was beginning to stir after the long hiatus of the war years. He joined the board in a staff position in 1949, and by 1953 he was executive secretary. In 1953 he moved to the smaller but feistier Merc, where he reigned for twenty-five years. The Merc was trading 250,000 contracts a year when he took the helm, and in 1978, when he retired, volume had swelled to more than 9 million contracts.

Harris's search ended with Dr. Mark Powers, a thoughtful and articulate thirty-one-year-old University of Wisconsin economist who had written his doctorate dissertation on pork belly futures. One of eleven children who had grown up on a Wisconsin dairy farm, Powers had a deep understanding of agricultural commodities. But over their first lunch together Harris looked Powers in the eyes and told him to forget about pigs and cows and to think gold and currencies. Changes in the world currency system were in the wind, and the Merc wanted to be ready to take advantage of them.

Powers was hired in 1969 as the first professional economist at any futures exchange. He immediately set about looking into the idea of trading futures based on money instruments, a concept he remembered from his college textbooks. His research included a casual call to Milton Friedman to get his ideas on the subject. Powers couldn't have found a better brain to pick—or a more sympathetic one when it came to currency speculation.

While Powers was doing his spadework, a bit of international monetary mumbo jumbo was taking place that would eventually play a crucial role in the IMM's future. In early 1971 tremors from a series of monetary crises were jarring the world's economies. The shadowy international currency speculators—whoever they were—mounted a massive attack against the already bruised dollar by shifting sums of huge amounts into stronger currencies, notably the West German mark and Japanese yen. To keep the values of their own currencies from rising beyond the fixed price "ceiling" set by the 1944 Bretton Woods agreement, West Germany and Japan were forced to sell unlimited amounts of marks and yen for dollars, amassing between them nearly 24 billion U.S. dollars.

As banker of the world the United States was learning a painful lesson: the vicious monetary cycle built into the Bretton Woods system. The nation was caught in an economic anomaly. The more currency it spent, lent, or gave away, the more the global economy became lubricated. But the more currency floating around the world, the less confidence other nations had in it and the sooner an international financial crisis was likely to occur. Unable to take the pressure any longer, West Germany and Japan cut their currencies' moorings to the dollar and allowed the mark and yen to float—to fluctuate in value in response to economic influences. In floating their currencies, the countries were in direct violation of the rules of the International Monetary Fund, the supranational agency that was the watchdog over the Bretton Woods agreement. Suddenly it was monetary anarchy and every country, including the United States, for itself. The entire system was collapsing.

On August 15, 1971, President Richard Nixon stunned the international financial world by announcing the United States would no longer honor its pledge to exchange gold for foreign-held dollars. The reason for such drastic action: In the first six months of the year the United States had reached an all-time record deficit in its balance of payments of $11.6 billion. That amount was more than the value of all the gold left in Fort Knox.

Four months later finance ministers of the leading industrial nations met in Washington's Smithsonian Institution to scrap the Bretton Woods agreement and hammer out a new agreement. It was give-and-take all around. The United States agreed to devalue the dollar by raising the official price of gold from $35 an ounce to $38 an ounce. That meant, in effect, that an American would pay more for a Volkswagen, a German would pay less for a roll of Kodak film. More U.S. goods would be sold overseas, and fewer foreign articles would be bought by Americans, thereby improving the U.S. trade balance. For their part, the other major industrial nations agreed to adjust their currencies upward, making them worth more in relation to the battered dollar. The financial tune-up was designed to relieve pressure on the dollar in its reserve-currency role.

The ten finance ministers also decided to permit the exchange rates of the world's major currencies to fluctuate against the dollar by 2.25 percent above or below the official exchange rate—a total of 4.5 percent, instead of the 2 percent total fluctuation previously allowed under the Bretton Woods system. Almost unnoticed among all the other historic monetary moves, this agreement caught the scent of the boys at the Merc, who reacted to it like a pride of hungry lions on the prowl. All the time they were doing the groundwork for establishing the IMM, they weren't fully convinced it was a viable concept because of the narrow price fluctuations allowed currencies. Now the wider range had set the stage for some decent price action from a trader's standpoint.

The timing was perfect. That summer Harris had telephoned Milton Friedman at his summer retreat in Vermont, persuading Friedman to meet him and Melamed in New York to discuss the IMM. The three of them spent two days trading ideas at the Waldorf-Astoria. Harris and Melamed were sellers; Friedman was the reluctant buyer. In effect, the two relentless salesmen were asking Friedman to put his reputation on the line. The exchange needed credibility, someone with stature and impeccable credentials who could give the IMM a stamp of approval. Friedman bought. But it wasn't because he had succumbed to salesmanship. The time was right for an IMM, he believed. In light of what was going on in the world's chaotic monetary markets, now more than ever the financial community needed a way to hedge currency fluctuation risk. The problem was clear. So was the solution. For a nominal $5,000 fee, Friedman agreed to write a study on the subject. To this day that $5,000 stands as the best investment ever made by an exchange. It spawned a multibillion-dollar industry in financial futures, the markets of the eighties.

13

The Legacy

Friedman's study was released in December 1971, just at the time the finance ministers were huddled at the Smithsonian Institution, trying to sort out the world's monetary mess. He did not produce a major treatise with hundreds of pages loaded with footnotes and a mile-long bibliography. Friedman said all he needed in only eleven pages he soberly titled "The Need for Futures Markets in Currencies." "Bretton Woods," Friedman wrote, "is now dead." He looked at the series of monetary crises that had shaken the world's economies that year and saw two things clearly: Although central banks would continue to set official exchange rates, a much wider band of fluctuation would be permitted, and official exchange rates would be less rigid and respond to much less pressure.

"The President's action on August 15 in closing the gold window was simply a public announcement of the change that had really occurred when the two-tier system for gold was established in early 1968," Friedman observed. "No one can be sure just what kind of a system will develop in coming years—whether the world will continue on a dollar standard or whether a substitute international standard will emerge."

Friedman was right. Almost at the same time the exchange officials were poring over his paper, news from Washington clattered over the teletypes. Just as Friedman had predicted, the ministers had permitted the wider range of fluctuations. Within two weeks the IMM received its charter to do business in the state of Illinois. The new exchange was set to open for business on May 16, 1972. And the Merc let the world know.

But even Friedman's warm blessings couldn't melt the ice in some circles. Major New York banks that viewed currency trading as the private domain of the banking community considered the idea of a currency futures exchange "too ridiculous to discuss" when Melamed approached them. Typical of the polite rebuke among the foreign bankers was a letter to Harris from Edmund de Rothschild of the great European banking family. Rothschild declined an invitation to attend the monetary conference sponsored by the IMM in February 1972, three months before trading was to begin. Rothschild's sentiment toward the fledgling exchange was obvious from his letter, which in part stated: "The extension of a futures market in certain foreign currencies could no doubt be of interest to small individual investors but, as you are aware, there is a very highly sophisticated international market for foreign exchange operations in which the major banks in the world participate. Banks are, therefore, able to offer their customers all the requisite services for futures trading in the major currencies and they are also able to arbitrage their own requirements with each other. . . ."

Another skeptic of the IMM's prospects was economist Paul Samuelson. He questioned whether the IMM could really offer users significant advantages over the current network of banks and money dealers. Samuelson went on to theorize that if the IMM proved successful, it could incur the wrath of both the U.S. and foreign governments by fanning currency speculation and thereby disrupting exchange rates.

On the day the IMM opened its doors for business, one New York bank foreign-exchange dealer told the *Wall Street Journal:* "I'm amazed that a bunch of crapshooters in pork bellies have the temerity to think that they can beat some of the world's most sophisticated traders at their own game."

The big Chicago banks, however, had a different attitude toward the IMM. They were friendly. But that was not out of sympathy for an underdog. It was strictly a matter of business. The Continental Illinois National Bank was the IMM's delivery agent;

the First National Bank of Chicago, an exchange clearing member through which the futures contracts were settled; and Dr. Beryl Sprinkel, a Milton Friedman protégé and senior vice-president and economist of the Harris Trust & Savings Bank, was a director of the IMM. A year later, after the IMM had begun trading British pounds, Canadian dollars, German marks, Italian lire, Japanese yen, Mexican pesos, and Swiss francs (lire were delisted in 1973. and Dutch guilders added, followed by French francs in 1974), some major New York banks were showing interest. Both the First National City Bank and Chase Manhattan, the number two and three banks in the nation, were doing business through the IMM.

The number of foreign-currency contracts nearly tripled from 144,928 in 1972 to 417,310 in 1973. Nearly 1 million contracts changed hands the next year. And when private ownership of gold was legalized on December 31, 1974, the IMM began trading a contract in gold futures that very day.

The boys at the Merc were on the fast track, and nothing could hold them back. Not even the red tape of the Commodity Futures Trading Commission (CFTC), the regulatory agency of the industry. In the winter of 1975 the CFTC refused approval of a newly proposed IMM contract to trade U.S. treasury bill futures. In the face of rising inflation and volatile interest rates, the time was right for trading such short-term instruments. Approval, insisted the CFTC, could come only from the then secretary of the treasury, William Simon. Once more Melamed and the exchange turned to their friend Milton Friedman for help, and once more he gave it. Friedman immediately got on the phone to Secretary Simon in Washington to discuss the matter. The contract was approved that day. Subsequently treasury bill futures became the most heavily traded contract on either the Mercantile Exchange or the IMM, with more than 5.6 million transactions in 1981.

At the IMM's tenth anniversary celebration in the summer of 1982, the guest of honor was none other than Nobel laureate Milton Friedman. Melamed, the aging Young Turk, summed up those early days in an after-dinner speech to an audience that numbered more than 1,400.

"Who were we?" he asked. "We were traders to whom it didn't matter whether it was eggs or gold, bellies or the British pound, turkeys or T-bills. We were babes in the woods—innocents—in a world we didn't understand. Too dumb to be scared. We were audacious, brazen, raucous pioneers. . . . Could the IMM have succeeded without the backing of Milton Friedman? I doubt it . . . his name was—and is—magical. . . ."

Currencies, gold, treasury bills were the legacy the Young Turks were leaving the new Gatsbys.

14

Pardon Me, but Is This Really Necessary?

Even the board games played in 1973 mirrored the frenzy of the new commodity era.

At Kroch's & Brentano's bookstore in downtown Chicago a new commodity game called Bull, Bears, N' Bellies had sold out by September, but Stocks & Bonds, a game based on the stock market, was long on supply. The venerable Parker Brothers, makers of the ever-popular Monopoly, found a new pocket of gold in a sixty-nine-year-old game—the oldest in its line—called Pit. Parker had come out with the card game in 1904, a year after publication of Frank Norris's classic *The Pit*, a tale of the wild wheat trading days on the floor of the old Chicago Board of Trade. Now the Parker people had repackaged Pit to include a front desk type of bell used to signal the start and end of trading. They also changed the description on the package from "The World's Liveliest Trading Game" to "Parker Brothers Frenzied Card Trading Game." In 1973 they sold a quarter of a million of the games nationwide. It was a sign on the times.

In the pits of the Board of Trade, the Mercantile Exchange, and the nation's other exchanges, the game was being played for real. While Paul Rosen and his fellow traders were basking in the glory of winning, the exchanges were turning slowly on the spit of congressional investigation. In the wake of the unprecedented price gyrations, the politicians in Washington wanted to know if the exchanges had merely served as gambling casinos with farm products and other commodities as the chips.

There was good reason for such concern. Farmers were upset and baffled by the wide gulf between the futures prices trading on the exchanges and the cash prices for on-the-spot deliveries of the actual grain. Normally the cash markets moved upward before the futures markets. But at one point they woefully lagged. And the usual 7-cent- to 8-cent-per-bushel spread between the two prices had grown to more than 60 cents on the average. In some cases it was a country mile more. When corn, for example, traded at $3.80 on the Board of Trade, the farmers in Iowa were offered just $2.38 a bushel in the spot market. The Chicago futures prices, exchange officials argued, were based on delivery in that city, and it was the freight costs of shipping the grains that accounted for the big price difference. But even at 60 cents a bushel, the critics countered, the difference in freight costs would not have accounted for the spread. Moreover, they noted, most of the farm products never even passed through Chicago.

Exchange officials mounted yet another defense. They pointed out that the massive grain exports had clogged the nation's railway network, blocking the fluid movement of crops from the grain elevators. The elevator operators were prevented from moving grain fast enough to accept new deliveries from farmers. Consequently, lower spot prices were offered at times of record future prices.

Consumers, too, urged their congressional representatives to jump into the centrifuge of criticism. They blamed the sharp increases in retail food prices on the speculators. But there was some evidence to challenge this contention. The markets were back in working order—that is, the cash price for *real* grain was moving ahead of the futures price. At one point in June 1973 soybeans for July delivery had sold for about $10 a bushel while the cash price for immediate delivery was more than $11. That meant more traders were selling futures contracts, thereby driving prices down, than were buying them. Thus, while supply and demand theoretically dictated that prices should go up, traders were holding them down.

Technically futures prices on the exchanges should not have directly affected the prices Americans paid for food. Why? Because the number of contracts traded on the exchanges are only a fraction of the total supply of any given commodity. The exchanges, however, do reflect the pricing risks already present in the economy. And those who don't use the markets still monitor the prices on the exchanges as a gauge.

Commodity prices, nevertheless, had slipped by a third from their August peaks. Yet, at the time of congressional hearings in late September and again in mid-October 1973, retail prices hadn't budged despite record harvests of corn, wheat, and soybeans. Exchange officials sniffed at the accusations that the markets had been manipulated by greedy traders and laid blame on the quirks of nature rather than on man for the run-up in food prices. The Board of Trade's well-oiled public relations machine kicked into high gear and churned out a booklet entitled *The Soybean Phenomenon.* It laid out the reasons why beans had zoomed to nosebleed heights of $12.90 per bushel, citing failure of the anchovy crop off the coast of Peru as a primary reason.

Testifying before the House Select Small Business Subcommittee on September 25, 1973, Frederick G. Uhlmann, then chairman of the Board of Trade, explained the bloated food prices this way: "The problem is the result of record worldwide demand at a time of shrinking surpluses at home. The buying spree that ensued can only be described as panic. Virtually every country of the world suddenly wanted to trade dollars, which were becoming less valuable, for food that was becoming more valuable, and the prospects of hunger only increased the eagerness of the buyers."

About three weeks later, on October 14, in his testimony before the same committee, Michael Weinberg, Jr., then chairman of the Chicago Mercantile Exchange, fashioned the defense in a more glib manner. "If an evil group of speculators pushed commodity prices to their recent highs," he told Representative Neal Smith, Democrat of Iowa and chairman of the committee, "then an equally good group of speculators theoretically pushed prices down the 35 percent that the livestock and other markets have dropped in recent weeks."

There was also a question about conflict of interest as a source of market manipulation. The conflict arose from traders wearing two hats, trading for their own accounts and as brokers for the public. They had the opportunity to "trade ahead of a customer"—to buy or sell for their own account when they had in hand a customer order that could be executed at the same price. It was impossible to police the situation in the pit unless someone sat on the shoulder of a trader.

The practice of dual roles was seldom an issue in the years prior to the Soviet purchases. There were often slack trading periods, and traders became brokers because there was not enough business. In 1965 the Securities and Exchange Commission eliminated stock exchange floor traders altogether to avoid conflict of interest. But there was a marked difference between the way stocks and commodities were traded and the function of floor traders. Stock markets were not used for hedging. Commercial firms didn't use securities to hedge against the prices of their products and services. Since stocks and bonds were purchased solely for investment purposes, the SEC considered everyone as part of a single class and sought to give every investor an equal chance by the ban on floor traders. In the commodities markets, as Chairman Uhlmann explained, "sometimes the flow of human bodies is vital" to assure a liquid market, where efficiency depends on the quick reaction of floor traders to mercurial developments in a closely related cash market. The message—for those who cared to read between the lines—was clear: The traders in the pits had the advantage over the public. They still do.

The exchanges had learned to live with criticism. Ironically, in 1848, the futures markets were created to protect the farmers. The posted prices on the exchange reduced the opportunity for middlemen to underpay farmers for their crops. While it may have kept the middlemen honest for a time, among the speculators who swarmed over the exchange floors it unleashed some of the tawdriest tendencies of free enterprise: greed; corruption; price manipulation. "The methods and techniques of manipulation are limited only by the ingenuity of man" was the way a federal court put it when it found the giant Minneapolis-based grain-trading company Cargill, Inc., guilty of manipulating the May 1963 wheat futures contract on the Board of Trade. From pesos to pork bellies and soybeans to silver, hardly a commodity has gone untouched by the hand of the manipulator. The number of documented incidents could fill a sizable bookshelf.

For better or worse, the exchanges can't seem to shake their rowdy reputation as indoor gambling spas where big spenders bet on commodity prices rather than roll dice (though traders love craps, too, as you'll later see) and where the traders and big commerical house brokers in the pits reap huge profits at the expense of the farmer, consumer, and public. To this day farmers are wary of the big-city boys on the exchanges. The exchanges spend millions of dollars each year going out into the heartlands to lure the farmers and ranchers with seminars on the fine points of hedging. Yet it is estimated that only one out of every fifteen uses the futures markets.

At times farmers have brought their gripes to the exchange doors. Blaming the futures markets, in part, for depressed farm prices, they rolled their tractors down La Salle Street to the Board of Trade in 1978. And in January of 1985, they picketed both the Board of Trade and the Mercantile Exchange in an effort to draw attention to their plight. Exchange officials told the farmers their beef was with the government and not them.

The exchanges were under attack from practically the first day they opened their doors. Reformers called commodity traders "merchants of misery," middlemen who stole from the farmer who grew the wheat and from the factory worker whose children ate the bread. Seven traders on the Chicago Board of Trade went to jail in 1876 after the Illinois legislature had passed a short-lived law that declared futures trading to be illegal gambling. By the late 1880s approximately 200 bills had been introduced into Congress to kill all futures trading or trading in one or more commodities. Extensive hearings, like those in 1973, were held, and the matter was debated, but despite the strong views of critics, Congress invariably decided against the abolition of futures trading. The reason all these proposed bills failed then and in subsequent years was simple: No one offered a better system to replace the futures markets.

The exchanges thrive on speculative risk, and about the only way to eliminate it would be to set a fixed price on each commodity by government edict. If you don't want government price-fixing, so goes the conventional wisdom, you must have speculation.

Risk taking has always been a part of American life. The very roots of America were based on a gamble. The thirteen original colonies were largely financed by lotteries, as were such schools as

Harvard, Yale, Princeton, Brown, Dartmouth, and Columbia. George Washington and Benjamin Franklin were staunch advocates of lotteries as a means of raising public funds. Agrarian Thomas Jefferson went so far as to endorse the lottery as "a salutary instrument wherein the tax is laid on the willing only." Today all but four states allow some form of public gambling activity, ranging from bingo to state lotteries. In a 413-page study a few years ago the National Gambling Commission reported that an overwhelming majority of Americans—more than 80 percent— regard gambling as an acceptable activity and that nearly two-thirds of the American people make wagers of one kind or another.

In view of our hearty appetites for a game of chance, it isn't surprising to find a gambling mentality among risk-oriented traders. "When I hear that trading bell ring," said scalper Rich Kramer, "I say to myself, 'Deal 'em.' It's a game." Ralph Peters, former chairman of the Chicago Board of Trade and a highly successful trader, admitted it a few years ago, when he told the *Chicago Tribune*, "It's like playing poker. But isn't all of life?" Administrative Law Judge George H. Painter best summed it up in 1976 in a ruling on a case that involved a group of traders on the Chicago Mercantile Exchange who cornered the frozen pork belly market:

> Futures markets perform a valid economic service to society, especially in the areas of price insurance and price stability, and nothing in this decision is intended to disparage that worthwhile function. There are striking similarities, however, between futures trading and pari-mutuel wagering. New money is not generated in the futures market. For every dollar lost on a losing contract, one dollar, minus commissions, is won on a winning contract. There is one winning contract for every losing contract. Winners buy low and sell high, or sell high and buy low. Losers do the opposite. The possibility of delivery on the exchange is the single element distinguishing futures trading from wagering. And to repeat, delivery is the exception, not

the rule, on most futures markets, including the Chicago Mercantile Exchange.

While no one was out to kill off the futures markets in the fall of 1973, the hearings caught the fancy of a growing number of influential senators and representatives who demanded more than a mild rebuke of the industry's inability to police itself. They saw the market machinery turning into some kind of monster capable of going on a lunatic binge without the ability to distinguish right from wrong. They wanted tighter control over the markets. "The system simply must be harnessed," insisted Minnesota Democrat Hubert Humphrey to the chagrin of his friends on the Minneapolis Grain Exchange. "It's like a train getting longer and longer and still being pulled by the same old tired locomotive."

Part of that "tired locomotive" included the Commodity Exchange Authority (CEA), a bureau within the Department of Agriculture, which then had jurisdiction over the industry but did little in the way of policing and disciplining. Desperately undermanned with a staff of 160—compared with the Securities and Exchange Commission's army of 1,600 to do its policing of the stock and bond markets—the CEA was as much in the dark about the futures markets and its players as was the public. CEA surveillance relied largely on reports from the exchanges and commodity brokerage firms, which tended to gloss over their own problems. Although the CEA had power to suspend or revoke the licenses of brokerage houses and brokers and to order violators to cease and desist from illegal practices, it was a reluctant enforcer. During the 1973 trading turmoil it only suspended the trading licenses of five floor traders and two firms for fifteen days to six months and issued fewer than a dozen cease and desist orders.

The Commodity Exchange Authority (critics said the title was a misnomer) was responsible for enforcing the Commodity Exchange Act, a federal statute that was confusing and disorganized. Nowhere in the statute, for example, is there a definition of *manipulation*—the very situation for which the statute was created in the first place in 1936. Nor did the statute even bother to define a basic futures contract. It left the defining up to the courts. (In 1978 the act was radically amended, but it still excluded the definitions.)

As it turned out, the exchange officials had put up a poor defense. Caught somewhere between smugness and despair, they had been too defensive. In fending off the congressional investigators, they admitted that indeed, some of the nation's futures exchanges were in the Dark Ages and that there had to be an overall agency to regulate commodities. "Once you've said that," Michael Weinberg later mused, "you can't be totally aggressive or on the offensive." By January 1974—four months after the hearings—no fewer than five bills had been introduced to strengthen futures trading regulations.

Eventually the bill that came out of the House Agriculture Committee (called the Commodity Futures Trading Commission Act) set up the Commodity Futures Trading Commission (CFTC) in April 1975, replacing the Commodity Exchange Authority. The CFTC's authority was extended to nonagricultural commodities. This newly refurbished commission promised to be to commodities what the SEC has been to stocks. But the CFTC has yet to gain the "full respect and confidence of the Congress or the other agencies with which it must work and compete," wrote former CFTC Chairman Philip McBride Johnson in his book on commodities regulations published in 1982.

It was also through the Commodity Futures Trading Commission Act in 1974 that Congress set the stage for a grab bag of exotic futures in the coming years by expanding the definition of a commodity. This was defined as anything "that is or becomes the subject of futures trading, intangible as well as tangible." With that scope, cat pelts could be back on the trading boards of exchanges someday. Or tulips. Or even jelly bellies. As for "intangible" commodities, they came on-line in 1982, when the exchanges began trading stock index futures contracts. It's like trading a fantasy because unlike a carload of wheat or $100,000 of treasury bonds, stock index futures can't be delivered. Speculators buy and sell contracts for the *imaginary* "delivery" of an *imaginary* portfolio of stocks at a fixed date. They hope to profit from the rise or fall of the portfolio's *theoretical* value, which is based on the movement of *abstract* indicators such as the Value Line Index of about 1,700 stocks, the Standard & Poor's 500 and the Dow Jones Industrial Average. As metaphysical as this may sound, it makes no difference to traders because the payoff is very tangible: the contracts are settled in cash.

15

Hyping the Future

Mike the Mad Russian dashed into the pork belly pit minutes before the opening bell, flailing his arms wildly like a man drowning. Clutched in his hand was a copy of the *Wall Street Journal.*

"Look," he intoned, "this story makes us sound like we're a bunch of crooks." Before anyone could respond, he reached into his pocket and pulled out a Lone Ranger mask and put it on. "I'm a highwayman, I'm a highwayman," he shouted, and proceeded to trade the entire day with his mask on.

Mike had been upset by a routine story out of Washington on the congressional hearings. The newspapers were following the commodity story closely in the fall of 1973, and some of the traders like Mike were becoming sensitive to the publicity. So were the exchange officials. It was around this period that the exchanges set out to do a little positive image building. They began pouring millions of dollars into public relations and advertising campaigns with the idea, in the words of E. B. Harris, that "business is show business."

Not surprisingly the Merc was one of the most aggressive in its ad campaign, hiring a small but highly creative agency to develop a series of clever, sassy advertisements. A typical Chicago Mercantile ad promoting trading in pork bellies showed a portrait of English philosopher Sir Francis Bacon with the caption "Sir Francis Pork Belly." Another Merc ad touting lumber futures even took a good-natured swipe at the larger and more somber Chicago Board of Trade with a picture of a two-by-four and the caption "The Chicago Mercantile Exchange presents the board of trade." In a more serious vein the Merc painted futures trading with a glossy coat of romanticism, likening futures trading to the last frontier. "Starting with little more than ingenuity, guts and the courage of his convictions, the frontiersman achieved incredible success . . ." the ad stated. It went on to assert that a commodity trader succeeded or failed on the basis of nothing other than his own abilities and that the "Chicago Mercantile Exchange is dedicated to preserving the spirit of the frontier." To round out this rawhide toughness, it might have said that a trader also needed a pair of leather lungs.

The ad hardly projected a modern image. But then Merc officials figured it was better to portray commodity traders as hustling pioneers rather than as hustling riverboat gamblers, the image already fixed in the minds of many.

The Merc wasn't exactly shooting from the hip with its ad campaign. It more or less had a feeling for its prospects. Outside the exchanges, then, who were the nation's commodity traders? An earlier ad in *Playboy* magazine gave the Merc an inkling when it drew some 900 responses. But the exchange wanted more specifics. So it did some marketing research. In a profile study of some 4,000 commodity traders, the exchange pegged a typical trader as someone between the ages of thirty-five and fifty-five with at least a bachelor's degree and an income of close to $20,000 a year. There were some 5 million people in the United States who fitted that description at the time, and according to projections, there would be 9 million such people by 1990. But only a fraction traded commodities.

The Merc study also showed that most of the commodity speculators lived in Illinois, California, New York, Texas, and Florida and were relatively new to the market; 73 percent of them had been trading for fewer than four years. It also showed the 70 percent of them had securities accounts as well as commodities accounts. The one thing that the study could not show, however, was the psychology of the people in the market, that fear-greed threshold that allowed them to take a risk during the day and to sleep at night.

The ad campaigns were only a small part of a giant effort to educate—and lure—the public. Meanwhile, the Board of Trade rewrote its jargon-choked commodity trading manual—to rave reviews. "Its lucid explanations and examples could go far towards breaking down the self-imposed mental blocks which frequently characterize the thinking of potential new participants in commodity trading markets," wrote one reviewer in the *Journal of Commerce.*

There were other educational efforts. The Mercantile Exchange, for example, cosponsored a Commodity Trading Institute with the Central YMCA Community College in downtown Chicago, where students could earn a two-year associate in business degree in commodity futures. It also offered a telelecture service to universities across the country, a telephone hookup between Merc spokesmen and the classrooms for question and answer periods. The University of Notre Dame even installed quote machines for Merc commodities prices for use in statistics, pricing, and M.B.A. courses. The Board of Trade set up its own school for prospective speculators, brokers, its staff, and government regulatory authorities who needed to understand the markets before they could oversee them. In addition, the board put together a series of lectures on cassettes while working with colleges to set up courses in commodities futures markets.

The combined push by the brokerage houses and the commodities exchanges was paying off. Although the number of commodity traders remained a tiny band compared with the number of shareholders (about 500,000 versus nearly 33 million), the dollar volume in commodities outpaced the dollar volume of all stocks traded on U.S. exchanges for the first time in 1972—$257 billion worth of commodities compared with $204 billion for stocks. The narrow gap widened into a canyon the next year. In 1973 commodity trading hit a record 25.8 million contracts, up 42 percent from 1972 and a startling 260 percent from 1962. The dollar volume doubled the previous year's, ballooning to $520 billion—more than twice the market value of all stocks traded. The thick-skinned aggressiveness of the Merc had paid off handsomely in the decade ended in 1973, when volume had soared 1,690 percent mainly as a result of the introduction of frozen pork bellies, live hogs, and live cattle, thanks to pressure from the Young Turks. The currencies had not yet taken off.

16

I'm OK,
You're Not

At the Board of Trade, Paul Rosen had undergone a change. As far as I could see, it wasn't for the better. There was a cockiness about him, a downright arrogance. You could see it whenever he entered the soybean pit to trade. Paul truly believed he had the golden touch. It was as if he had received some great prophetic vision that he could do no wrong. I suppose it was possible since Paul talked to himself. If you looked closely, you could see his lips moving every so often after he'd made a trade. He'd psych himself up with little pep talks, the way professional tennis players do whenever they miss easy volleys. They sort of roll their eyes upward and mumble insulting remarks to themselves. Sometimes it works, and they bounce back. Sometimes they crumble under the pressure regardless of all the self-flagellation.

With nearly $700,000 in his trading account, Paul had also become guarded. It stemmed from a certain shyness about wealth, from the fear that attention could bring a tax audit, and from the pressure that he had been right. In the pits those who were right got stronger and those who were wrong got weaker. It was social Darwinism at work.

Ego was also involved. Once you were right—and everyone knew it—you took on the pride of a samurai ready to challenge anything. Your mere presence in the pit forced some traders to stop and watch. But it was a double-edged sword: A big winner was held in awe by his fellow traders, but if that same winner suddenly became a big loser, it was a quick shot of confidence to those around him, a vivid reminder just how vulnerable traders really are.

No one knew how high soybeans were going in the spring of 1973. Paul thought he did. How high could beans go? Nothing ever went straight up. There were always market corrections, periods when things cooled off and prices drifted lower or leveled off. How much were soybeans worth? Was it $5 a bushel? Or $8? Or $10? Nothing seemed to make sense, except that Paul had nearly three quarters of a million dollars in his trading account. On paper he was worth a small fortune. And he was convinced soybean prices had reached their peak.

Paul was no longer a scalper. Nor was he a spreader, a trader who works two future months simultaneously—buying one futures contract, selling another—in order to cover the market movement up or down and thereby reducing the risk of loss. There is the expectation that the price relationships between the two contracts will change so that the subsequent offsetting sale and purchase will yield a net profit. This could happen, say, if the current crop of soybeans is in short supply but the next year's crop is expected to be large. Hedging, however, never fitted Paul's temperament. By reducing the chances of losses, he argued, you limit your opportunities for profits. Paul had his own trading technique.

Basically it boiled down to his watching the market and awaiting his conviction that he could predict which way it was heading. Then he took a position—usually a big one—and held it until his hunch proved right or wrong. Nothing scientific, just gambler's instinct. The second he realized he was wrong he'd get out to minimize his loss. Paul followed what some call the first law of commodity trading: Cut losses short, and let profits run. It is the most quoted maxim in the business—and the most ignored. The Commodity Exchange Authority had examined the trading activities of 8,782 speculators over a nine-year period, and only 2,184—25 percent—had made a net profit. The main reason for such weak performance, the CEA noted, was "the small speculator's characteristic hesitation in closing out loss positions."

The CEA study more or less confirmed what the experienced commodity traders had been sagely saying for years: The speculator who dies rich dies before his time. For even following the first law to the letter was no guarantee that losses wouldn't get out of hand. In a fast-moving market you could lose thousands before you got out. And even the seasoned pros get locked into limit-up positions for days on end. It happened to Leo Melamed in 1973, when he was trading Swiss francs on the IMM. To this day he shudders when he talks about it. He sold francs short, unaware that the United States was about to devalue the dollar for the second time in fourteen months. The Swiss franc had appreciated in value from the previous devaluation because historically it was one of the world's most stable currencies. On February 12 Washington devalued the dollar, and not long afterward the Swiss franc began to move higher. In fact, it kept going straight up, locking itself into limit-up position for ten painful days, painful for those, like Melamed, who were short Swiss francs. By the time the market cooled somewhat and Melamed was able to get out he had lost upwards of $100,000. "It was an awful hit," he recalled. "I had my tail between my legs for a long time."

That was the kind of market it was in soybeans, too. There was no time for a planned strategy in the 1972–73 fast-moving soybean market, only time to react. But it was with the tide, the flow of the market that moved upward. All along Paul had been a buyer, a bull on soybeans. Now he would go against the tide. Paul convinced himself that soybean prices were on their way down and that the other traders were far too optimistic. He began selling soybeans short when most everyone else, including the public, continued to buy them.

Paul sold 300,000 bushels of soybeans—sixty contracts—at an average price of $6.45½ per bushel. No sooner had he sold the last contract than the market proceeded to move straight up. As prices rose, he held on to his losing position as if he were paralyzed with panic. Four days later, when soybeans reached $6.95½, Paul got out of his position, buying back into the market with a loss of $75,000. That was only the first blow. The very next day he was back in the market, again selling short. He was indignant, single-minded, determined to be right.

Shortly thereafter Paul isolated himself from his friends and family as the markets continued to determine his schedule for living: up early because of anxiety; to sleep early because of mental exhaustion. He was angry and disappointed in himself for listening to his emotions. He had been trading on wishful thinking instead of on facts. That had made him more vulnerable to tips and rumors, which helped him justify his losing streak. There was total lack of trading discipline. Everything he had learned in the previous year and a half of trading now meant nothing. Eventually he turned his anger inward and became depressed, overtaken by a feeling of existential despair, the crumbling of his universe.

Somewhere along the way Paul's greed had exceeded his fear. When that happens, say the pros, a trader can never remain solvent. Paul was caught in the shifting market like a jet traveler soaring through three time zones, hurled into a kind of future shock—too much change in too short a period. There was a negative energy he just couldn't overcome. It seemed that whenever the market slipped a few cents, he was long, and when it rallied, he was short. He was being whipsawed. Paul no longer had a feel for the market; his timing was totally off, his edge lost in panic.

I ran into Paul one Friday morning in the trader's lounge, where he sat in the corner, sipping a cup of cold coffee. A cigarette dangled from the corner of his mouth. He had lost a good deal of weight in the two months since I had last seen him. A three-day-old stubble could not hide his pallid and haggard face, which seemed frozen in a perpetual pout. The eyes were mournful slits.

"I heard you lost a bundle," I said bluntly.

Paul took a deep drag and blew twin plumes of smoke out of his nose. He nodded. "You heard right. They got me. I got burned on those fucking beans," he said without once looking at me. "But I'm not out yet."

Knowing what I knew of traders, I wasn't surprised that Paul still had some fight left. There was something about the pits that grabbed a trader's mind and wouldn't let go. He sat there forlornly with the shame of a defrocked priest. His only sin was that he had guessed wrong. In doing so, he had lost a lot of money. If for nothing else, he had to make it back in order to recoup his stature.

Two weeks later the word on the floor was that Paul had taken another big hit. It was soybeans, sold short again. He had tried to make his comeback on a more conservative bent. In an effort to hold down losses, he traded for the first time with stop-order limits—that is, he set specific prices at which his contracts would be automatically liquidated and gave the order to another broker to execute. This way, he figured, if the market went against him, it wouldn't be disastrous. But as the price of soybeans continued to ascend, Paul became more irrational. Like a reformed alcoholic who suddenly jumped off the wagon, Paul began canceling the stop orders to avoid being stopped out of his losing trade. His Maginot Line of discipline crumbled; it was the beginning of the end. He found himself chasing the market again, trying to make bigger trades with the hope of getting even. This time he lost everything, including his Board of Trade membership, sold to pay off part of his losses.

Three weeks after his last trade Paul tried to commit suicide. Mentally he had done it long before. Through mutual friends I tracked him down at Weiss Memorial Hospital and paid a visit. That was the last time I saw him. Several months later I left Chicago for a job as a foreign correspondent. Paul, I'm told, is currently working as a stockbroker somewhere in the La Salle Street district, the financial heart of Chicago anchored at the south end by the stoic Board of Trade Building. Paul shucked his friends and past, maybe out of shame or a need to start new.

There is an ironic footnote to Paul's demise. As it turned out, he had been right. But his hunch was premature. Soybean prices did fall fast and furiously. They eventually peaked in mid-July and then plunged by a third in September, just five weeks before he bellied up.

Exactly what happened to Paul is impossible to say. That's probably for some psychotherapist to probe. Perhaps he had made it too fast and too easily and was feeling pangs of guilt over it. That feeling is not uncommon among traders. And, like Paul, a good number end up giving their winnings—and then some—back to the market. Why? It's a question traders are hard pressed to answer. Even the losers don't know. In any case, Paul's experience emphasizes perhaps the single most pressing problem among successful traders: the tendency to self-destruct. Richard Dennis realized it early in the game. "It is far more important to know what Freud thinks about death wishes," he said a couple of years after he had left the MidAmerica Exchange for the Board of Trade, "than what Milton Friedman thinks about deficit spending."

Paul didn't know from Freud or Friedman. All he knew was his passion for trading in a game too hard to walk away from once you tasted victory. That's why I wouldn't be surprised to find him back in the pits someday.

PART II

What Does It Take to Win?

Jeff: What're you so happy about?

Mutt: I'm happy because my business is so good!

Jeff: What business?

Mutt: My business! I started with ten bucks—I bought a horse! Then I swapped the horse for a motorcycle. Then I traded the motorcycle for a washing machine. I swapped that for a radio. Traded the radio for a car and sold the car for ten bucks!

Jeff: Ten bucks? But you didn't make anything on all those deals!

Mutt: Maybe not. But look at the business I done!

—Bud Fisher

17

A Psychic Battlefield

I have a friend who likes to remind me that there's logic in any economic system—if you want there to be. I think of that every time I observe the pandemonium of the trading pits, where hundreds of traders are wailing, writhing, wringing hands, and drumming heels on the floor. The scene calls to mind poet Edwin Arlington Robinson's definition of America: a sort of spiritual kindergarten where hundreds of bewildered infants are trying to spell *God* with the wrong blocks. But in that "playpen" the game is deadly serious.

For an anthropologist a commodities exchange could be a laboratory in the wild, the province of economic combat where winning, à la the late Vince Lombardi, isn't everything—it's the only thing. The pits are a psychic battlefield, where the open outcries echo the primal screams of the most ancient bazaars along the most ancient camel routes. . . .

Walk down La Salle Street, through the gray canyon of Chicago's financial district, on any early morning. Attorneys and bankers, with their attaché cases, and stockbrokers, with their *Wall Street Journals* tucked under their arms, are briskly but somberly heading for their offices. There is a quiet dignity about the street, a calm, steady flow leading to the august corridors of financial power, where dealing and haggling take place behind closed doors.

At the foot of the street, along West Jackson Boulevard, stands the Board of Trade Building, a forty-five-story gray limestone edifice built in 1930. Atop its pyramidal roof, a thirty-two-foot aluminum statue of Ceres, the Roman goddess of grain (designed by sculptor John Storrs), watches over the business kingdom like the divine eyes of Doctor T. J. Eckleburg staring out from a billboard in *The Great Gatsby.*

The revolving doors of the Board of Trade open onto low entrance corridors, flanked by shops and the Sign of the Trader, a popular watering hole for the commodities crowd, that lead into a three-story Art Deco lobby. It is a masterpiece of the period, sleek and polished surfaces finished in several varieties of contrasting marble that mirror a diffuse light cast from translucent glass and nickel reflectors. You hear muted conversations as people head for the elevator banks. The elevators fill up fast, especially the ones heading for the fourth floor, where the trading pits are located. As the elevator moves up to the second floor, there is an unidentifiable droning, a churning and muffled rumbling sound. At the third floor the sound is louder but still incoherent, like a chorus of moaning voices chanting a mantra. When the elevator doors open onto the fourth floor, the drone explodes into a frightening, tumultuous crescendo of noise: agonized, screeching human shouts, as if some cataclysmic disaster had befallen hundreds of people.

Here are the pits.

The pits are the mirror, not the cause, of a trader's complexity. Take a peek into the pit—any pit—and you see men and a few women with glints in their eyes, facing off only inches apart, set to do battle. With the bong of the trading bell, it's as if the "go" in the nervous system had been turned on full throttle. The traders flex their instinctive expressions—the smile, the grin, the frown, the fixed stare, the panicked face, the angered face—as the adrenaline pours into the blood pumping up the entire circulatory system. In order to reduce the chance of mistakes, most novice traders practice their moves in front of mirrors before they enter the pits for the first time. Some faces are red and openmouthed; others, white and tight-lipped. Some mouths are salivating; others are dry. Their jaws jut forward; their eyes narrow to the gaze of people at the limit of their endurance. The faces are mottled with exertion. These are the faces of war.

Traders lunge forward. Others pull back. Some bob and weave and sway as if they were caught up in a primal rhythm of some tribal ritual dance of seduction. And there are those who jump up and down to attract the attention of their demands like frustrated children pleading with adults to be heard. Aggression and fear, threat and counterthreat erupt with each one-eighth of a cent tick of a trade.

When buyer and seller clash, you see postures of threat and intimidation. "Every move to withdraw is checked by a move to attack," observed zoologist Desmond Morris of the aggressive nature of the "Naked Ape." "The intention movements have become stylized, the ambivalent jerkings have become formalized into rhythmic twistings and shakings. A whole new repertoire of aggressive signals has been developed and perfected." He could just as easily have been describing the pit.

Like the Light Brigade, the commodity traders charge into the Valley of Greed—the pit—with adversaries to the right and adversaries to the left, all screaming their lungs out. A trader's scream can hype the adrenaline and unnerve an opponent: It's all part of the trader's battle plan, a strategy of intimidation and aggressive one-upmanship.

"I work out my aggression on the floor," the Merc's Melamed once admitted to a reporter. That was an odd admission from a trader who has a poster on his office wall that reads: "Be a lover—not a fighter!—credo of a commodity trader." Aggression, of course, does not necessarily mean hostility.

The pits legitimize conduct that in other times and places is irrational. And in an era when people eagerly use personal computers for impersonal communication, the pits are an anachronism. They are alive with a physical and emotional energy that can't be programmed in a memory chip. "Trading is 98 percent emotional and 2 percent intellectual," conceded Ronald Manaster, a partner in Goodman-Manaster Inc., a commodities clearinghouse located at the Board of Trade Building.

Traders make up in grit what they may lack in gray matter. That's why there is sweat—a lot of it. It's the sweat of perseverance, determination, endurance, of the brow. But it is not the sweat rising out of the puritanical elements of human character, the sweat that built a nation, that prompted Thomas Alva Edison to define *genius* as "one percent inspiration and ninety-nine per-cent perspiration." And it isn't the jock sweat that soaks football jerseys and drivels down the legs of joggers and around the arms of tennis players. It's another kind of sweat, a "psycho" sweat pumped from the dark wells of anxiety, produced by depression, insecurity, bad news, bad tempers, bad luck, and broken dreams. It's a nervous sweat that soaks palms, foreheads, and armpits even in cold weather. It's a volatile sweat like the business that pro-duces it, a sweat that constantly reminds the trader that every-thing he does in the pit either takes money out of his pocket or puts it in. It's the sweat of fear.

"Essentially the successful trader has learned to cope with fear—primarily, his fear that what is wanted most—money—can be lost or denied," observed Richard Teweles in *The Commodity Futures Game.*

18

Pit Diplomacy

How about the untried trader, the neophyte who is about to step into the pit for the first time? He sweats a lot, too. A new man in the pit is like a fresh recruit sent up to the front lines. He knows the principles of combat and how to use his weapon, but until he has been in his first fire fight, he's nervous, unsure, scared out of his wits.

Jerry Michaels knows the feeling. He had been looking forward to that first day of trading in the Standard & Poor's pit at the Mercantile Exchange. He saw himself as a natural. And why not? Jerry was a supersalesman, his company's top insurance salesman nationwide. But the cutthroat insurance business had choked premium commissions to a trickle. He could always go back to insurance when the economy picked up. Meanwhile, he would try commodities. Michaels had all the confidence in the world and the size to go with it. A strapping six-foot-two-inch 240-pounder, he certainly would have no trouble being seen or heard. In fact, given his mass, he appeared to be a sure bet to bully his way in the pit. Jerry Michaels had not knuckled under to many people in his life. It was only after he walked into the pit, he says, that "It hit me." In soft, measured tones Jerry recalled: "Suddenly I felt very insignificant, scared, apprehensive. I was no longer confident. I had doubts. It looked a lot harder. I couldn't even understand what people were saying. It sounded like one blend of yelling and everything appeared chaotic. For me the pit was disorganized confusion." And when the forty-one-year-old Michaels looked into the faces of his trading opponents, "I felt old."

All that happened before he attempted his first trade. After a short time he regained his composure and even managed to overcome the self-consciousness that comes with that first outcry. He bought one contract from another trader. But in his anxiety Michaels didn't close the trade according to Hoyle. "I forgot to say 'Buy it!'" he recollected. That small oversight brought on the wrath of the surly trader Michaels had dealt with, a mean and nasty person, all five-feet-six-inches, 140 pounds of him. "You dumb son of a bitch," the trader roared. "Okay, sold!"

"He called me every name he could think of, the worst street language imaginable," Michaels said. "Then he told me I had no business trading here."

For the first time in his memory Michaels found himself taking verbal abuse, a tongue-lashing from a runt. A punch would have cost Michaels a $3,000 fine. But that's not what restrained him. Michaels gave in to pit diplomacy. As a pit newcomer he could not afford to make enemies. The only advice a fellow trader had given him before stepping into the pit was to make friends. If you happened to pick a fight with a trader, order filler, or broker who had a lot of friends in the pit, you could be ignored. So Michaels bit down on his lip and said he was sorry. He knew it was going to take time before he was accepted, before he could get used to his new life in the pits.

Some traders never get over the pit jitters. For two years Dr. S. Jeffrey Garfield traded on the Merc's International Monetary Market. And all that time he couldn't handle the pits. There was the tension and the nerve-racking speed of the markets to cope with. And there was the scalper's peculiar trading knack, always baffling and elusive to Garfield.

"I was extremely nervous," he remembered. "I used to stand in the middle of the pit. I'd look at the board and couldn't figure out what was happening. Scalpers are born, not made. Some can trade ten and twenty lots at a time the very first month they step into the pit. I can't write that fast or hear that fast. I'm not that quick."

Rather than enter the pits, Garfield stayed on the sidelines and traded through order fillers. At the end of two years, he sums it up,

"I didn't make or lose two thousand dollars." Even his timing was off when he sold his membership for $70,000 in 1977. The very next year in late October IMM memberships were selling at $165,000. "It was a lousy trade," he said with a shrug. "I sold that seat too early."

But Garfield, a psychologist with a thriving practice, didn't give up on commodity trading. He remains a serious trader to this day. That's apparent if you call his office before 1:15 P.M. The message recorder answers: "Hello, this is Dr. Garfield. I'm sorry, but I'm not available right now. You can reach me at this number during my regular working hours Monday through Friday afternoons. . . . I check for messages at nine A.M. and nine P.M. seven days a week. Thank you for calling."

Garfield, a slight, balding fortyish man with a statistician's mind, spends his mornings charting and trading commodities. In the late afternoons he counsels troubled persons. About half his clients are commodity traders of every type from every Chicago exchange. Garfield trades from a distance now, the scalper's life well behind him, somewhere in his psyche's catalog of shaky experiences. Up by five-thirty every morning and on the phone to check the currency markets around the world, Garfield is a position trader, a strict technician who copiously charts the ups and downs of commodity prices. On one wall of his office hangs a huge point-and-figure chart used to trade Swiss francs and other currencies. (Point-and-figure technicians record only price changes, unlike bar chartists, who record a commodity's price range, close, and volume.) But he had just closed out a two-month-long position in orange juice at the time I met him for an interview in his office located on Chicago's posh North Michigan Avenue. He still makes more money in psychology than in commodities.

Why do traders flock to him, shelling out $100 for a forty-five-minute visit? Because he knows them better than any psychologist or psychiatrist in the city. For more than a decade he has counseled traders: traders who couldn't handle success; traders who couldn't handle failure; traders who couldn't handle anything. Perhaps he knows them too well.

A solid oak-stained door opens to the narrow waiting room of Garfield's office. There are clues that he knows what makes commodity traders tick. Opposite the couch on the wall hangs one of those clever Chicago Mercantile ads, this one of a pig wearing sunglasses. The headline: GLAMOUR ISSUE. "The celebrity shown here," the ad copy says, "just happens to be the world's most actively traded commodity." In the 1960s and early 1970s pork bellies were the darlings of the pits, but that was before the advent of financial futures. On the table next to the couch was a rather odd assortment of reading material: a copy of *Real Men Don't Eat Quiche, Original Teachings of Ch'an Buddhism* and a couple of Garfield cat books. But two stacks intrigued me the most. One was a pile of *Playboy* magazines; the other, a heap of comic books. What were *Spider-Man, Conan the Barbarian, Captain America, Superman,* and all the other superheroes doing in Dr. Garfield's waiting room? Itching to be read, of course. Garfield himself is an avid reader of comic books, maybe forty a month.

"The most intelligent trader and the biggest money-maker I see both read comics," Garfield explained.

Before I could pursue the point further, the door to the waiting room opened and a client walked in. My forty-five minutes were up. The client was a scalper at the Board of Trade. Blue jean-clad and in his stocking feet, Garfield showed me to the door. Earlier I had asked him how cerebral successful scalpers were. He turned to the waiting client and asked, "Are scalpers bright people?"

"You have to be dumb to be a scalper," the man answered. "You have to be dumb."

19

Pit Culture

With psycho sweat comes psychobabble, a flurry of phrases—many with sexual overtones. Interestingly for a number of traders—both men and women—the market has a female persona. After all, it isn't mighty Zeus perched atop the Board of Trade Building, presiding over the commodity kingdom. It's Ceres, the goddess of agriculture, a mythical Mother Nature whom you don't fool around with unless you want hail on your soybean crop or worms in your pork bellies. There's a respect for this raucous and angry market lady, an awe for her sheer power that can turn a man financially impotent in the blink of an eye. Perhaps that's why photographs, sketches, paintings of the exchange floors and pits hang like pinup girls on the walls of traders' offices and homes. There is a love-hate relationship here. Like so many Sky Mastersons, traders want to woo Lady Luck and to conquer her, too.

"Traders try to make the market, like going to bed with a woman who won't submit," observed Jake Bernstein, a clinical psychologist, author, and seasoned commodity trader. "It's sexual. It's a macho thing."

For many traders the market is a "bitch," a "cunt," a "whore," an "old lady." Speculated one trader looking over his pricing chart: "She could give it another burst, but she's drying up." Every trader knows that you try "to get a leg up" when you short the wings "on a butterfly spread." Or you can "goose" the market, "massage" the market, "make" the market, "ride" the market, "hump" the market, "pump" the market, "squeeze" the market, "bleed" the market, "scratch" the market, "claw" the market, and "fight" the market. But if you "fight" it or "go up against it," chances are you'll be "screwed" by it or maybe "fucked over." If so, you'd better "pull out" fast. Or else it's "down the tubes!"

The market's female aura isn't just an outgrowth of the trader's fantasies or a spillover from the sexual revolution of the sixties and seventies. It's always been that way in the commodities markets. Frank Norris saw the sexual innuendo back at the turn of the century in *The Pit.* The market was something human then, too, something his hero could fondle and manipulate: "He could feel—almost at his very finger tips—how this market moved, how it strengthened, how it weakened. He knew just when to nurse it, to humor it, to let it settle, and when to crowd it, when to hustle it, when it would stand rough handling." In the end, though, Ms. Market won.

To be sure, the market is no primate; it doesn't nurture. From that first day in the pit, the birth of a trader's life, it's everyone for himself, young and old, man and woman alike. The floor of the exchange defies meritocracy as well as motherhood. Credentials mean nothing in the pit. Nobody cares if you got 800 on your Scholastic Aptitude Test or were a Rhodes scholar or were first in your class at Harvard. "The pit is a total equalizer. It doesn't care who you are or what you are," the Merc's Leo Melamed has said.

This equality even extends to the way traders dress. The dress code of the exchanges suggest a classless society, a culture without social distinctions, a melting of different sizes and shapes into the same uniform. A tie for men is mandatory, blue jeans are out, and everyone, man and woman, wears the unisex trading jacket like a uniformed student in a parochial school. The colors of the jackets may vary, but otherwise, everyone in the pit is a duplicate.

Former Chicago Mayor Michael Bilandic kind of summed up the pit's lack of meritocratic culture in 1978 at the Board of Trade's 130th birthday celebration. Standing before a cake five feet high and weighing 300 pounds in the shape of the Board of Trade Building, Bilandic sliced off a section of a yellow door trimmed in chocolate and marveled: "You have M.B.A.'s from Harvard, and you have people who walked in off the streets. . . ."

High school dropouts face off against doctors, lawyers, Ph.D.'s with an irreverence similar to that of the city editors in the old newspaper days who turned their noses down at graduates of journalism schools. Once I overheard a trader passing himself off as a Rhodes scholar. It turned out he was a former construction man who had spent a lot of time working on roads before working the pits. Then there was the trader who tried to muscle his way with his résumé and had a quick comeuppance. Knocked to the floor in the heat of trading, he locked fists and wits with his assailant. After the apologies somehow the exchange between the two touched on credentials.

"I have an M.B.A. from Stanford," he boasted.

"Big deal. So I'm a Ph.D.," the assailant shot back.

"In what?" the Stanford man challenged.

"In finance, man, what else?"

"Bullshit. I don't believe you."

"It's the truth. I'm a P-H-D: Parents have dough."

The pit culture ignores not only credentials but civilized amenities as well. There are no handshakes in the pits. Or thank-yous. Or pardon mes. Or you go firsts. There isn't time. Just a quick nod to seal a buy or sell. And not only do these adversaries trade buys, sells, and gibes, but they often trade jabs, too. Tears, sweat, and, yes, blood ooze from the pits as overzealous traders vent their aggressions and frustrations in hand-to-hand combat. They push, elbow, slap, punch, kick, bite, wrestle, step on toes, spray one another with saliva, and parry and thrust their pencils like sabers, jabbing a hand here, an arm there, and sometimes even a face—all in the name of communication.

"Vicious" is the way soybean trader George Seals once described the trading pit. "It intimidates me." It was a startling statement from a man of sequoia proportions who spent ten years living dangerously as a tackle in the trenches of the National Football League. Seals stands six feet three inches and weighs 255 pounds. The former Chicago Bear retired after the 1973 season with a medical chart of injuries that included missing teeth, knee surgery, shoulder separation, broken fingers, and severed nerves. But his emotions were intact. Seals—the first black man to become a member of the Board of Trade—gave himself three years to see if he could make it.

A decade later he was still in the pits. "I've learned not to be sensitive and that you can do everything right and still be wrong," he said in the den of his Hyde Park home on Chicago's South Side. From his surroundings and the Mercedes 450SL he drove, it looked as if Seals had been right more often than wrong.

Nevertheless, for a man used to teamwork most of his life, Seals's adjustment to the pits has been slow in coming. "I don't think I'll ever be comfortable in the pits," he murmured. "The whole business is an enigma to me. When that trading bell rings, it's every man for himself." And the battle rages.

Every exchange has its wounded veterans of the pit wars. In a pit about thirty feet in diameter with as many as 300 gladiators of high finance crowding onto eight narrow steps, anything can happen. And it usually does: close encounters of the unkind.

Laurence M. Rosenberg, former chairman of the Mercantile Exchange, has a black spot on his right palm where he was accidentally stabbed with a pencil. Harry ("the Hat") Lowrance, a Merc broker, cried once in the treasury-bill pit when another trader's pencil punctured him in the right cheek. He saw rage, blind rage. Harry, in fact, became so furious that a friend escorted him off the floor for the day because his timing was totally "off." Ron Morris still has a weak wrist from the time he landed on it. A female trader had grabbed Morris by the collar and swung him clear out of the pit—right after he had called her a bitch. From then on she was known as the ball breaker—but not to her face. It's impossible to tally up the bruised toes, shins, and ribs in the course of a hectic trading day.

But such injuries in the line of duty pale against what happened to Fast Freddy's finger. They called Fast Freddy the motor-mouth of the bond pit at the Board of Trade. To listen to him, you'd swear that he was a 33 record at 45 speed and that he probably should have been trading with chipmunks. In some respects many commodity traders are like chipmunks, a nervous, restless, and suspicious breed that survives by industry, has acute hearing, and is highly vocal. But to make matters worse, Freddy was a chronic *kvetch*, forever complaining about the market and the "rotten" trades he'd make. Naturally it was always the other guy's fault whenever Freddy was on the losing end of a trade. Freddy was the kind of person who got on almost everybody's nerves, a bore best summed up in three words: prompt, precise, and punctual. He was a walking compendium of market facts and figures, a chartist who had memorized dry statistics and could spit them out like a baseball trivia nut. He would analyze the market, project and use swing calculations, estimate point-and-figure moves, scrutinize divergences from one market to the next, and watch the shifts in open interest—the number of futures contracts outstanding—in order to figure out where the public stood in the market. Each day at exactly four minutes before the opening bell Freddy would haul out his charts for one last look. Then, with one minute and ten seconds left, he would put the charts away and begin to psych himself up with the verve of a professional athlete. "Think market," he'd tell himself, "gotta get into the flow." If it was a winning day, you could tell by looking at him. He would strut around and mumble, always in earshot of other traders, "I'm on top of the heap now." But when he was a loser, you could tell that, too. Freddy would lapse into "mellowspeak."

"I gotta get my act together," he'd stammer. "I gotta-gotta stay cool. Can't let the market get away. I need space. I gotta get out of here." And he'd disappear.

One day Fast Freddy did let the market get away. He was down nearly $40,000. In his frustration he lashed out against another trader. Freddy accused the trader of selling him five treasury bond contracts at a price higher than Freddy thought he paid. The difference in price would have pared Freddy's loss by $10,000. Haggling over mistrades is frequent in the pits and guarantees boiling tempers. First Freddy turned on the 45 speed, letting go a barrage of profanity capped off with the finger. Then he turned his back on the trader. The rebuffed trader rushed Freddy and tapped him on the shoulder. Freddy spun around in a paroxysm of anger and poked his finger in the trader's flushed face. The trader jerked his head back, paused, then lunged and snapped at Freddy's index finger like a chained dog that had been taunted by a sadistic child. He got him. The teeth sank right into the tip of Fast Freddy's index finger. No blood was drawn, nor did Freddy need rabies shots. But it hurt like hell. Swollen and bruised, his bandaged finger pained him for days. Never again did the two trade with each other. Fast Freddy, traders say, was never quite the same after that incident. He became a bit withdrawn, even docile, and reluctant ever to fight it out in the pit with a trader. But his mind still remained taut when it came to the market.

As Fast Freddy and the others will tell you, there are no friends in the pits, not when your house, your kid's education, and your beloved Mercedes are on the line. Clearly the force that binds the pit society together—indeed, all economic worlds—is self-interest. "You do not take prisoners in here," a trader who deals in gold on the Mercantile Exchange told *Esquire* magazine in 1981. It boils down to the simple fact that when a trader is right, he wants all that is coming to him for being right. But if he's wrong, sometimes he wants mercy. There have been traders who have fallen to their knees, crying like babies, begging for another chance or another ten grand to keep them going. "I can't take the fucking pressure," a burly pork belly trader once screamed, jumping up and down on the top tier of the pit. In another instance a frazzled cattle trader leaped into the middle of the pit, dropped to his knees, and began pleading with the heavens to end trading—and his painful losses.

"I'm losing everything. I can't lose any more. I'm going broke. Stop trading," he roared, his eyes rolling back toward the ceiling of the trading room for a zap of lightning to end the day. Trading, of course, continued. He, of course, went broke.

20

Pit Falls

When the going gets too rough, certain physical attributes help. Take height, for instance. A tall trader can have a definite advantage. That's what Jeffrey Greenberg found out trading gold on the Mid America Exchange. At five-feet five-inches Greenberg was sandwiched between two six-footers at the opening bell. Had he been taller, he reckoned, he probably would have ended up with merely a bruised chest. Instead, it was a broken nose. In the frenzy of a moment at least one of the men, and possibly both, accidentally elbowed Greenberg's face. Wham! Greenberg didn't even realize he had been hit until the trading day was over. Others came up to him to ask what was wrong with his nose. Nose? What nose? "I looked in a mirror," he recalled, "and it was all over my face."

The expectation of "making it" can keep a trader in the pit, concentrating too hard. And at times not even the call of the wild—or the call of nature—can deter him from opportunity. During the midst of a furious trading session in the Board of Trade bond pit, a trader actually defecated in his pants. It wasn't the result of a traumatic trading loss, but a loss in bodily control. The trader was so caught up in the action that he wouldn't leave the pit until the contracts he was holding turned a profit. Embarrassment aside, he stood his ground. Fortunately for those around him, he made his profit and high-tailed it for the nearest rest room. At least no one was hurt.

One afternoon in the Board of Trade's soybean pit a trader lay helpless with a broken leg at the close. He had been caught in no-man's-land, a point somewhere in the middle of two screaming walls of bodies hurling toward each other, firing off their last trades on the last bong of the closing bell. He wasn't discovered until the sea of bodies parted. Another time a trader passed out in the corn pit from an allergic reaction to some medication he had been taking. Not a tick of a trade was missed. The others continued trading around him until he was removed by the paramedics and given oxygen. No one is known to have died in a pit yet. But in recent years the exchanges have hedged that risk with paramedics and oxygen tanks on standby.

Some wonder why there aren't more injuries. At least every couple of days a trader on some exchange gets thrown out of the pit on his ear by another trader who has been pushed too hard or crowded. Territoriality is the law of the pits: I stay on my turf, and you stay on yours—and God help you if you try to inch me out. You really want to rile the sympathetic nervous system of another trader? Try taking over those few square inches on which he or she makes a living. Some traders have stood on the same steps on the same spots in the same pits for decades. Asked why he likes his spot, one veteran trader wryly quoted an old Chinese proverb: "If you stand by the river long enough, you will see the bodies of all your enemies float by."

Nate Feldman was certainly attached to his spot on the old trading floor at the Board of Trade. And when he died it was immortalized by poet and fellow grain trader John Dickson, who dashed off this elegy to Nate called *Immortality:*

> Five times a day
> Nate Feldman,
> ooh, ahh,
> massaged his piles
> on a
> round brass post
> at the
> Grain Exchange
> When he died,
> seven brass posts

were dull and corroded,
but Nate's brass post,
ooh, ahh,
shone as bright
as the
moon.

There are, of course, more practical reasons for finding a "right" place in the pit: to be seen and heard. In a pit jammed with shrieking bodies, the trader in the rear has to fight harder and use more energy and is prone to lose out on more trades than those in the center. He's like a patron in a seat behind a pillar in the upper balcony at a musical, craning to hear and see. Position in the market and in the pits is crucial. Speculating can be a hard and trying business, and if you're not on the job all the time—on your spot—you'll soon have no job at all. Some traders have even graced their spots with fanciful sobriquets. One trader fondly refers to his place in the gold pit as the G spot. A soybean trader calls his the sinkhole. Whatever name, those tiny claims staked out and held by squatters' rights can be the most valuable few square inches anywhere on earth.

Just ask those brokers who sent their faithful runners down to the Board of Trade at 6:00 A.M.—nearly two and a half hours before the opening bell—in December 1981 and January 1982. Interest rates were climbing, and the treasury bond pit was a wild roller-coaster ride with limit-up moves. To ensure an advantageous spot in the pit, the runners were ordered to find places and hold them until the brokers arrived. Possession of a spot is nine-tenths of pit law, and most abide by it.

"I was the new kid on the block," recalled Erika Lautman. "I didn't want to fight, but I made it clear I wasn't going to move." It was April 22, 1982, the first time she stepped into the pit to make her first trade. "You could feel how territorial it was."

You could also feel the masculinity. At the time Erika was twenty-seven and one of fewer than 10 women in the Merc's treasury bill pit packed with some 250 hungry traders. "I felt stark naked," she said. "There is a lot of intimidation." All of her pert five-foot-three-inch body began to shake, and her voice quavered with fright.

"What's wrong with your chest?" the trader next to her asked. Erika swallowed hard and looked down at her open neckline to see huge red blotches creeping up from her chest. Nerves, opening day jitters: Call it what you want. The result was the same: a bad case of hives.

There was a guy who kept telling her to move, a trader with whom she will never do business again. But Erika stood her ground. By the end of her first day she had bought and sold twenty treasury bill contracts, chalking up a profit. Her shaking had stopped, and the hives were gone, too. But the very next day in the gold pit nobody would trade with her, "just to give me a hard time," she said. That kind of snub didn't last long, however. It never does, Erika found out, as long as someone in the pit thinks he can make a profit off you.

"One of the things that greed does is blind you to things," she said. "It makes no difference, you'll take it [a profit] from anybody whether it's a man, woman, hunchback, blind person."

A few years ago, in fact, there was a blind trader in the corn pit at the Board of Trade. He'd stand in the pit with his Seeing Eye dog and an assistant who would quote prices. He'd buy and sell, screaming with the best of them. Obviously, in the pit a twenty-decibel voice is more important than twenty-twenty vision or no vision at all. the voice is the trader's most important asset, and if it gives out permanently, he may as well turn in his badge and hang up his trading jacket. Laurence Rosenberg, a former chairman of the Chicago Mercantile Exchange, once had polyps removed from his vocal cords. The doctor told him the polyps had come from abuse. Rosenberg was more fortunate than Steve Peterson, who traded at the Chicago Board of Trade for five years before he was forced to leave because of voice and hearing problems.

Some traders pop as many as fifteen cough drops in a four-hour trading session to keep their throats lubricated, but that doesn't prevent those red, painful, blisterlike little nodules which form on overused vocal cords. Like a pair of rubber bands stretched tightly between two fingers, the vocal cords of a normal male voice snap together 100 to 150 times (200 to 250 for the female voice) each second to create the noise traders communicate with. The faster the market, the more hectic the trading, the higher the velocity at which the vocal cords snap. Nodules on the cords create breathy sounds, the kind easily muffled by the roar of the crowd.

Short of bringing megaphones into the pits and pounding their chests in Tarzan fashion, traders have tried all sorts of ways to rev up their outcries. Some cup their hands around their mouths to create echo effects. Others screech in falsettos. And like football players who take ballet lessons to improve agility, traders have sought help from experts in lung power; they have paid $90 an hour for radio and television voice coaches who train celebrities to do commercials. A few have even gone further—into the parlors of operatic voice teachers who offer the fine points of vibrato by projecting and breathing through the diaphragm.

At least a score of traders have enrolled at a speech therapy program at Northwestern University offered by Dr. Hilda Fisher, a tall, robust woman recognized internationally for her speech work. She regards commodity traders as professional voice users, just like singers or actors, and she reeducates them on how to use their voices. Breathing from the diaphragm helps. So do relaxation exercises designed to relax the muscles of the neck and, in turn, ease tension on vocal cords. With bigger—and louder—markets, the problem appears to be getting worse. In 1983 University of Illinois researchers completed a random study of traders on the Mercantile Exchange, showing that 5 percent of them had voice or throat disorders. The initial findings are part of a larger project on the effects of background noise on the human voice.

Traders insist that people with distinctive voices in the pits get more buys and sells because they are recognized more easily and that women have a problem competing with booming male voices. They're probably right. Even men with high voices have a hard time.

Then there are those who think it better to stimulate the brain instead of the lungs. They have gone to psychologists and psychiatrists in order to become more assertive. By loosening up in the pit, they believe, they will vocalize better. One trader who was down on his luck suddenly found that he couldn't swallow every time he entered the pit. He went to his doctor for a checkup. There was nothing physically wrong. Perhaps it was a psychological problem, the doctor suggested. The befuddled trader went to a psychiatrist. No help there either. Swallowing is an involuntary action, and no doctor could explain why the process just stopped. Within minutes after trading started his throat would go bone-dry. He'd begin to think about swallowing and would lose his concentration. Was it too much pressure? Too much anxiety? He never did find out the reason for his strange malady. But it stopped once he got out of the pits. He has since traded only through brokers.

Traders will take time off just to give their vocal cords a rest. There is nothing sadder than to hear the once-robust voice of a trader turn into a chirp, a rasp, a croak, a hoarseness that reduces his sounds to a whisper, his words to a murmur.

Yet it's more than voice over matter. The situation becomes a case of being both heard and seen. Pit diplomacy calls for walking loudly and carrying a big stick. That's why traders will don wardrobes like carnival barkers on a midway, hoping to create step-right-up attention with gaudy polyester ties and wild-patterned trading jackets. One of the Merc's pork belly traders sports a tie festooned with—what else?—pigs with little gold halos and white wings. But it's usually his red-and-white candy-striped jacket which catches the eye from across the pit. Sometimes it's his navy jacket with bright white stars. Another trader wears a different polyester tie each day—with a jacket that, of course, doesn't match. Others sport blazers with big blue daisies or huge plaid checks or jackets of many-hued madras. No one has yet shown up dressed like a sideshow geek, but once a Merc trader, for one reason or another, saw it fit to wear a gorilla mask during a trading session. "Dress ugly" could well be the code of attire for those traders who believe that loud façades go with loud lungs.

Nevertheless, it is sound that reflects the emotional state of the pits. The entire trading floor is a huge echo chamber, blaring one gigantic voice fractured into a million deals.

"Three for Deece, three for Deece," bellows a trader in a red jacket, thrusting his arm in the air palm outward like a *Sieg heil* to indicate he has three contracts or 15,000 bushels of soybeans for December delivery to sell. The trader next to him in the orange jacket fulminates even louder: "Ten for Deece, I've got ten for Deece. Ten for Deece." Yet another trader chimes in with manual shorthand (a fist means one cent; four fingers, three-quarters of a cent; three fingers, a half cent; and two fingers, a quarter of a cent) and a Donald Duck voice. Bobbing up and down, he looks at the man who yelled, "Ten for Deece," and then he delivers a *Sieg heil*, showing the back of his hand. "Five for five, five for five," he roars. Sold! That means he is a buyer, a bidder wailing and willing to pay five-eighths of a cent for five of those ten soybean contracts. (If beans, say, had been selling for $4 a bushel, the new bid indicates the price has just moved up to $4.000625 a bushel.) At precisely the same moment a blue-jacketed trader is thundering, "Six for Oct! Six for Oct!" with October beans for sale.

Offers to sell and bids to buy explode from anywhere in the pit at any time. A buyer one second may be a seller the next. So buyers and sellers aren't separated, and that only intensifies the noise, the emotional fervor, and the acrimony of the pits.

21

If It's Raining on La Salle Street, Soybeans Must Be Long

The sky was black, and the boys on the floor of the Board of Trade were stirring. Trading in the soybean pit had come to a halt because prices were bid limit up. There was drought in the Illinois Soybean Belt. And unless it ended soon, there would be a severe shortage of beans. With limit up, there was no play in the beans. If you had bought, or gone long, you were cool and making money. But if you had sold, or gone short, you were sweating.

Suddenly a few tiny drops of water slid down a window. "Look," someone shouted, "rain!" More than 500 pairs of eyes shifted to the big windows along the cash grain tables at the south end of the trading floor. Then came a steady trickle. The milling in the soybean pit froze as the traders came alive. The steady trickle turned into a steady downpour. It was raining in downtown Chicago. It was raining on La Salle Street!

Sell. Buy. Buy. Sell. The shouts cascaded from the traders' lips with a roar that easily matched the thunder outside. And the price of soybeans began to budge. Soon they were down half cent from their highs. Then a penny. Then two cents. Then three. The price of soybeans had broken like some tropic fever. There were buyers and sellers, and both were sweating. There was action in the pit. Why shouldn't there have been? Wasn't it raining on La Salle Street?

It was pouring in Chicago all right, but no one grows soybeans

122

in Chicago. In the heart of the Soybean Belt, some 300 miles south of Chicago the sky was blue, sunny, and very dry. But even if it wasn't raining on the soybean fields, it was in the heads of the traders, and that's all that counts. To the commodities market nothing matters unless the market reacts to it. The game is played with the mind and the emotions. And the pits, where that game is played, is a "neitherworld"—neither all reality nor all fantasy.

As for all that talk about supply and demand, a grizzled trader once explained it to me this way: "It's just a bunch of numbers. And we all know that people use statistics the way dogs use lampposts—for convenience rather than illumination."

Nevertheless, many traders are "news" and "nose" buffs when it comes to supply and demand factors. They like to know what's happening in the world that could affect the markets and to sniff out what's going on in the pits before trading starts. Every event, every tragedy, or every disaster is judged by its impact on the market. The traders' callousness grows thicker the longer they stay in the pits. Some even begin to see black humor in disasters. "Ski Brazil—go long coffee" was the advice on the exchange floor when Brazil lost 50 percent of its coffee crop a few years ago. And at the time of the Honduras earthquake in 1978, Harvey Tillis remembered one of his trader friends rushing up to him and saying, "First of all, I feel sorry for those people in Honduras." Before Harvey could comment, the mournful trader immediately added, "Second of all, is there any place we can trade bananas?"

"If the H-bomb dropped," Tillis noted with a shrug, "traders would want to know if they had time to go long gold." But that's all part of commodities. Fortunes are made and lost on quirks of nature, on wars, on peace, on forecasts, on panic, on rumors, on the whims of the mind.

American presidents have sometimes become irritated by this fact of trading life. It happened in 1948, for instance, when the United States was feeding a starving Europe through the Marshall Plan. The need for food naturally meant more demand, and there was a run-up in grain prices on the Board of Trade, incensing President Harry Truman. Commodity traders, he said, "are merchants of human misery." On that emphatic note he promptly proceeded to embarrass the traders by making public a list of those who held positions of 2 million bushels or more. At the time big positions had to be registered with the Commodity Exchange Authority. Truman demanded that the CEA release the list to the newspapers, and it did. "It was like the Internal Revenue Service pulling your tax return," recalled Ben Raskin, a young grain clerk at the time. "There were some very mad and embarrassed traders."

22

Pssst!

When there aren't Malthusian possibilities to trade on, there is always rumor. Rumors represent opportunities, manna for the speculator. Gossip, hearsay, unconfirmed reports—they circulate in the pits like a contagious virus, often triggering market moves long before big sales that affect the market are formally reported. The exchange floor saying "Buy on rumor, sell on fact" is a maxim that you won't find in any of the hundreds of commodity how-to-trade books and manuals that have flooded the bookstores in recent years.

"Rumors," said Alan Becker, a thirty-one-year-old trader at the Merc, "rumors are the lifeblood of the nation, so why shouldn't they be the lifeblood of the pits?" A rumor on the floor of an exchange spreads by jungle telegraph: You don't hear it; you feel it if you're one of the natives. A good rumor can be worth its weight in gold or pork bellies or orange juice concentrate. And although rumors can never keep the market going straight up or down for a sustained period, they do cause bulges in the market and quick chances to make big money. There are, of course, big fines and threats of temporary expulsion from the pits if a trader is caught rumormongering. But to the best of anyone's recollection, no trader has been penalized because it is virtually impossible to track the source of a rumor. It's like going after the elusive yeti in the Himalayas: The tracks are there, but try finding the body. Besides, nobody really wants to squelch a "hot" rumor because you never know when it could be a cold fact. In the backs of many traders' minds is the memory of that fine year of 1972, when grain prices shot to unprecedented heights, first on rumor, then on confirmation that the Soviets were buying. By grabbing at the rumor, some traders teetering on the brink of disaster ended up as millionaires.

Rumors can start anywhere; some grow out of sheer desperation. On the Mercantile Exchange once, when the price of eggs was hitting new highs daily, one of the big traders had sold short, thinking there would be a break in the price at any moment. But there was no sign of relief. He was caught in a classic squeeze, and it was beginning to hurt. Then came the rumor, one as hard to swallow as a raw egg. During a coffee break the big trader told several of his colleagues about the new and unpublished discovery by the Cubans. The Cubans? Discovery? A friend of his in the Food and Drug Administration, he whispered, had called him with the report that the Cubans had discovered that eggs were a primary cause of cancer. As preposterous as it was, it worked. Within a half hour the selloff had begun. All the traders had really heard were the words *egg* and *cancer.* That was enough. The egg trader who started it all managed to buy back his short position at a hefty profit for the day.

For a time in the summer of 1981 there was a wild trading spasm in the Merc's pork belly pit. Word had filtered into the pit that McDonald's was going to be a big buyer of pork. It had been selling pork sausages on its breakfast menu for years. But this was something different, *they* whispered among themselves, one of those rumors just nebulous enough to whet the speculative appetite of a trader, something about a new kind of sandwich. There was more meat to the rumor, as it turned out, than bone. The following spring McDonald's introduced its boneless pork McRib sandwich.

Some rumors can start inadvertently. It happened with orange juice. Every trader knows that when a hard freeze hits the Citrus Belt in December, orange juice concentrate futures get hot, and prices run up. That's what happened on the old New York Cotton Exchange one December when it was located on Beaver Street. Here's how the Great Orange Juice Squeeze came about:

A pit broker sent a runner to get him a can of orange juice from the machine in the traders' lounge. During the night, it seems, the machine had gone awry, and all the cans of various juices had frozen solid. The dutiful runner returned, uttering the words *The orange juice was frozen.* The broker acknowledged the report with a shake of his head, but over the trading din the other brokers heard only the words *orange* and *frozen,* and the buying spree was on. Within a half hour orange juice concentrate futures were limit up. Traders were convinced that there was a freeze in Florida and the crops were ruined (after all, temperatures in Manhattan that day had dipped well below 32 degrees). When reality finally set in, prices had closed lower than the previous day's close.

Even the *Wall Street Journal* acknowledges the reality of rumors. No more euphemisms calling those rumors unconfirmed reports. Turn to the section called "Futures Markets" on any business day, and you'll get the point. It's the *Journal*'s recap of trading activity in most of the commodities on the nation's exchanges. It can also be a roundup of rumors. Take, for instance, the headline on a story that ran on December 15, 1982: RUMORS OF POSSIBLE CUT IN GILL'S CROP ESTIMATE RAISE PRICES OF COCOA. The story began: "Rumors that Gill & Duffs, a London-based trade house, may lower its cocoa crop estimates because of a continuing drought in Brazil sent cocoa prices sharply higher...." Another story on the previous day, December 14, noted: "Prices rose modestly, partly because of rumors that Russia bought two million metric tons of U.S. wheat. The rumor caused the strongest run-up at the Kansas City Board of Trade, which trades futures in hard red wheat, the type that the Soviets were said to buy. But the expectation also fueled buying in Chicago, which trades soft red wheat.... But the outlook for U.S. grain exports remains bearish, said Robert Lekberg, an analyst with Shearson/American Express Inc., and as 'negative thinking' revived, prices fell from their highs at the close of trading." (It would appear, then, a rumor is only as good as the positive mental attitude behind it.)

Just one week before, sugar had had its turn: "Prices jumped, partly on rumors of Soviet buying. March-delivery sugar climbed 0.22 cent to 7.89 cents a pound. Analysts said buying by dealers and a dearth of sellers helped spur prices. 'The trade is getting bullish,' one analyst said."

Sometimes rumors come in clusters. On April 18, 1984, gold and silver prices rose sharply, while interest rate and stock index futures fell. The reason? A rumor-plagued day that had President Reagan being shot, Federal Reserve Board Chairman Paul Volcker resigning, a big bank taking a large loss on a Government National Mortgage Association securities position, and Iraq sinking an oil tanker in the Persian Gulf. All those rumors, the *Journal* somberly noted, had "caused confusion."

As if rumors aren't enough to move prices in one direction or another, there are always "negative psychological and technical factors," as one analyst explained the "thinly traded soybean market." And don't forget about the "no news is good news" notion of life. On December 16, 1982, "corn and wheat prices fell slightly in the absence of any news." But trader-psychologist Jake Bernstein will tell you that news "tends to be the enemy of most traders since they know not how to use it." It's not the news itself but the way the news is interpreted that matters. Nearly every trader knows that it takes months for economic news to become economic fact and that the period between those points accounts for most of the price activity.

So, when traders are short on either news or rumors, they are long on *expectation* and *anticipation,* probably the most prevalent conditions that move markets. "The pessimists were squeezed out of the market," said one analyst, who had commented on the reason why prices of stock index futures closed sharply higher during a trading session, according to the *Wall Street Journal.* "He said," the *Journal* continued, "anticipation of lower interest rates and a possible cut in the discount rate added fuel to the fire." A week later treasury bill and treasury bond futures closed slightly higher as a result of falling interest rates. Analysts concluded that the initial euphoria of falling interest rates "was dampened by continuing expectations" of a depressed business economy.

For lack of anything better, analysts even speculate about *feelings.* "It's still too early to tell. But there's a feeling in the market that the crop will be smaller," said one analyst about Brazil's cocoa crop. Analysts hedge their views with enough ifs and buts to fill a grain elevator, and if you want a reason for something, there is always an analyst to oblige. Take the time in early December 1982 when wheat, corn, and soybean prices fell sharply. The analysts were hard pressed to explain price gains in terms of supply and demand. They were stumped. The Illinois and Mississippi rivers were too high at certain points to allow the grain barges to navigate effectively. The big shippers know that in the end, the movement of a commodity from one point to another affects its price more than anything else. (It's something akin to how World War II capitalist Milo Minderbinder of *Catch-22* fame operated when he bought eggs in Sicily for 1 cent each, moved them secretly to Malta, where he sold them for 4½ cents, then bought them back for 7 cents and resold them to the air force for 5 cents—at a tidy profit of 1½ cents each.)

One analyst theorized that the high-water situation on the rivers obviously would boost grain prices. He argued that if supplies weren't available from river ports in the interior of the United States, then exporters with commitments to deliver supplies might buy futures contracts for protection. Naturally that would push prices higher. Right? No, wrong, if you listened to what another analyst had to say. He saw the river problem as one that would depress prices. This analyst reasoned that an exporter who loses business because he doesn't make good on his delivery commitments soon gets a reputation as an unreliable supplier. Consequently, his business may not pick up once conditions have improved.

Disagreements among analysts have spawned a whole new endeavor among certain analysts. Their sole business is to keep tabs on the views of their colleagues. I first found out about the curious art of analyst watching when I ran into Big Wally at the Board of Trade. That's what I called him, all 220 pounds of this man mountain. With his watery, sad puppy-dog eyes and fleshy jowls he reminded me of a forlorn St. Bernard that was lost in a blizzard. What do you call a thirty-two-year-old bachelor, pulling down $120,000 a year, who favored sneakers, black socks, and string ties? Eccentric, I suppose.

Whenever he saw me, he'd drape his paw over my shoulder, pull me toward him, and bellow, "There are no small trades, just small traders." And he'd roar a belly laugh.

But Big Wally wasn't a dummy. He was, in fact, a quick-witted trader riding a hot streak in soybeans at the time, and everyone knew it. There was still a bit of the naughty boy in him, a devilish prankster who loved to unnerve other traders. Most mornings, shortly before the opening, he'd sidle up to a group of traders, distort his Silly Putty face, and whisper out the side of his mouth in an authoritative bass, "Did you hear that . . ." He was a tease, and like the others, he savored every tidbit of rumor. Oddly enough, he ignored them all for his beloved charts. He charted soybeans, corn, wheat, treasury bonds, silver coins, gold, and a number of commodities on other exchanges. He even had a chart on analysts.

Wally had been reviewing the previous day's closes for corn and soybeans when he began to mumble to himself, shaking his head ominously. It looked like another one of his ploys.

"What's up?" a fellow trader asked.

"The beans are gonna break," he cautioned.

"Impossible," the fellow trader replied. "Exports are up, and beans still have a lotta play. Everybody's talking lower yields."

"Yeah, but the Sentiment Index doesn't agree," Wally insisted.

"The what?"

"Sentiment Index, Sentiment Index," Wally repeated. "It's my secret weapon, a kinda last resort, my ripcord when nothing is working right."

The Sentiment Index, it turned out, was not a figment of Big Wally's trading imagination. He had the charts to prove it. There's an outfit in Portland, Oregon, called Commodity Outlook, Inc., that actually surveys the opinions of professional advisers and the scores of brokers' market letters. It then consolidates all the opinions into The Market Sentiment Index for dozens of commodities. Although it was intended only as a guide, Wally swore by it whenever he had a feeling the market was in for a turn. The Sentiment Index worked on the theory of contrary opinion, which holds that when 85 percent of those analysts surveyed are bullish, the market is overbought. That means a drop in prices is likely to occur. Conversely, if 75 percent of the analysts are bearish, the market is probably oversold, and a rally is on the way.

I never bothered to find out the accuracy of the Market Sentiment Index, but it wouldn't have made any difference to Big Wally. It was the idea of analysts' being analyzed that intrigued him. "I look at it this way," he boomed, parting his lips with a smile. "It's like one psychiatrist with a set of neuroses treating another psychiatrist with the same neuroses."

23

We Love You, Conrad

For every commodities analyst who hedges his comments with an "if," "could," "perhaps," or "only time will tell," there is one who lets the figures do the talking. The magic name among grain traders for more than twenty years has been Conrad Leslie, the swami of the private grain and soybean forecasters who is able to predict the nation's crop with startling accuracy long before it's in the silos—and three or four days before the U.S. Department of Agriculture prediction comes out. To those traders who swear by him—and there are hundreds—Leslie, as one of his fans put it, is the "grandfather of fundamental analysis."

Leslie's forecasts can and often do cause hundreds of millions of dollars to change hands at exchanges in Chicago, Kansas City, and Minneapolis. It sends commodity traders and brokers bolting into action across the country. Just before a Leslie report comes out, only the gutsiest of traders will take a big position. Most take a wait-and-see stance before jumping into the market. Since a number of grain traders live by the intelligence they gather, when a forecast with a track record like Leslie's is circulated, it can have an impact on the grain markets. With the surpluses of the 1980s and the sophisticated communications network, it's hard to come out with a surprising crop report. But situations can still change fast, thanks to drought, floods, exports, and government programs that cut back production.

During the 1960s, when grain prices moved up or down 2 cents a bushel, depending on the government's price support levels, crop forecasts didn't pack the wallop they do now. The price of, say, soybeans might change no more than 40 cents a bushel in a year. After 1972, as surpluses dried up, there were limit moves—up and down—of 20 cents (10 cents for corn) occurring two and three times a week. Commodity prices moved in dollars over a year.

There were times, however, when Leslie was well ahead of the government on the situation prior to 1972. In 1970, for example, he beat the government by accurately forecasting the extent of a corn blight that sent the price of corn up from the government's support level of $1.05 a bushel to $1.40.

He still fiercely competes with the government forecasters. His office on the seventeenth floor of the Chicago Board of Trade looks like the inside of a modern airport control tower that tracks planes with one of those computerized alpha-numeric systems. Leslie uses computers, too, among other things. The office is crammed with computer terminals charting price trends, five television screens flashing the latest grain quotations from the pits, high-speed teletype machines hammering out economic and agricultural news from around the world—and a tank of tropical fish. He also receives weekly weather summaries from twenty-six states where corn, wheat, and soybeans are grown.

But it's a little white postcard that makes Leslie tops in the crops outlook business. Each month from May to November Leslie and his wife, Cynthia, mail out a postcard questionnaire to some 3,000 grain elevator managers across the country, asking one simple question: How are the crops doing in their respective areas? Leslie's approach is very different from that of the Agriculture Department, which queries about 90,000 farmers. Leslie believes elevator operators are more sensitive to month-to-month changes than farmers. Since the operators buy the grain, store it, and borrow the money from banks to finance operations, they will usually visit the farms to see the situation at first hand. They are constantly trying to determine just how much the farmers will be trying to sell and how much they can take.

The Leslie crop estimate report comes out seven times a year. Early in January there is a report on the number of acres the nation's farmers have already planted in winter wheat and what they expect to plant in the spring. The March report is another "planting intentions" survey on corn and soybeans. In May comes the first actual estimates of wheat production. Thereafter are monthly forecasts on the progress of wheat, corn, and soybean crops that continue until the harvest is over in November.

Both government and private surveys are tabulated with the hush-hush of the Manhattan Project. The government's results are collated in each state and then sent to Washington, where the totals are calculated in great secrecy. Leslie collates his 3,000 inquiry cards in the privacy of his suburban Chicago home. He compares the current results with those of both the previous month and a year earlier. He puts together each state's total for a national forecast. It is printed and mailed to his firm's clients (Leslie through his Leslie Analytical Organization acts as a consultant to Thomson McKinnon Securities Inc.), to the newspapers and wire services, and, free of charge, to each of the correspondent elevator operators. Leslie takes precautions to make sure nobody gets his forecast before release. Some people have tried or seriously thought about getting an early look at the report. Leslie once discovered a clerk had been offered $1,000 to slip out the report ahead of time. Over the years I have run across more than one trader who considered tracking down the printer of the survey with hopes of sneaking a peek. Up until about six years ago Leslie was a partner in the brokerage firm of Mayer, Gelbart & Leslie, and not even his partners saw the forecast before the general readership. The report is usually mailed on a Thursday in plenty of time for the Monday markets.

How about Leslie himself? Does he use his findings to trade before anyone else? Leslie says he takes a neutral position in the market twenty-four hours before he issues a forecast and will make no comments on market conditions for a day before the forecast is released.

Leslie scans some sixty periodicals each month to keep abreast of the latest shifts in international politics, fluctuations in currency values and interest rates, and changes in agricultural policy. Yet although he is a fundamentalist, he believes it's the chartist view that has grown in importance in recent years to the speculator. (There indeed has been a rising fraternity of analysts who ignore fundamentals by charting market trends from historical experience, working under the assumption that over long enough periods there will always be a historical pattern. But finding that pattern in a cycle can be as tough as finding a gas station that still gives green stamps.)

Chartists plot the future by plodding through the past. They try to find the correct short-run moving average of a commodity in order to apply it to a long-term historical pattern. They use the same skills and methods as do their more visible counterparts (the Joseph Granville types) who attempt to forecast stock market trends. Take, for example, the pecuniary historians, those who chart currencies around the world. When two lines cross—as when the average value of, say, the Japanese yen contract over eight days crosses its average of twenty-five days—it's a signal to buy. Similarly, when the two lines diverge, it's a signal to sell. By contrast, a fundamental forecaster of currencies is a far more pragmatic fellow. He, of course, is concerned with things that appear real, such as the four factors that comingle to determine exchange rates: a country's trade balance, inflation rate, interest rates, and the money that flows in and flows out. Both groups cast their skills on markets with varying success.

What happens when those two little lines cross one way or the other on every technician's chart? Naturally there's either a great deal of buying or selling. Over the past few years, in fact, chartists as a group were thought to be moving the foreign exchange markets over short periods. How? By arriving at "consensus" for key currencies such as the U.S. dollar, the deutsche mark, and the Japanese yen. Currency chartists were heroes of the day in the wake of Ronald Reagan's presidential victory in 1980. The fundamentalists then had predicted a halt in the rise of the dollar. The chartists saw the dollar's value increasing faster than it had in the previous several years. They were right.

Unfortunately glory is short-lived in the commodities business. In January 1981 the same technicians had smugly predicted the dollar would peak out at 2.20 to 2.30 marks to the dollar. Two months later the dollar fell to 2.05 and then turned around and peaked at 2.57 by August.

To find out more about such things as charts and cycles, I looked to Nikolai Dimitriyevich Kondratieff and Jake Bernstein.

24

Around and Around

Jacob ("Jake") Bernstein was thirty-five years old and had been a millionaire for at least a half dozen years. He made his money trading commodities and dealing in coins and oriental rugs. He also was the author of a successful commodities newsletter and several how-to books on trading. As for Kondratieff, well, he had been dead for at least fifty years, a victim of one of Joseph Stalin's prison camps somewhere in the wastelands of Siberia.

Bernstein looked more like a student than a commodities adviser. He wore blue jeans, and his black collar-length hair jiggled as he talked with animation, bouncing in his chair. His glasses clung firmly to a full face. Behind the wire frames were darting brown eyes. In soft, measured tones he talked about his favorite subject, cycles.

"Everything moves in cycles," he said. "I have never seen markets running contrary to the fundamentals. Fundamental analysis tells you what the markets have done, but the technical approach looks into the future."

Bernstein is a staunch advocate of the Kondratieff wave, or so-called K-wave, named after the Russian economist whose only crime was thinking aloud. Bernstein's newsletter, rated the best in the field in a reader survey by *Futures* magazine a few years ago, bases its advice on the Kondratieff theory.

Kondratieff was disavowed by the Kremlin because of his cycle theory of capitalism. Sometime in the early 1920s he had begun studying cycles of commodity prices as a scholar at Moscow's Agricultural Academy. He concluded that commodity prices, from a historical perspective, predictably hit peaks and valleys over long periods. These periods, which he called waves, were cycles that lasted for decades. The upswing of the first long wave was from 1789 to 1814; its decline began in 1814 and ended in 1849 to complete a sixty-year cycle. The rise of the second wave began in 1849 and reached bottom in 1896 for a forty-seven-year cycle. Then in 1896 prices moved upward again in a third wave that lasted until 1920, just prior to the Great Depression, which hit the American farmer in the early 1920s.

Consequently, Kondratieff saw the capitalist economy as being on a roller-coaster ride, dropping from boom to bust and back to recovery, at which time the cycle would repeat. Russian officials, it seemed, loved the boom-to-bust part of the theory. But when it came to the recovery, they lowered the sickle on Kondratieff. A recovery? The comrades wouldn't hear of it. That simply did not hold with the Marxist line that capitalism was doomed to collapse completely. And Kondratieff was banished into the footnotes of economic history.

As for his theory, some prominent American economists, such as Nobel laureate Paul Samuelson, don't buy it. They dismiss the K-waves as absurd. A few even liken Kondratieff's theory to astrology. But there are also many scholars who see some validity in Kondratieff's cycles. The late economist Joseph Schumpeter, who was Samuelson's professor at Harvard during the 1930s, accepted Kondratieff's evidence. In 1939 Schumpeter published *Business Cycles*, basing his theory on short, medium, and long-range time periods. He, however, saw technical innovation as the key to rising waves. Once that technology had matured, the decline began. The era of the Iron Horse, for example, produced investment and prosperity. But once the railroads had been built, investment dropped sharply, causing the downswing.

Schumpeter explained it in 1942 in *Capitalism, Socialism and Democracy*. "The process of industrial change," he wrote, "provides the ground swell that gives the general tone to business. . . . Thus there are prolonged periods of rising and of falling prices, interest rates, employment and so on, which phenomena constitute parts of the mechanism of this process of recurrent rejuvenation of the productive apparatus."

Communism notwithstanding, Kondratieff (along with astrology) has since become food for hungry capitalists. Jake Bernstein's M.B.H. Commodity Advisors, Inc., newsletter has 1,000 subscribers, each of whom shell out $415 a year. He also runs well-attended seminars at $300 per head, explaining the Kondratieff fifty-year cycle concept to commodity hedgers and speculators and its impact on the thirty various commodities Bernstein tracks. And there is steady demand for his *Handbook of Commodity Cycles.*

But for the majority of the pit locals who swing with the market action, K-waves and Schumpeter hold about as much appeal as do quantum mechanics and particle physics. To them a couple of seconds is long term. Fortunately there are enough Kondratieff watchers to keep Bernstein very busy. His computer is loaded with data on price movements and trading volume in an attempt to project the future. Who knows why the cycles are there? No one really does. Yet analysts such as Bernstein are convinced the cycles are constant and identifiable like the rings in trees and the moon and tides. Everything, he believes, moves in cycles. Gold? Moves in a cycle of some 6.8 years, top to bottom to the start of a new upward cycle. . . .

Jake Bernstein doesn't talk easily about his past. Like the Merc's Leo Melamed, he learned something about survival as a child. He was born in 1946 in the rubble of Germany in a refugee processing camp. His father had been released from the horrors of Dachau and his mother from Auschwitz. The family moved to Montreal, patiently saved, and waited to emigrate to the United States. In 1959 the Bernsteins were admitted to the United States and settled in the North Shore Chicago suburb of Winnetka, where Jake still lives and works. The son of a tailor, Jake attended New Trier High School, a highly competitive place geared to upper-middle-class students. He was an average student with no particular burning desire to make millions. Then came college.

Oddly, he followed Melamed's path there, too, though, of course, unknowingly: He attended the University of Illinois and majored in psychology. But after college their paths parted. Jake was determined to become a clinical psychologist. He went on to do graduate work at Roosevelt University in downtown Chicago while working at Chicago Read Mental Health Center. But, he recalled, "I realized school had nothing to do with making money. It just hit me like a bolt of lightning one day."

Like many others before him, he got into commodities more or less by accident. One day a fast-talking commodities broker convinced Jake to put up $1,000 to speculate in the market. The broker ran the $1,000 up to $20,000 in a year, speculating in eggs during a hot market on the Mercantile Exchange in the late 1960s.

Smug and flush with success, Bernstein convinced himself that he, not the broker, was the speculative genius. Jake's winning streak was matched only by his amateur's streak. He grabbed the $20,000 and plunged head-on into pork bellies. He lost everything.

The market had burned Jake, just as it had burned me and just as it burns others, amateur and pros. Jake also took a break from the market, but it wasn't to nurse his wounded trading ego. Rather, it was to learn: about commodities, about markets, about cycles, about the psychology of trading, about anything and everything in the puzzling cavalcade of elements that affect supply and demand. He even began investigating the deep pathology in the minds of traders. Jake spent three years "reading every book I could find and developing what I thought was a good theory of trading on cycles." He did not trade during this period. Finally, when Jake was ready to test his theories, he couldn't. He was broke.

Jake turned to a couple of friends, borrowing several hundred dollars from each. But instead of playing the market, he founded a newsletter and a firm, M.B.H. Commodity Advisors (partners M. and H. are no longer with Bernstein). As soon as he had enough money, he got back in the market again. This time he traded with a single-minded purpose. "It was the last place I could make the Horatio Alger story come true," Bernstein said, his lips knotted into a smirk of confidence. "Besides, there was more leverage in commodities than in anything else."

The entrepreneurial appeal of the market grabbed Jake's mind. "The commodity market struck me as just the right thing," he noted in his first book, "particularly for a young Jewish kid who grew up in a poor home with parents who had instilled in him a high degree of motivation."

So it was off to the markets with motivation and Kondratieff. Both have served Bernstein well. There is some trouble fitting Kondratieff's half century into exact dates, he has admitted, but that makes little difference. "The last bottom was between 1947 and 1949, five to six years before it was supposed to have happened," Bernstein said reflectively. "This cycle was too short, so Kondratieff was wrong." Nevertheless, what he did see in Kondratieff back in January 1980 was a very painful collapse into severe deflation. "It is possible that I may be a bit early in my forecast," he told his clients then. "Perhaps the disastrous downturn won't come until 1982." As it turned out, the 1980 recession took hold and wouldn't let up until well into 1983.

Bernstein doesn't know why the cycles are there, but he claims they are constant and identifiable and different for each of some thirty commodities he follows with a computer jammed with data on price movements and volume of trade in order to identify the ups and downs and to project the future. As it happened, though, Bernstein's cycles, computers, and market intuition proved wrong in his call of the 1979–80 surge in gold and silver prices. He thought that silver at $29 an ounce was "crazy" and that gold was too high at $500 an ounce. He told his clients to cash in at those prices. Subsequently silver went to $45 an ounce and gold to $800. Why the cautious bent? One reason may have been that gold and silver had been traded on the commodities markets for too short a time to create the most accurate of cycles. Another reason may have stemmed from his own fears, which caused him to misjudge the cycles.

Bernstein wasn't alone in his judgment. Most of the technicians couldn't believe their own charts when bullion went berserk. It was a classic case of panic buying, the sociologists and psychologists agreed, a fear of being too late and left out on a good thing—a stampede set off by greed. Even crooks latched on to the commodity scene. The entire complexion of burglary changed as burglars passed up TV sets and stereos, heading straight for the silverware and gold jewelry. One San Francisco victim, trying to salvage a bit of humor out of the metals madness, told a *Newsweek* reporter, "At least, I was burglarized by someone who keeps up on current events."

There was no doubt that gold and silver had lost touch with reality. At $850 an ounce of gold was worth more than 500 pounds of hamburger. And 7 pounds of gold was enough to buy a typical American single-family house. How about a suitcase of bullion? That could have paid for a tanker of crude oil. The run-up in gold seemed to bode well for the U.S. government at the time. It was sitting with a gold hoard of 8,600 tons, worth $220 billion, more than enough to cover all the U.S. dollars held as official reserves by foreign central banks. On the other hand, gold fever fueled the fires of inflationary psychology. A growing number of people figured that if the dollar was worth only one eight-hundredth of an ounce of gold, then it was hardly worth anything at all. That kind of thinking prodded people to spend their dollars faster, rather than to save them, thereby pushing prices even higher. The inflation-fanning gold rush eventually petered out with the hard knocks of recession. But it served to remind Bernstein and his fellow analysts that charts and computers are one thing, psychology is another. Listen to the "father of fundamental analysis," Conrad Leslie, explain his business: "An analyst today has to rely on charts and computers 60 percent of the time and fundamentals 40 percent of the time. But he has to be 100 percent psychologist."

25

Bullion, Bulls, and Bubba

So the gold market runs, in good part, on the disorganized state of the world—and mind. Both are seemingly unpredictable. Naturally gold is, too. Even in the early days of the inflation-fanning gold rush, doomsters and analysts were baffled by the capricious yellow metal. The gold story unfolded through a set of spontaneous circumstances well beyond the calculations of a chart or a computer. It began with a classic short squeeze in August 1979.

Up until then the United States had been chipping away at its stockpile of gold through monthly gold auctions in an effort to slow the rise of prices. But in August it changed its strategy. It decided to reduce the monthly gold sales to assure itself that there would be enough gold to support the dollar in case of a monetary crisis. Just at the time the U.S. Treasury was holding back, the Arabs, flush with petrodollars, were starting to increase their purchases of gold. The supply of gold going into private hands had been sharply reduced.

Meanwhile, across the Atlantic in Germany the gold trap was about to be inadvertently set off. At the request of an Arab buyer the Dresdner Bank of Frankfurt took 96 percent of the August 21 gold auction. The massive purchase put this overwhelming amount of gold in the hands of one buyer, and that left bullion dealers without gold they anticipated buying. Many of the dealers had already sold the gold, in effect going short. They were being squeezed and forced to cover their commitments in the open market by buying back. That, in turn, drove the price of gold higher. Following the August 21 auction, gold spurted from $307 an ounce to $375 a month later.

Most of the analysts at the time were bearish. They could see no apparent reason for gold to rise. Several days before the squeeze most forecasters scoffed at the notion that gold could hold above $250 an ounce. "This is the type of action you see at the top of a big bull market," one commodities analyst smugly stated on August 16. Said another after the spurt in gold: "The potential of a decline to $270 an ounce within the next four to six weeks is quite good." And one of Wall Street's most respected international finance experts advised clients to sell at $277 because the price is "likely to drop below $250 an ounce" within six months and possibly as low as $235. Defiantly gold promptly shot up to $440 per ounce. Five months later gold was selling at $835 an ounce in London and Zurich.

Speculation had gotten so out of hand that U.S. Treasury Secretary G. William Miller declared no more U.S. gold auctions would be undertaken while the market remained unsettled. The edict only sent everyone scrambling for more gold. Traders concluded that the administration was now willing to see bullion prices rise freely to higher levels. So they bought still more. The Soviet Union, the world's second-largest gold producer behind South Africa, played the gold game like a shrewd speculator. It depended on sales of gold to pay for imports of everything from American grain to Western European high technology. But in 1979 the USSR cut its sales from 500 tons to less than 250 tons and sat back to watch the glittering rise in its reserves. Like the big oil-exporting countries, the Soviets discovered that leaving a commodity in the ground rather than exporting it helped drive the price up. It was a simple yet highly profitable lesson. War has always been the best excuse for hoarding gold, and some cynical analysts accused the Soviets of invading Afghanistan in early 1980 in order to push the price of gold even higher.

But hoarders playing Armageddon with copper? A spontaneous run-up in one commodity can also set off a wave of speculation in other metals markets. The week gold hit $800 an ounce, silver jumped from $39 an ounce to $47, while platinum, the costliest of all precious metals, leaped to a record $918 per ounce. The wave of speculation in silver was predictable. It and, to some extent, platinum have, like gold, become a traditional store of value. But copper? Against all odds and all reason copper took off in the wake of gold's ascent. If any metal should have been in a tailspin, it was copper. The metal's two biggest users—the automobile and construction industries—were in deep recession, pounded by high interest rates and inflation. Yet copper, too, ran up from just 88 cents per pound in mid-1979 to $1.48 in February 1980. It shouldn't have, but it did. Obviously it was the numbers game all over again. Remember, soybeans had a spin in 1973, sugar in 1974, coffee in 1977, orange juice in 1978, gold and silver 1979–80, treasury bills and treasury bonds 1980–81, and stock index futures 1982–83. All rose. All tumbled. All rose again.

In an effort to cope with such hair-trigger volatility, many analysts and traders have turned to the computer in recent years. Before 1973 commodities were short on computer research because the markets were relatively docile. Once prices had become volatile, though, the slick application of computerized trading began to take hold. Big food processors and grain shippers began using computers to keep track of their extensive commodity needs and related positions in the futures markets. Soon traders and commodity advisers were plugging market statistics into their computers. At times the computer calls for rapid-fire trading, which could mean a couple of dozen buy-sell decisions for a single contract. Other times it may instruct the trader to hang on to a position for the life of a contract. Reliance on crop and weather information, export business, and other such factors goes out the window.

The computer is a mere extension of the chart. The price history of a particular commodity and its trading volume are plugged into a computer that has been programmed to yield the maximum investment strategies for that contract. The information is then applied to a current contract.

Computer science is easily thwarted by the market, too. What does a floppy disk know from a flip-flop market? Obviously very little in view of the dismal performance of most commodity mutual funds in recent years. Like stock and bond funds, commodity funds pool investor money and then speculate in a string of commodities on the basis of a computer readout. Psychology often gets in the way of computer logic. "The performances of these funds have been so uninspiring," said analyst Conrad Leslie. "It creates an itch among analysts to start one themselves."

To the purists, those fundamentalists who cling to the whims of supply and demand, the proliferation of computer commodity programs is a mindless venture. One thirty-five-year veteran at the Board of Trade explained it this way: "To the best of my knowledge, there are still charts in the hold of the *Titanic*. In a static market where there's relatively little to move prices one way or another, computer programs do nothing more but sell breaks and buy bulges. It reminds me of the book *Fate Is the Hunter*. The author describes an airplane flight that took off. The instrumentation was perfect, the weather was perfect, the pilots were experienced, and the plane crashed. From that the writer concluded that 'Once again, fate urinated on the pillars of science.' "

People who trade in large quantities for a period of time can exacerbate price movements, forcing them higher or lower. But once they have ceased their efforts, the market settles back to where it should be. The market, as any purist will tell you, tends to conspire against the single biggest interest.

It's a view similar to that held by a number of economists who scrutinize the nuances of the stock market. In academic circles it's called the efficient market theory or random walk theory. You can fill a trading pit with the studies that have been done (with, of course, computers) showing that stock prices charted over long periods move in unpredictable ways or random walks. They seem to follow chance. The same could be said for commodity prices. Both the stock and futures markets rapidly digest any information that becomes public. Thus, the experts conclude, markets are as random as future events and are inherently unpredictable.

You won't find any of the pit locals subscribing to the efficient market theory or any other. They know that emotions and reflex override theory in the heat of trading and that greed and fear rather than efficiency move markets. If you don't believe it, just ask any *bubba*, a Jewish grandmother who can always add a dash of common sense to her chicken soup. That was the suggestion of a pair of Columbia University psychologists a couple of years ago. Any *bubba* worth her European accent, they argued, could refute the efficient market theory. The *Wall Street Journal* reported that the audience at Columbia tittered when Stanley Schacter, professor of social psychology, explained that "bubba psychology is the study of what Jewish grandmothers know without benefit of graduate training."

Schacter went on to say that in economics and other social sciences, "If it doesn't seem right to your grandmother, it probably isn't." He and his *bubba* theory collaborator, Professor Donald Hood, an expert on visual perception, contend that whether the market is a raging bull or a raging bear, either condition clouds the mind and tends to interfere with rational thought. It seemed axiomatic to the professors that even if a person becomes euphoric in a bull market or glum in a bear market, either of his reactions will result in his grabbing at straws. Handy straws can be an analyst's recommendation, a rumor, even a horoscope. To prove their point, Schacter and Hood analyzed the stock market from 1972 through 1979 (there were two bull markets, three bear markets, and three stable markets in the period), discerning the different ways people acted from one type of market situation to the next. Their conclusion: People aren't coldly rational, much less "efficient," about investing money or anything else. Although their study dealt only with the stock market, Schacter told me, "I suppose the same could be true of the commodities market."

Professors Schacter and Hood could have easily proved this by spending just five minutes in any active commodities trading pit where indeed energy quotient triumphs over intelligence quotient. Academicians are constantly venturing into the pits for first-hand looks at capitalism in the raw to bolster some trading theory of one kind or another. Invariably they walk away either satisfied or scratching their heads. "Once a year the professors come down here, and we tell them what we do in twenty-five minutes," said a veteran corn trader at the Board of Trade, "and they leave thinking we are a bunch of assholes. Nobody can teach trading in the pit."

26

The Eye
of the Mind

As farfetched as it may sound, the *bubba* theory has as much merit as any of the other rationales in the commodities markets. There are traders who have turned to the moon, the stars, even the extrasensory perceptions of the mind as well as hypnosis. In the 1920s a speculator by the name of Burton Pugh based his *Science and Secrets of Wheat Trading* on lunar phases. Pugh would buy wheat on the new moon and sell it twenty-eight days later on the full moon. His moonbeam strategy supposedly made a great deal of money. Another advocate of lunar cycles was G. D. Gann, who employed a series of "magic charts" to trade from.

There are still plenty of moonstruck traders around. They reckon that if the moon can move oceans, surely it can move stock and commodity markets or at least the people who trade in these markets since the human body is 80 percent water. In April 1983, for example, a market letter titled *Deliberations* cautioned subscribers to be wary of the moon. Its author, Ian McAvity, a Toronto investment analyst, explained it this way: "You could argue that the market tends to lose points around the full moon, and gains during the new. In theory, you should short the day before a full moon and cover the third day after. You should go long the fifth day before a new moon and sell the fifth day after." Some dismiss such theories as lunacy, an oddity to banter during cocktail chatter. Others swear by lunar cycles and even live—and trade—by them.

One grain trader (who prefers anonymity) on the Chicago Board of Trade constantly scans the heavens for a buy or sell sign. Every March he consults his astrologer. If the moon and Jupiter are within eight degrees of each other, he explained, that's a bearish sign because it's an indication of a potentially big harvest. He then becomes a big seller of corn and soybeans. Or, "If Venus transits my natal sun," he said, "or is good aspect to my natal moon, that's potential for good fortune." Nonsense? How do you argue with a man who refuses to buy a pair of shoes on the full moon because obviously they won't last? Without a revved-up psyche he may as well trade through a computer. This trader also walks away from the pits whenever his Mars is "constricted" because that is a "clear" sign his energy level is too low. Sometimes he'll take a couple of days off until there's order in the planets again before jumping back into the chaos of the pits. Although he's not a millionaire, his astro-trading has kept him comfortably in the futures game since 1977.

Then there's Joseph DeLouise. His approach to commodities is a synergistic blend of mind and matter that combines cycles, charts, fundamentals, and deep self-hypnosis. DeLouise is a swami, fortune-teller, psychic extraordinaire who calls himself Chicago's Nostradamus and is founder, editor, and chief analyst of a newsletter on commodities, stocks, and options called *Prophet Sharing.* "I also use horoscopes," said DeLouise, the good-natured, bearded Svengali of forecasters.

DeLouise divines the course of a market or the direction of gold or silver or interest rates with a methodology that is definitely not in the mainstream. In his promotional material DeLouise describes his daily routine in this way:

> Mr. DeLouise is one of the few successful psychics who is registered with the Securities and Exchange Commission and the Commodity Futures Trading Commission. . . . He begins his day by checking the Wall Street Journal to confirm his previous day's predictions, he then goes to the Board of Trade to get a personal view of the market's activity. From there he visits Brokerage Houses to check volume trend and a host of other indications to determine the movement of the Big Money Trader. With the

information he has learned and the impressions he has formed, he returns to his office where he will put himself into an altered state of consciousness, receiving images and feelings that enable him to make his final decisions for the markets. . . .

An altered state? To get there, he explained, he must reach "way up into the eye of my mind." That takes relaxing, a lot of it. The route can be slightly different each time. He dims the lights of his small office on South Michigan Avenue, not far from the Board of Trade, the Merc, the MidAmerica Exchange, and the Midwest Stock Exchange. He lies down on the green couch near the large bluish crystal ball resting on a glass stand next to the globe. He then takes a series of long breaths as if he were about to go underwater for a time. Or he may sit at his desk, eyes closed, breathing deeply while he listens to the soothing and familiar message on his tape player; it's his own voice telling him to relax. He writes the word *gold* on a piece of paper, massages it for a moment, folds it, places it on the desk (if he is lying down, he places the paper on his forehead), and concentrates.

He ponders. DeLouise, his eyes tightly closed, begins to conjure an image. "I see a ram or a billy goat," he says with a hint of urgency in his voice. A ram? A billy goat? Obviously gold is going higher; both the ram and the goat are signs of strength. The images vary, and DeLouise never knows which one will be plucked from the eye of the mind. If he sees the image of a sinking ship, then he knows gold is moving lower. But if a train appears and begins gathering speed, it is going up. Sometimes it can be rain cascading down a gutter, a sure sign that a particular commodity or stock is a loser. And there was the time he saw a bumblebee slamming on its brakes; naturally DeLouise concluded that interest rates would drop sometime in the next three weeks.

Once a client asked DeLouise if corn futures were a good play. The eyes closed, and soon the image appeared. It was the prospective trader rowing out too far in a boat and getting lost. DeLouise tried to persuade him to stay ashore. Rowing? Boat? The client shrugged, thanked DeLouise, paid him $50 for the forty-five minutes of financial vision, and later plunged into that vast sea of corn futures, where, according to DeLouise, he drowned. "He over-committed," DeLouise recalled of the corn trader, "and wound up in a mess."

It's on the subject of cycles, though, that a conversation with DeLouise begins to sound truly bizarre. "There are seven-hour cycles, seven-day cycles, seven-month cycles, seven-year cycles," he said, his voice sounding urgent. "Cycles are determined by your glands and the people and things around you. . . ."

DeLouise wasn't always a financial mystic, though for years he made his living working on heads. The only thing his customers wanted from him in the 1950s and 1960s was a shampoo and a cut. DeLouise was a hairdresser. He gave up his blow dryer and scissors in the early 1970s shortly after forecasting the run-up in gold. In 1973 he predicted that the price of gold would double from about $40 an ounce in the early part of the year. He was right. Before that, in 1968, he had predicted in a newspaper article that the Dow Jones Industrial Average would drop below 750 in 1969–70. Right again. In another newspaper article in late 1971 he forecast that the market would break 1000 in September 1972; it did so in November of that year.

DeLouise was doing so well he gave up Mr. Joseph's Style Salon to become a full-time forecaster. But with his newfound career came the wrath of the Securities and Exchange Commission. He still had amateur status as far as the SEC was concerned. "The SEC moved in and told me if I didn't stop doing this, I'd go to jail," recalled DeLouise, a small and wiry man who once had visions of becoming a jockey. He had gotten in trouble, he said, with his views on IBM and Polaroid. DeLouise ended his feud with the SEC by meeting the agency's requirements as a registered investment adviser. In doing so, he made sure the SEC was fully aware that he used everything his mind and imagination could draw from to make forecasts. He also registered as a commodity trading adviser with the Commodity Futures Trading Commission. Neither of the two agencies requires advisers to have any level of financial training or any knowledge of economics or business. Both are concerned only that an individual's background be disclosed accurately.

DeLouise, the youngest of three brothers, was born in 1927 in a mountain village on Sicily. His initial psychic experience occurred at age four, when he found $3,000 in coins and gold that an uncle had buried long before he died. The find turned out to be the stake the family needed in 1931 to come to America, where they settled in Chicago's Cabrini Green area, a warren of narrow streets on the Near North Side heavily populated by Italian immigrants in pre-World War II years.

It is obvious that in the world of commodity newsletters and stock market newsletters anything goes. DeLouise is the first to admit it. But as with any profession, he pointed out, "It's success that counts." Back in 1981 his newsletter was free to anyone who would send a stamped, self-addressed envelope. Now, for $195 a year, a subscriber can obtain the prognostications of DeLouise twice monthly.

In 1983 DeLouise added a new type of client to his financial and personal counseling list: brokers. "I work with stock and commodity brokers who have lost their edge," he explained in a matter-of-fact tone without any trace of show-biz theatrics. "I use hypnosis to bring them back to their winning ways. I take them back three and four years and then teach them to project the future." A psychic consultation for personal enlightenment costs $25 an hour, double when the subject touches on money and investments. There is a day rate, too: $500, which includes breakfast, lunch, and dinner with DeLouise, who spoon-feeds his psychic intuitions to hungry millionaires. "Some individuals will fly in from the West Coast," he said. "These guys have millions, and they want to figure out as many ways as they can to hedge against inflation."

Regardless of his methods, DeLouise is part of a highly successful and largely unregulated mini-industry that's in a boom cycle. There are more than 200 independent investment seers who are unaffiliated with either a commodities or a securities firm. And while there are no hard statistics available, these free-lance forecasters were estimated to be pulling in $35 million a year in 1983 from more than a quarter of a million subscribers. Some of these newsletters have considerable influence. In January 1981, for example, the "sell everything" bulletin flashed by Joseph Granville was said by analysts to be one of the main reasons for triggering a $40 billion one-day stock market sell-off that temporarily turned the investment world on its ear. To the pros in the commodities pits, however, none of this should be surprising. They have come to expect anything.

27

Billy and
the Imitators

There are times when commodities simply ignore the charts, the chartists, the mystics, the psychics, the astrologers, the tides, the moon, the fundamentalists, anything that may or may not affect prices. They terrorize and glamorize markets, setting off reactions that are like good news, bad news jokes. Take, for instance, what happened when world oil prices broke sharply in February 1983. It indeed was good news for the consumer, longing for those days when gasoline at the pump was $1 a gallon. It was bad, however, for stock market investors, especially those who held shares in oil explorers, oil producers, and oil service companies, and for major banks (Citicorp, Chemical Bank, Continental Illinois among them) with big loans to oil-producing countries. Good if you were an owner of bonds because lower oil prices gave investors more reason to expect lower inflation rates. Bad if you held gold or gold futures or gold-mining stocks since gold is a hedge against inflation. And so on.

Gold had taken a drubbing in the wake of falling oil prices. In the previous summer and in part of the winter of 1983 it had rallied some $200 an ounce. But the first sign of lower gold prices unleashed a torrent of sellers, who obviously anticipated even lower prices. The selling snowballed, setting off a minefield of stops—orders to sell—and prices tumbled. During the hectic last week in February gold had lost more than half its $200 gain. (A week later, on a Friday, soybean prices on the Board of Trade rallied fifteen cents a bushel within a fifteen minute period, and gold on the Mercantile Exchange shot up $10 for the day.) Why the sudden and sharp rally despite falling oil prices? Perhaps rumors? I checked with Conrad Leslie to confirm my suspicions. Leslie, who meticulously tracks both soybeans and gold, gave this explanation: "The strength [of soybean and gold prices] reflected rumors that North Korea invaded South Korea and our Alaskan troops had been placed on alert. That was accompanied by another rumor that more U.S. soldiers were going to be committed to El Salvador. Somebody was getting hurt in the market, so somebody started rumors. There's a law against it, but no one's ever been caught."

To find out just how bad a hit some of the traders had taken during the gold sell-off, I called Billy Bullion, one of the pit locals at the Mercantile Exchange.

"It was a crazy market," he said. "In five days it went from a bull to a bear market. That kind of change rattles your brains. It was too fast, too hard to reverse your psychology. There were a lot of losers. There was blood in the pit."

Fortunately Billy didn't shed any. A seven-year veteran, he knew how to survive in the pit. He had made nearly $1 million during the gold rush of 1979 and 1980, when the contagion of gold fever pushed the price from about $220 to $850 an ounce in a year. But a bitter divorce settlement had cost him a sizable chunk of his winnings. He was thirty-four.

Billy had a scalper's knack, and over the years he treated the gold pit like a mother lode. Whenever he needed money—a lot of it and fast—he'd return to the gold pit to do some prospecting. Trading 50 and sometimes 100 contracts at a crack, he'd move in and out of the market like a hummingbird darting from flower to flower, pausing just long enough for nectar. When he wasn't trading, he dabbled at business. His portfolio of investments included a quarter interest in a restaurant, a minor interest in a metal smelting concern, three apartment buildings, two condominiums, and some land in Arizona. The tax man was breathing down Billy's neck, and he needed $170,000 to make past amends with the Internal Revenue Service in connection with the sale of some farmland and back taxes. So, after a six-month layoff, it was back to the pit in the summer of 1982. He still had the touch. From August to mid-October Billy Bullion managed to add $200,000 to his trading account.

Billy knew all the trading tricks and trader types. He had learned the early lessons at the MidAmerica Exchange, where he had bought a membership for $3,000. Fifteen months later he traded up, at the prodding of a friend who was a member of the Mercantile Exchange. Billy sold his MidAmerica membership for $8,000 in order to buy a seat on the Merc's International Monetary Market. It was the winter of 1977, a good eighteen months before double-digit inflation and an unsteady American dollar set off the gold stampede. When Billy bought the IMM membership, gold was selling at around $130 an ounce, well below its high of $200 an ounce, reached in 1975, when a renascent gold rush petered out. Billy's IMM seat cost him $48,000, of which he put up $8,000. Another $15,000 came from his friend, and he borrowed $25,000 from the bank on a note cosigned by the clearinghouse that would handle his trades. The clearinghouse was readily willing to accommodate Billy, knowing full well that the seat was undervalued and eventually would be worth a lot more than $48,000 (in December 1982 the asking price for an IMM membership was $200,000).

Billy was a tall, gangly fellow, skinny from his neck to his toes. An "advance man for a famine" was the jocular way someone once described him. He laughed when I told him of the description, vigorously nodding his head with approval. Billy was always in a joking mood outside the pit. But once the gong sounded, it was serious, no-nonsense business. His lightheartedness and slapstick aura turned into a kind of acerbic exaggeration. His furrowed eyebrows and tightly clinched jaw said it all. Nobody ever really knew what Billy was thinking once he was in the pit. But they knew he thought only of himself. There was more than a bit of Fred C. Dobbs in him, the half-crazed, paranoid prospector in *Treasure of Sierra Madre* who turned against his two pals and made off with their share of the gold. Nobody, but nobody, was going to pull a fast one on ol' Fred C. Dobbs—or on Billy Bullion either.

Billy, in fact, had a scheme of his own. He decided to use a ploy learned from one of the big "gunslingers" who had long retired from the pork belly pit. It was a variation on the old shell game. Billy's victims were the small, insecure traders, the vulnerable ones, craning their necks and straining their eardrums to see

153

and hear which direction the big traders were swinging in the market. "Imitators" was what Billy called those traders who bristled with envy every time a Billy Bullion entered the pit. Here's how his ploy worked:

Billy entered the pit knowing that the imitators' eyes were focused on him. Without dallying or showing the least bit of hesitation, he immediately began to buy with an air of confidence that suggested that perhaps he knew something that no one else did. He bought ten cars, then twenty cars, then fifty, screaming his lungs out. He was priming the imitators, luring them on. Sometimes it was only a matter of seconds before they followed, buying their ones and twos with the confidence that they were backing a winner. Nobody, they were convinced, would jump into a market and buy big unless he knew precisely what he was doing. Billy knew all right. But what the imitators didn't know was that Billy Bullion was a seller, too.

That's right, a seller. Shortly before the opening Billy had casually placed a number of sell orders with four different gold brokers. The orders totaled some 300 contracts to be sold at specific prices as the market moved higher. Billy had only to make sure that the market advanced by nudging it just enough. Gold moved in ten-point increments or $10 per tick. Billy's buying coupled with that of the imitators squeezed enough ticks out of the market to push the price of gold $50 higher within the first fifteen minutes of trading. Then Billy unloaded. He began selling everything he bought in the name of profit taking. Naturally the others followed. They wanted profits, too. But some of them couldn't get out fast enough. The sudden rush of selling helped reverse an already faltering market that had been momentarily propped up. Now the momentum shifted downward as gold prices fell more swiftly than they had risen. The ticks rattled off with the sound of a Geiger counter in a hotbed of uranium. Billy even took a loss on some of his contracts, but that hardly mattered. By shorting the market as it moved up, he made an even bigger bundle when it came tumbling down. Markets always seem to drop faster and farther on the way down as if pulled by the force of gravity.

Billy's timing had been superb. He had used his ploy three days running and walked away with more than $210,000 in his trading account. Within that week the market had turned from a bull market to a bear market. Gold, which had stood at $505 a troy ounce the week before in European bullion centers, fell steadily down to close at the end of the week at around $400 an ounce. The weeklong retreat had toppled bullion by more than $100 an ounce, or 20 percent. Nearly 7 million ounces of gold changed sweaty palms that week on the Mercantile Exchange alone. It had taken gold three months to climb $100 and only one week to get down.

The price swings during that hectic week were excessive even by the volatile standards of bullion trading, and most analysts saw it as panic selling. The nerves of officials at New York's Commodity Exchange were as volatile as the price of gold. Noting gold's volatility, they increased the minimum cash down payment—the margin requirement which is generally a reflection of the risk involved—on a 100-ounce contract of gold by 60 percent from $2,500 to $4,000. It wouldn't have made any difference to Billy Bullion because, in a sense, he operated like the exchanges themselves with that Machiavellian rationale that anything goes if it worked—provided, of course, that it was all legal.

Was Billy's ploy illegal? No, just sneaky. Anyone can pump the market up for a few furious moments if he or she has the trading muscle to do it. That, analysts such as Conrad Leslie believe, is what has given the futures markets their mercurial nature in recent years.

"The biggest deterrent to stability in prices is granting traders bigger positions than in the past," said Leslie. "It encourages price determination through power. The evidence to me is the wide differential between the market's closings and its openings. That kind of instability causes commercial interests to increase their markups. And of course, it also makes public trading a great deal more difficult. Then both commercial and public interests stay out of the futures markets, and it becomes more of a professional trading pit." Whenever that happens, you have the traders, as one local put it, "picking each other's pockets."

When it comes to volatility, even stocks—those boring bits of paper that are supposed to be far less risky than commodities— aren't immune from trading vagaries. Back in October 1980, for example, a four-year-old genetic engineering outfit called Genentech, Inc. offered its stock to the public. Genentech's engineers were biologists who created new microorganisms to do specialized tasks. Genentech was a glamour stock with the promise of futuristic breakthroughs—and futuristic profits as well. On October 14, 1980, 1 million shares of Genentech were offered to the public at $35 a share, or some 3,500 times the estimated annual per share earnings (Genentech had made money the previous year, earning just $81,500, or 1 cent a share, for its scientist-owners and some venture capital firms, but it had had an operating deficit amounting to nearly $1 million since its inception). Genentech was discounting, as the analysts say, the hereafter.

Nonetheless, speculators saw Genentech as the Rolls-Royce of genetic engineering companies and its stock as a "pure play," meaning they went for it in a big way. The stock indeed gave them the action they craved. In the first twenty minutes of trading the fledgling issue shot up to $89 a share, and it settled at the closing to $71.25. By the end of the week it was selling at $56 a share. By March 1982 Genentech was selling at $17.

Billy Bullion didn't care about stocks. Nor did he really care about gold. He didn't care that a gold mine cost about $2 million to start in the 1890s and $200 million in the 1970s. And you could bet that he didn't lose any sleep over the fact that it took nearly 80 million tons of rock to yield just under 1,000 tons of gold. Billy wasn't interested in facts or statistics. But he had given some thought to a gold-colored booklet put out by the Mercantile Exchange entitled *Understanding Trading in Gold Futures.*

"This is what I believe when it comes to gold trading," he told me one morning over breakfast at Lou Mitchell's, a popular restaurant among traders, just a block from the Mercantile Exchange.

He flipped to page 15 and shoved the booklet at me, urging me to read the section under "Factors That Determine Gold Prices." It was a quick read. "Prices and price fluctuations of gold," it stated in bold letters, "are not the result of chance, but are determined by powerful economic and psychological forces that continuously change. . . ."

"What's the point?" I asked.

"You notice the phrase *psychological forces*? Well, that's what I believe in when it comes to trading gold or any other commodity," he said, shoving a forkful of hash browns into his mouth.

"Look," he continued in between methodical bites, "it's easy to psych out a bunch of imitators, vultures and weasels and shle-miels."

Billy, it turned out, had mentally categorized the trading types he had encountered over the years. It was a string of characters that belonged in the coda of a Fellini movie. They all seemed to cling to that fear of losing. There were hundreds of traders in the pits, Billy observed, whose fear of losing was associated with disapproval: from other traders; from friends; from lovers and wives and family.

"That's why we're a bundle of insecurities," he growled. "Who the hell wouldn't be?"

At first, he explained, money was for show. "You gotta remember, this is a group that likes to see others fail. It's a very competitive group, and you measure yourself according to your peers. You see an ass making seven hundred thousand dollars a year, and you know that you can do it, too."

But how?

28

Hocus Pocus

Commodity traders are like gamblers who partake in such rituals as kissing the dice before they roll them, or switching seats at the blackjack or poker tables, or carrying lucky rabbits' feet or some other charms. Trusting luck and superstition has a natural appeal when people feel powerless. Those who read horoscopes, sociologists tell us, find life to be too complex, too uncertain, out of control—similar to the nature of the commodities markets themselves. "So they say 'nuts' to rationality," explained Cornell University sociologist Edward C. Devereux, Jr., in a *Business Week* article a few years ago.

Some traders wear the same old lucky shoes for years patched up by the skill of a shoemaker's needle, or wear lucky ties shredded with age, or scribble orders with inch-long lucky pencils, or wear lucky trading watches, or sport lucky buttons, or carry lucky coins, or chew lucky brands of gum, or hum lucky tunes, or use lucky runners, or gulp predawn breakfasts at lucky restaurants, or follow any other number of lucky routines.

You won't catch Maury Kravitz entering the old Mercantile Exchange from the Canal Street entrance. He always comes in from the Jackson Street side. Nor will you find him lighting his cigarette with a lighter because that's unlucky, too. You won't see him driving down a street called Western Avenue either. It's a wide Chicago thoroughfare, but an ominous one for Kravitz. Once he drove down Western Avenue and lost $60,000 in two straight days of trading. He's never been down Western since. And for nearly three years, not rain, sleet, or snow could keep Kravitz from parking his Mercedes 280E outdoors. Parking in his garage was unlucky.

"A good commodities trader is superstitious," Maury Kravitz said. A rotund and good-natured bearded man who in the late seventies wrote a commodity newsletter on gold called *The View from the Pit*, Kravitz had turned in the tailored pinstripes of an attorney for the loosely fitting trader's jacket back in 1971. Kravitz, with his predilection for the romantic (a trait uncommon to the pragmatism of the pits), began to philosophize. He told the story of the time Leo Melamed left his lucky lighter in a restaurant. "The two of us and our wives were vacationing on St. Martin's Island at the time," Kravitz recalled. After a relaxing dinner the four returned to their hotel. As the taxi pulled up, Melamed realized he had left his lighter at the restaurant. It was a cheap lighter, hardly worth the worry. The affluent Melamed could buy a carload of them back in Chicago. But it was his *lucky* lighter.

"Go back to the restaurant to get the lighter?" one of the wives said wonderingly. Melamed couldn't—or didn't want to—explain. He turned to Kravitz and said, "I'm in the market!" Kravitz immediately knew what Melamed meant. He had a position in the market and had misplaced his lucky lighter, his trading lighter.

"We turned around and drove clear across to the other side of the island back to the restaurant to get the lighter," Kravitz said. Melamed found it. Kravitz doesn't know if Melamed ended up a winner on the trade, but he did know that Melamed was a lot more relaxed once he had his lucky lighter back.

Sometimes traders in search of that lucky charm are even willing to bank on someone else's superstition. Nick Farina found that out. Farina at the time was a Chicago financial reporter whose beat was the Chicago Board of Trade. A corn blight was playing havoc with the nation's crop, and that meant a severe shortage of corn and higher prices not only for corn products but for the country's cattle and other livestock that were raised on corn. Farina was making his rounds as usual, roving the trading floor to find out just how well the pros were holding up. One of his key sources had been long a million bushels of corn and understandably was anxious. Trading was in progress that Monday morning in June, following a weekend of rain in the Corn Belt, which was good for the longs. Outside the corn pit Farina began conversing with his source.

"It always rains when I leave my top down," Farina casually remarked.

"What kind of car you got?" the source asked.

"Mustang convertible," Farina replied, hoping to get the small talk out of the way so he could get on with reporting the corn story.

"Does it really rain every time you leave the top down?" the source queried, grabbing Farina by the arm and pulling him closer so no one else could hear. Then, in a very firm and somber voice, he whispered, "Leave the top down all summer, and I'll buy you a new Mustang."

For a few moments Farina gave the offer serious thought, but then he politely refused it. "He really meant it," Farina said. "That's the kind of money some of those traders have. And some will spend it on anything if they think they can win."

Most traders would never go that far because deep down they know what it *really* takes to win in the pits. As a youngster growing up on Chicago's tough West Side, Maury Kravitz was a sort of Peck's Bad Boy with a brain, the kind of kid who got As on tests and Fs in behavior—and took pride in both. He was a kid with street smarts, a survivor who always knew what he wanted.

At eleven it was a bicycle. But the hard knocks of reality hit quickly when his parents sat him down with the blunt message that they couldn't afford one. That wasn't going to stop Maury. "I didn't understand," the raspy-voiced Kravitz recalled. "That's when I decided I wouldn't be left out of the American Dream. I would do anything to get myself a chunk of it." A year later, at twelve, he became an entrepreneur in the lucrative auto parts business. He stole hubcaps from neighborhood cars. It was a short-lived venture when he made his first and last mistake. One set of hubcaps belonged to a fellow down the street who happened to be a policeman. "He ended my career," Kravitz said, cracking a boyish grin. "I've been straight ever since."

Kravitz, an only child, had great admiration for his father. "He was a scholar with a capital *S*," Maury said. Nathaniel Kravitz, by his son's account, was a child prodigy in the tiny town of Calis, nestled along the Dnestr River in a buffer zone between Romania and Russia known as Bessarabia. By age seven Nathaniel had memorized the five books of Moses along with parts of the Talmud, an effort which won him plaudits from the rabbi and village elders and the nickname *Zaidehle* ("little grandfather"). In the wake of World War I Nathaniel left home on his own, exploring other parts of Europe, learning and teaching along the way. He made his way across Hungary and Czechoslovakia into Germany, where he stayed just long enough to earn his passage across the Atlantic. At fifteen Nathaniel had left Europe behind forever. The rickety freighter he shipped out on was bound for Cuba. Eventually he met and married Maury's mother, who had emigrated to Havana from Kiev. They moved to Philadelphia in the 1920s, and Nathaniel began a serious career as a journalist, writing and editing for a number of Yiddish-language newspapers. In 1939 Maury and his parents moved to Chicago, the haven of Jewish journalism west of the Hudson, where Nathaniel continued to edit Yiddish newspapers for three more decades. It wasn't the easiest way to scratch out a living, especially during the Depression years, but money had always been the least of Nathaniel Kravitz's concerns.

"He spent his entire seventy-six years garnering knowledge," said Maury with awe in his voice. "He had a working knowledge of some thirty-five languages, including Sanskrit, Urdu, and Swahili. He was not a superstitious man."

Maury wanted more than intellectual wealth. That wouldn't guarantee him the tangible slice of the American Dream he had yearned for as a youth. He decided to become a lawyer. It was while attending John Marshall Law School in 1952 that he got his first taste of the commodity market as a part-time $18-a-week messenger for Merrill Lynch, Pierce, Fenner & Bean at the Mercantile Exchange. Merrill Lynch, too, was a novice in commodities then with only two brokers, two telephone clerks, and one messenger on the floor. It was a stark contrast with the battery of phone clerks and platoons of runners and brokers it uses today.

Kravitz had just entered law school after a three-year hitch in the United States Army, spending most of the time in Germany. The American Dream meanwhile simmered on the back burner of his desires. There were more pressing matters like eating. His financial condition, as he put it, was "extreme insolvency." Looking back, he recalled, "I had enjoyed that precarious financial status at least sixteen times that year."

One afternoon Kravitz was having a cup of coffee in the restaurant across the street from law school when a friend and fellow student, Leo Melamed, joined him. Kravitz was about to put on his most desperate "I gotta have ten bucks look" when Melamed broke the good news. Leo was being promoted from a runner at the Merc to a phone clerk for Merrill Lynch. That meant the job of runner was available. "Leo was still talking as I bolted out of the chair on my way to the exchange to apply for the position," Kravitz said. He was hired. It was a convenient job since school was only several blocks from the Merc.

Eventually Kravitz became the personal telephone clerk for the top Merrill Lynch broker on the Merc floor, a big, burly, heavy-jowled Dutchman named Joseph Sieger. He could be a hydra-headed monster and an angel. "He was loud, profane, and one of the best brokers that Merrill Lynch ever had," Kravitz insisted, the kind of person you could swear at and swear by. Sieger would scream at Kravitz, call him names when he didn't respond quickly enough, and lecture and insult him. Yet he was a good friend, and on occasion a benefactor. For instance, when Kravitz didn't have the tuition for the next semester's law school, Sieger paid it without telling him. When Kravitz tried to thank him for the help, Sieger bellowed, "Mind your own business, bud."

The egg and onion markets were in full bloom then, and for a young man who saw a certain magic in risk, the prospect, as Kravitz said, "stirred the nettles of the soul." Before hanging up an attorney's shingle, Kravitz was impelled to try his hand at trading. He had been on the floor for three years and observed the action firsthand as a runner and phone clerk, but until you entered the pits faced off against an adversary, you were still an outsider looking in. Kravitz borrowed $5,000 to buy a membership and got Joe Sieger to sponsor him.

"OK, dummy," groused Sieger, "I'll help you get the membership, but why any membership committee would approve a dummy like you is beyond me." The seat cost Kravitz $3,850, leaving him with about $1,200 to begin his trading career.

162

First he sought the advice of his mentor. There was no one who knew the ins and outs of trading better than Sieger.

"Now here is what you have to do," Sieger told an attentive Kravitz like Aristotle instructing Alexander the Great. "I want you to read all the books that are available on commodities, particularly on chickens and eggs. At the same time start studies on charts, and learn everything that you can learn on charting the commodity markets. When you have completed that, I want you to talk to these three traders [he named them] and ask them to describe their trading techniques to you as best as they can. When you are in the pit, do exactly the same thing Harold does. When Harold buys, you buy, and when Harold sells, you sell. Don't neglect to subscribe to these two advisory services. Start a statistical study program on the basic fundamentals of the egg market. Make a study of weather trends because as you know, when it is cold, the chickens don't lay eggs as frequently, and if it gets too snowy, the trucks can't get the eggs to market. Watch the open interest numbers and the spread relationships in the egg options. Day-to-day volume is an important consideration. When you have done all these things, then you are ready to start trading."

Kravitz was soaking it in, scribbling notes on a pad as if he were back in law school in a torts class. He was ecstatic. There he was at the feet of the master being led down the Eightfold Path to trading Nirvana. That is, until Sieger threw in the kicker to his trading dissertation like a well-timed punch line.

"If you have done everything I have suggested," he told the wide-eyed Kravitz, "then I think that in, oh, let's see, in about four to five weeks, you shouldn't be down more than about four to five thousand dollars."

The hell with it. He would prove Sieger wrong. Into the egg market Kravitz charged, aiming to become a ninety-day wonder. As it turned out, Sieger was indeed wrong. It took only three weeks for Kravitz to lose $4,000. The losses continued to mount, and in less than three months he was out $15,000. Kravitz borrowed more. Lost again.

Maury Kravitz had had enough. Whatever the key was to successful trading, he couldn't latch on to it. He could yell as loudly as the rest and bully his way into the crowd, but he couldn't win. Frustrated over the losses, Kravitz resumed his legal career. He kept his membership for four years, periodically dabbling in the pits, but the trading knack still evaded him. Finally, in 1957, he sold his seat for $19,000. At least, he told himself, that trade was profitable.

While those early trading years were expensive, those forays into the pits were to pay off in later years. He had learned to respect and fear the markets and that to survive, a trader had to cope with the emotional swings that could take him to the heights of elation and the depths of despair—with no time in between. Any veteran trader could have told him that, but it was something *he* had to discover on his own, something *he* had to feel deep in his gut. And as for all the prepping Joe Sieger had provided, those gems culled from decades of trading, it meant little when he got down to the realities of the pit. "There is no way to learn the art of trading in a vicarious manner," Kravitz said, stroking his chin with his pudgy fingers.

Kravitz practiced law successfully over the years, but the lure of the market remained a constant temptation. He gave in to it in 1971 and decided to return to the pits for one more try. Times had changed. Now there were more commodities to trade and a new generation of traders. His longtime friend Leo Melamed was now a political force on the exchange. The markets were heating up; this time it cost Kravitz $87,000 to get into the game. Everything had changed, including Kravitz. It had been fourteen years since he had last been in the pit, a long time to ponder mistakes, to set strategy, to mature. This time, he convinced himself, he was ready. He would give himself time; if he couldn't cut it in five years, that would be it.

Kravitz started out trading pork bellies and then swung over to gold in 1975, riding a wave of fortune and, to some degree, fame. Maury Kravitz became the Goldfinger of the gold pit, eventually buying and selling more gold yearly than anyone in the Merc, in the United States.

Kravitz traded more gold in a year than the 53 million ounces annually mined throughout the world and became a broker for other clients as well, among them his first employer, Merrill Lynch. Only one other trader in the world did as much volume as Kravitz, if not more than he. That was Samsanov, the chief Soviet gold trader who works in Wozchod Handelsbank in Zurich. "That little fellow," Kravitz said of Samsanov, "is nobody's fool." The Soviet Union is the world's second-largest gold producer behind South Africa, and Kravitz respects the way the Russians trade gold.

Kravitz's prodigious gold trading earned him international recognition of a kind. In June 1981 he was invited to participate in the prestigious international gold conference at Montreux, Switzerland, an annual event that draws the world's leading economists and presidents of the European central banks. Kravitz doesn't hide the fact that it was a high point in his career; his face lights up with animation when he talks about it. There was Maury Kravitz, the alumnus of the streets of Chicago's West Side, the scholar's son, the *enfant terrible* of the gold pit whom one of the Merc elders had called "a mischievous kid." Kravitz spoke authoritatively on the role of gold futures, discussing the myriad of economic and political factors that affect markets. What he didn't tell the dignitaries of high metallic finance, however, was what it took to survive the pits. He told me one afternoon in his office. Economist John Maynard Keynes once dubbed gold "a barbarous relic." To hear Kravitz tell it, you have to be a barbarian to trade it.

"A good floor broker," he snapped, "isn't a turn-the-cheek Christian. He should have qualities similar to Genghis Khan's Mongol horsemen. You have to be built like an animal. The successful brokers are almost vicious. The sedate person finds himself at the tail end of things."

A half-empty bottle of Pepto-Bismol sits on his desk as a warrior's tribute to the gut-wrenching world of the pits. There are more obvious battle scars. For instance, there is the permanent sandpaper hoarseness of his voice, which mellows into a whisper when he's not in the pit. It is a voice damaged by the years of daily outcries, a price hundreds of other traders would gladly pay to become millionaires. Physically the pits haven't been all that kind to Kravitz, who once reviewed a list of nineteen characteristics of a coronary profile and concluded, "I qualified for eighteen out of nineteen." He is constantly fighting his weight, starting a new diet practically every week. He is also a heavy smoker and a poor eater, who will grab a quick hamburger and a couple of Bloody Marys for lunch at the Iron Horse in the basement of the Mercantile Exchange Building. Or he'll stop in at the Union Station Restaurant, across from the Merc, for a 6:45 A.M. bacon and eggs special awash in grease with plenty of black coffee. The restaurant feeds capitalism on the run, catering to the tastes of commodity brokers, railroad men, postal employees. And there's the pressure, sometimes vise-tight. Kravitz feels it every time he walks into the pit, especially on those days when he's behind from the opening bell and, as he once put it, must "grovel like an animal to catch up." But sometimes all the groveling and aggression can't make up for the mistakes, which come too often in a fast-moving market. All the feel and instinct dissipate, giving way to the pandemonium of the moment: paper from orders flying like confetti; the shrill ringing of phones; the cursing; the hollering; the whistling; the clapping; the shoving; the gesturing—anything to connect buyer with seller and seller with buyer. Anything. Only at the close, when the smoke clears and the calm sets in and the hearts beat normally again, only then do traders tally up their profits, losses, and mistakes.

29

Sorry, Wrong Trade

For a trader like Kravitz who bought and sold a daily average of 800 to 1,000 gold contracts worth more than $30 million, mistakes were bound to be made. Those mistakes, or so-called outtrades, can be small or large. No matter what size, they all are painful because they put extra pressure on a trader to make up for his carelessness. Often in the anxiety to play catch-up more mistakes are made, the kinds of mistakes that sometimes made Kravitz want to board his 38-foot, teak yacht and set sail in the usually calmer waters of Lake Michigan or to dash home, down a glass of white wine, gulp a quick dinner, and splice the trading day together in the would-have, should-have, could-have hour.

Stories are common about outtrades running into thousands and even hundreds of thousands of dollars. Nearly every trader has an outtrade sooner or later, and Kravitz was no exception. During one stormy session he thought he had bought fifteen contracts from another trader. It turned out to be a losing trade. But Kravitz didn't realize just how big a loss it was until the next morning, when the previous day's trades were settled. To his utter dismay, he had bought fifty contracts, not fifteen. Amid the screeching outcries of the pit "fifteen" often sounds like "fifty" and vice versa. Even a hesitating "uh" can sound like an "eight." Kravitz's outtrade was a $110,000 mistake, the kind, he said, that made him pull in his horns in a bit. It was a painful and costly mistake, to be sure. And while there's not much solace in numbers, Kravitz was not alone in his agony.

When a market goes berserk, the normal trading structures simply break down. The following morning the wall of an exchange can look like the white cliffs of Dover, plastered with computer printouts listing more than 10,000 transactions that failed the overnight clearing process. Since the 1960s Wall Street has learned to handle the paper work blizzard with relatively few mistakes that come with record 100-million-share days. But the futures exchanges still have a hard time coping. Their computers work well. It's the human element that seems to short-circuit. The combination of speed and confusion jolts the system. The exchanges pride themselves on speed in handling and executing an order—two to three minutes, they claim, from the time the order reaches the floor. The scene has the aura of Eisenhower's war room on D-day. In those few minutes here's what happens: buy and sell orders are received by constantly ringing telephones or clattering teletype machines located around the periphery of the trading floor. The orders are time-stamped and given to a runner, who dispatches them to the broker in the pit. The broker fills the order. As each order is filled, the broker reports price changes to a price reporter, glaring at a video screen from raised pulpits. The reporter, in turn, programs the quote into a central computer. The computer transmits the price onto electronic price boards over the trading floor and to tickers around the world. The filled orders are then picked up by runners, who return them to the telephone and teletype desks, where they are time-stamped and immediately confirmed to the customer. It's hardly a well-oiled machine.

What the exchanges don't mention is the fact that in those few moments when the order is received and filled in the pit, all hell can break loose, and the world can turn upside down. Many an order becomes a loss before it hits the pit because the market moves so quickly. It works, of course, the other way, too. Regardless, it's the traders in the pit who have the edge over the public.

Pit trading has always been error-prone whether it's 5,000-bushel lots of soybeans, 100-ounce contracts for gold, or $1 million certificates of deposit. The more crowded the pit and the faster the action, the greater the chances for a misread hand signal, a misheard word. A flick of the wrist to indicate a sale (an outward palm) is often mistaken for a buy signal (inward palm), and there is always the possibility of mistaken identity. That often occurs when a trader can't be sure whether someone on the other side of the pit is signaling to him or to the lurching traders on either side of him or to the one hanging over his shoulder. Some traders often shout "Sold!" to mark completion of sales even when they are buying, resulting in "sale-against-sale" outtrades. And in the crush of a wild closing, when the trading madness reaches a crescendo, many brokers don't have time to write down their transactions. After the trading bell they scramble about, trying to figure out what they have traded and with whom.

Out of this chaos anything can happen. In the summer of 1982, for instance, so much paper was flying around the Merc floor that some got caught in the lights around the perimeter and actually started a fire. The traders hardly noticed, and a couple of fire extinguishers handled the situation. The floor of an exchange at the end of a trading day is carpeted with paper refuse that tells a thousand stories of wins and losses, of mistakes and shenanigans.

Starting the day with an outtrade is like going to a wine-tasting party with a hangover. The morning is the time when the pit broker who made $6,000 in commissions the previous day finds out he lost $10,000 to a single trading mistake. The cost of making a trade good comes out of the broker's pocket. The mistakes turn up each night in the exchanges' clearinghouse computers, where each sale is matched against the opposite buy. The data from a pit broker or trader are recorded—often illegibly on trading cards emblazoned with the trader's name or brokerage house at the top—and put into the computers. The computers reject all buy trades that can't be matched to a sale, and vice versa, as outtrades. Mornings in the wake of fast markets brokerage firms send their battalions of clerks scurrying across the floor on missions of hide-and-seek. Their job is to identify the missing sides of outtrades. Sometimes it can be Mission Impossible. There are enough finaglers to start a bureau of missing persons, traders who disappear when it comes time to even up. They simply refuse to acknowledge their money-losing trades, thereby robbing the winners of profits. Some traders can get away with it once or even twice, but sooner or later nobody will trade with them. But most traders take their outtrades with the spirit of the Victorian British soldier who bit the bullet with a sense of duty, discipline, and stoicism. The sweet thing about commodity trading is that for most, there is a next time. Nevertheless, trading snafus are increasingly costly to the pit brokers who fill orders for brokerage house customers. In an active pit the tension these cause can explode into physical combat. More than once a pit trader has turned on a pit clerk who misshuffled a stack of orders during a fast price swing. The result has been bruised chins, bloody knuckles, and huge fines—all for a few seconds of satisfaction.

Somebody is always ready to take advantage of the confusion. Every so often an outtrade clerk will pull an outright scam at the expense of an unwitting broker. For instance, after the close of a turbulent market the clerk simply makes up a profitable trade and puts it in the broker's account without his knowledge. The trade is in the name of a friend of the clerk. They split the profit; the broker loses. If the broker's loss isn't too great, chances are he will let it go, knowing full well that he can't keep up with every trade he makes in a fast market. Some such phony trades have gone all the way to arbitration, and the broker has often lost.

30

Trading a Fantasy

In the summer of 1982 the futures contract based on the Standard & Poor's Index of 500 stocks took over where gold had left off a couple of years earlier. The S&Ps, as they are called, took off with the bull market in stocks in August 1982. Introduced in April 1982, it was one of those novel contracts the exchange had, in effect, thrown against the wall like a plate of spaghetti to see if it would stick. The exchange needed a winner. With inflation seemingly in control, gold had lost its luster, and the activity in the gold pit had mellowed considerably. In fact, trading in the Merc's gold pit became dormant, and Maury Kravitz, along with others, turned to the S&P pit for action. The market for gold trading had moved to the Commodity Exchange in New York, where much of the real gold was stored in bank vaults. Things had begun to ease off in the once-hectic treasury bill pit, too, as interest rates became less volatile. That pretty much left S&Ps to take up the slack. The contract provided a lot of action and attracted hordes of young, inexperienced brokers and traders.

The exchanges argued that stock futures would actually make stock trading safer. Banks, insurance companies, and pension funds were encouraged to use the new contract to protect their stock portfolios from a bear market just as a grain dealer would use commodity futures to insulate himself from a sharp drop in the price of wheat or corn. A portfolio manager would sell stock futures, and then, if stock prices dropped, he would offset the loss on his real portfolio with his profits on the futures contract. Or if the market rallied, he would chalk up the losses on his futures contracts as the equivalent of an insurance premium. The rationalization that stock index futures were a "safer" gamble was like asking a person to give up cigarettes by smoking cigars.

Nevertheless, speculators flocked to the Merc's S&P pit, partly enticed by the contract's low margin requirements (a $6,500 down payment, or 10 percent to buy a contract of imaginary stocks worth about $65,000) and the prodding of Merc officials. Not only would the Merc be competing with the Kansas City Board of Trade, which traded its contract based on Arnold Bernhard & Co.'s Value Line Stock Index, but also with the New York Futures Exchange and its New York Stock Exchange Composite Index. Even more threatening was the intention of the Merc's archrival, the Chicago Board of Trade, to offer contracts based on the popular Dow Jones Stock Averages.

The pressure was on the 2,600 Merc members to participate in the S&P pit, built so hastily that the top stairs remained unpainted more than a year later. The Merc hyped the doctrine of S&Ps with missionary zeal. As traders entered the exchange floor, each was handed a button with the slogan "15 Minutes, Please," to urge them to spend at least fifteen a day trading the new S&P contract. And intermittently through the day an authoritative voice over the loudspeaker reminded traders to try the S&P pit for just fifteen minutes. At the same time the Merc reached out to the public with full-page advertisements in the *Wall Street Journal* and hired Louis Rukeyser, the host of public television's "Wall Street Week" program, to narrate two sixteen-minute videotapes that explained the S&P contract. It couldn't have picked a better endorsement than Rukeyser, whose show was watched by millions each week. Commodities brokers used the S&P tapes to win customers.

But it was the personal touch that really made the difference. Strolling among the pits as if he were a politician working the neighborhoods was Leo Melamed, former Merc chairman, pioneer of financial futures, symbol of the drive and success of the exchange, the man whose diplomatic finesse had become his trademark. Weaving in and out of the crowd, he pressed the flesh, patted backs, exchanged cursory remarks, made his presence felt. If there had been babies, he would have kissed them to win S&P

converts. As special counsel to the Merc board and chairman of its financial instruments steering committee, Melamed constantly circulated among traders, drumming up enthusiasm for new contracts. Supporting new contracts, he'd remind them, was in their self-interest. Most traders viewed Melamed's stewardship as having put money in their pockets over the years. After all, hadn't seats in the Merc's financial futures division climbed from $100 to $190,000 in eleven years? And hadn't the Merc steadily and dramatically increased its market share of trading volume (30 percent of the industry) since 1972, reaching a point in 1984 at which it was breathing down the neck of the Chicago Board of Trade.

Whatever his faults, it was the way his colleagues perceived Melamed that mattered. Leo, they believed, had got them this far, and he was far too shrewd to blow it on some frivolous venture. He was the guy with class, and the rest were 2,000 used car salesmen, as one of his fans put it. "My enlightened self-interest says I should be willing to give a pint of blood so that this contract can grow and grow," one trader later said after losing $10,000 trading S&Ps. In fact, the dues were high for many traders in the S&P pit, and it wasn't long before members turned the "15 Minutes, Please" slogan into "$1,500, Please." But Melamed was a magnet, one of the few who could rally the members, and when he walked into the pit and started trading S&Ps, the others did, too.

The push paid off from the very beginning. June 1983 S&P 500 contracts shot up from 105 in August 1982 to 144 in early October, a price increase worth $1,950 per contract. By January 1983 the Merc's S&P contracts accounted for nearly 60 percent of all stock index trading. Even those newcomers of the late 1970s, interest rate futures—contracts based on treasury bonds, bills and notes along with Government National Mortgage Association securities (Ginnie Maes), bank certificates of deposit, and Eurodollar deposits—had taken a good three years to reach the kind of volume S&Ps had in the first year. The trading floor of the Merc became so crowded that telephone and work stations were moved into lounge areas. And the city fire ordinances prevented the needed hiring of more clerks and runners in the summer of 1983, a situation that was remedied in the fall of 1983, when the Merc moved into a new $350 million forty-story carnelian granite-clad building just a few blocks from the old site on the Chicago River.

The Merc, meantime, had spiced up trading in the S&Ps by

removing the daily trading limit from the contract. That made the game far more treacherous. The previous limit on S&P futures had been five index points, which meant the value of the contract could rise or fall a maximum of $2,500 a day. The rationale for dropping the limit, explained exchange officials, was to bring the contract more in line with stock market practices, which have no limits to daily price moves. Before traders could get their bearings, the Merc followed up with a couple of new wrinkles in the commodities landscape. The first was an options contract on the S&Ps futures, which are the right, but not the obligation, to buy or sell the futures contract within a certain time. In effect, it was a futures contract on a futures contract for the imaginary delivery of an imaginary portfolio of stocks. And for those who were just as imaginative, but with smaller pocketbooks, the Merc came up with a second contract called the S&P 100. This contract consisted of a group of stocks plucked out of the S&P 500, an S&P microcosm as it were, designed to appeal to the smaller speculator with the hearty appetite for risk. These were among those "intangible" futures commodities which the federal regulators had OK'd, on the basis of their economic justification.

It wasn't long before the S&P contracts, which had all the volatility and drama of the usually raucous pork belly pit, became known as pinstripe pork bellies. Besides trading euphoria, the index futures created a so-called shadow market where traders bet on where the *real* stock market was headed. Index futures weren't a case of the tail wagging the dog, proponents argued, but rather making the dog itch for a while. Critics dismissed the contract as one big office football pool, and some tried to convince the commodity regulators that there was little economic purpose to index futures. A year before trading in index futures began, for example, Walter E. Auch, chairman of the Chicago Board Options Exchange, wrote a letter to the Commodity Futures Trading Commission warning of the potential for "sophisticated manipulative schemes" and that index futures are a "dressed up form of wagering."

If stock index futures were a form of wagering, it wasn't the first time someone had used stock indexes to make book. Ladbrokes of London, one of the world's largest bookmaking operations, has been accepting bets in Britain on the Dow Jones

Industrial Average since 1964. In fact, Ladbrokes welcomed index futures as a way to hedge its bets. When its "book" becomes too bullish or bearish, Ladbrokes may buy $10 million worth of index futures in the United States. It can still make a profit on its index futures even if it has to meet a heavy payout to British gamblers.

Outright betting on commodity moves was the vogue in America at the turn of the century. That's when the old bucket shops proliferated across the country. The bucket shops were run by potboiler operators who accepted bets on the movement of grain prices that were reported by the Chicago Board of Trade's ticker. The action became so hot and heavy that one federal judge proclaimed, "Gambling in grains may be said to be the national pastime," giving baseball an early run for its money.

Bucket shops were a highly unsophisticated, manipulative scheme. No grain was ever actually delivered on any futures contracts in a bucket shop. Orders were not executed on a legitimate exchange, and no commercial interests used bucket shops for hedging. A bucket shop was a betting parlor where anyone could bet against the house on price changes of either stocks or commodities. It was pure gambling, and the bucket shops hated losing. Whenever the shops became lopsided with bulls betting on one particular stock, they hustled up their cadre of brokers, who then sold the stock short, driving the price down. The cost to each bucket shop was usually no more than a couple of points on several hundred shares. The rare times when customers did manage to make a killing, the bucket shops would fold up their operations like Bedouins and move on or vanish without paying off. In his youth, fabled speculator Jesse Livermore earned the reputation of Boy Plunger in the Boston bucket shops. He'd beat them so often that they banned him. His bucket shop adventures are chronicled in the autobiographical *Reminiscences of a Stock Operator,* which was first published in 1903. Livermore, who had won and lost millions in stocks and commodities, boasted throughout his lifetime that he was a "60-40" player—content to clear his 20 percent. As it turned out, the 20 percent wasn't enough. Livermore lost once too often, and in 1941, frustrated and broke, he committed suicide.

Bucket shops came in all sizes, appealing to all classes. Some were hole-in-the-wall dives that accepted $1 bets. Others were set up as brokerage houses with businesslike auras of respectability.

Regardless of façade, their objective was the same: to fleece the customer. The first bucket shop, Rumble & Company, appeared in Chicago as early as 1876. One of the most pretentious was the Metropolitan Grain and Stock Exchange, located in Chicago's classiest hotel of the era, the Palmer House.

Some sharpsters added their own variations to the bucket shop scam. Foxy William Shakel, a bushy-browed, fast-talking promoter came up with the tape game. Each night Shakel would have a fictitious tape made up with prices of wheat, oats, and corn. The tape was then wound up tightly and placed inside a box. The next day the tape was drawn slowly from the box as if the latest prices from the Board of Trade were being relayed to the office. The bets piled up, and Shakel made a fortune. Shakel had four offices in Chicago's downtown Loop, and they were loaded each day with bettors. If there was ever a con man who knew how to *sting* a sucker, it was Shakel.

Such con games went on for years until the Board of Trade literally pulled the wires on the bucket shops. From 1910 to 1915 it was open season on the bucket shops. First, the board removed its tickers from the shops and all saloons. Without the quotations, the board reckoned, there could be no betting. But that hardly stopped the duplicitous bucket shops, which began bribing board members and employees of board firms. It worked for a while. One firm would hang a plank out the window and move it up or down with the market. Employees would signal out the window in a special hand code. Like plugging holes in a dike, the board then moved to seal itself shut by barring all entrances but one, removing all telephones, preventing messengers from leaving the building until after trading hours. And in a fit of frustration, it soaped all the windows.

The seesaw battle was finally settled in the courts in a series of suits by the board against the bucket shops. The board argued that the shops were in the business of stealing quotations from it, a practice that was undermining the entire futures market. In their defense, the bucket shops countered by asserting that the Board of Trade itself was a gambling institution. The case went all the way to the U.S. Supreme Court. The board won, severely crippling the future activities of the bucket shops. In the majority opinion, Justice Oliver Wendell Holmes commented on speculation:

As has appeared, the plaintiff's chamber of commerce is, in the first place, a great market, where, through its 1,800 members, is transacted a large part of the grain and provisions business of the world.

Of course in a modern market contracts are not confined to sales for immediate delivery. People will try to forecast the future and to make agreements according to their prophecy. Speculation of that kind is the self-adjustment of society to the probable. Its value is well known as a means of avoiding or mitigating catastrophes, equalizing prices and providing for periods of want. It is true that the success of the strong induces imitation by the weak, and that incompetent persons bring themselves to ruin by undertaking to speculate in their turn.

But legislatures and courts generally have recognized that the natural evolutions of a complex society are to be touched only with a very cautious hand, and that such coarse attempts at a remedy for the waste incident to every social function as a simple prohibition and laws to stop its being are harmful and vain.

31

Vultures, Weasels, and Mice

Justice Holmes might well have reconsidered his statement in light of index futures had he been around in the 1980s. Dealing with an undeliverable bushel of imaginary stocks is far different from dealing with a deliverable bushel of wheat. "For many," the *Wall Street Journal* observed of stock index trading in 1983, "the action holds all the thrill of an investment video game." That observation was based on a peek the *Journal* took over the shoulder of a trader who had been seemingly mesmerized by his price quotation computer, lapsing into a *Star Wars* monologue that lasted less than a minute: " 'The market is at 146.75, OK. . . . 80, .85, .90. . . . $100 in 10 seconds. . . . Now it's breaking back. Oh, my God! Now it's making new highs. . . . Gee, it picked up another $200.' "

Indeed, for many traders, bridging the gap of securities and futures in the S&P pit was entering an alien world. "There was a certain indignation, a lack of discipline, a rowdiness," said an exasperated veteran pork belly trader who spent those suggested fifteen minutes in the S&P pit and never returned. There were too many new faces, new names, new strategies. The action was the same as it was in most active pits, but the pockets had changed.

One element that never changes, however, is the trader. Regardless of which commodity is the darling of the crowd, traders bring into the pit extensions of themselves, and like a baseball organization, there is a pecking order of players: the stars, the rookies, the substitutes, the bush leaguers all wanting to score. They exist in the S&P pit, and in the pork belly pit, and in the wheat pit, and in the bond pit, and in every pit on every exchange—traders eager to make a buck any way they can. There are, for example, the mice, those traders who are constantly running scared, the nickel-dimers content to trade one or two contracts. Some are so intimidated by the maddening crowd they can place their orders only through pit brokers.

The mice are ruled by the intimidators, the flashy group that can size up the action within seconds of entering the pit. An intimidator is not a big trader but, rather, the bully on the block who can sniff out a situation with the sixth sense that comes with trading savvy, the kind of sense that produces a shark out of nowhere when a piece of bloody meat is dangled in the water. If, say, the market drops a couple of points with no apparent volume, the intimidator knows the locals are selling it down, shorting the market, as it were. That's when he makes his move. He'll start buying one, two, three contracts in order to begin nudging the market higher in an effort to force the smaller traders to cover their positions. It's a minisqueeze, but with just enough pressure to cause a scramble among the scalpers who have no intention of holding on to a position. The intimidators are the nomads of the pits, scooting across the sands of the Merc a few steps in any direction to trade gold or treasury bills or Swiss francs or cattle or pork bellies or hogs or eggs or potatoes or lumber, their speed increasing in direct proportion to the distance of the nearest pit.

On the heels of the intimidators come the vultures, who know how to pick the leftovers clean, to pluck those last few ticks away from the groveling crowd. For the most part, they specialize in the play at the close of a market, when things become chaotic, when the trading world seems to cave in to the sheer impact of human emotion. A few I came across actually nap in the traders' lounge or in a broker's back office and are awakened by runners just five or ten minutes before the closing bell, fresh and ready to race the stretch. They make a Jack Armstrong dash into the pit as if they were some all-Americans in a desperate bid to save the game in the last few moments. They'll buy ten, twenty; sell ten, twenty, nimbly dumping the contracts as if they were vials of nitroglycerin about to go off. While the intimidators profit on insecurities, the vultures corner panic.

Not to be undercut by either the intimidators or the vultures are the weasels, traders who stand at the elbows of friendly order fillers. The weasels are tipped off by the order fillers, who can treat their order decks like a tray of hors d'oeuvres during a happy hour. With the knowledge of what's in a deck, a weasel trades ahead of the order filler. If, for instance, a weasel knows there is going to be some heavy buying that will drive up the price, he'll go long, and vice versa if the deck is loaded with sell orders. Nothing complicated, just a little impropriety pegged to a subtle signal, such as the sound of a voice, the nod of a head, the scratching of an ear, or even code words. In exchange for the inside tidbits, the order filler uses the weasel as a sort of straw man to match customers' buy and sell orders. It violates the rule of competitive outcry.

Traders often get involved in a number of improper practices. Brokers have been known to take the opposite side of a customer's trade by buying for their own accounts a futures contract without first obtaining the customer's permission. There are the so-called accommodation trades, those through a third party. Here's how it works: The transaction is carried out through an accommodator, who agrees to buy from one trader and sell to another trader at the same or a slightly different price. The procedure is commonly known as a wash sale because there is little or no price advantage or disadvantage for either buyer or seller. But such activity creates artificially high trading volume that, in turn, gives outside speculators the impression of an active market, stimulating order flows from which traders profit.

Traders, of course, are tight-lipped about discussing floor practices when reputations and livelihoods are at stake. But some practices that are part of the unwritten code of pit ethics do nudge traders along that fragile line of legal and illegal trading. One such practice was common in the wild treasury bond pit at the Chicago Board of Trade in 1983. The practice was called ginzy, one of those arcane trading terms shrouded in mystery. No one knows exactly where the word came from, but some linked it to a former trader named Ginsburg who pioneered the practice, which was hardly mysterious. A ginzy took place when a broker sold part of his customer's order at the offer price and the remaining part of the order at the lower bid price. The orders were sold to the same trader. Thus the execution of the trade meant that the customer paid an average price for his contract somewhere between the bid and offer. Proponents of the art of ginzying argue that the customer isn't harmed unless the broker and trader agree on a price beforehand. Moreover, they reasoned, the trader who buys some contracts at a high price deserves to get a break at a lower price.

Not everyone in the bond pit ginzied. It was confined mainly to the southeast corner of the pit, where traders worked their spreads, or the simultaneous buying and selling of contracts covering different delivery months. Ginzying had heated up because of fierce competition among brokers. Spread business had become more competitive in the wake of a change in the tax laws in 1982 that wiped out the loophole, known as a straddle, which was used by traders to defer taxes on their profits. It left the brokers competing for less business, especially in the later-delivery months affected most by the tax change. The pressure was enormous on brokers to bend Board of Trade rules by filling orders between the ticks. The bond contracts—each with the face value of $100,000—are supposed to be traded in a minimum price increment, or tick, of one thirty-second. Each tick is equal to $31.25 a contract, or 1/32 of 1 percent of the face value. If, say, a contract had changed hands at a price of 781/32, or $78,031.25, the next highest price it could trade would be 782/32, or $78,062.50. The brokers claimed it was their customers who demanded executions between ticks to ensure the best possible price. Shaving half a tick off the purchase of sale price could mean a big difference in total profits. Spreads weren't very volatile, and the ticks were relatively large: $31.25 compared with just $12.50 for grain contracts. So a half tick off the price of 200 contracts, for example, could save $3,125.

Meanwhile, the Board of Trade's conduct committee warned the traders that anyone caught violating rules against noncompetitive trading would be suspended, fined, or even expelled. It was a hard line, but it hardly stopped ginzying. The only solution, some traders suggested, was to cut the minimum tick in half to 1/64. But that wasn't likely to happen because of the board's long-standing position: Large ticks make it easier to make a living.

Ginzying is a perfect example of traders doing what they have to in order to survive—just like the exchanges themselves. More than one broker has confided that a fast market is a license to steal. It seems that every time exchange officials or federal regulators come down hard on the boys in the pits, someone comes up with a new scheme. It brings to mind the conversation a retired exchange official had with a new chairman. The elder cautioned that one of the pits was getting out of hand with too many wild traders and too many questionable trading practices. The new chairman shook his head in a nod of resignation and sorrowfully replied, "I can't do anything about it. Let the evil fly."

32

The Best Laid Schemes . . .

The atmosphere was heavy with sweat and capitalistic hope as traders in the Merc's cattle pit milled about like so many anxious and fidgety kids waiting in line at a Saturday matinee. Jack Sandner was one of them.

It had been one of the roughest trading weeks in his life. From the outside, Sandner's pixieish face, framed by a strawberry beard, gave no hint that he was on the brink of disaster. But on the inside, welling up beneath the surface, he was feeling a volatile mix of emotions: desire; resentment; remorse; panic. At times he wanted only to go into his office, shut the door behind him, bury his head in his hands, and cry. For a brief moment, in the still of one evening, he had even looked down from his fifth-floor office on the empty street below, contemplating another way out. But that wasn't his style. He was too tough, too scrappy to cave in on sheer emotion.

Or was he?

If Jack Sandner was anything, he was a fighter. A former top-notch amateur boxer who had racked up fifty-eight wins against two losses as a wiry, fast-moving featherweight, Sandner was entering the pit for one more round; those who knew the situation were nervously calling it the final round. Sandner wasn't taking any bets on it, given the odds against him. He was down by more than $1 million, and his position was getting worse.

Only five days before, he had been poised at the summit of the commodities world. He had money, prestige, and, as the newly installed chairman of the Mercantile Exchange, power. Clearly he was a man on the move. How could everything so right have gone so wrong so fast? That's how it was in the commodities markets, and every trader knew it. One minute you could be leading the pack; the next, the pack could be baying at your throat for the kill. . . .

Sandner's journey to the top elected post of the world's second largest commodities exchange in January 1980 came largely by chance. There had always been a spontaneous side to Jack Sandner's life. As a youngster he seemed destined more for a life on the street than in the trading pit.

A steely, intense individual who grew up on Chicago's South Side, Jackie was a scrappy kid with quick fists whether he was defending himself or a friend. That wasn't to say he was a trouble-maker—not yet. He was too small to be a bully, but he was gutsy enough not to back away from one. His Irish father was a merchandise manager for a major downtown women's retailer, and his Italian mother, as he described her, was a "Back of the Yards girl who worked two and three jobs" as a housewife, secretary, and part-time dancing instructor. Back of the Yards got its name from the stockyards where Chicago earned its reputation as hog butcher of the world. The area was typically ethnic Chicago, a politically powerful Irish bastion, bordered on the east by blacks and west by Slavs, where the late Mayor Richard Daley was born and lived in a section called Bridgeport. Jack's was a strong and secure family for the first thirteen years of his life, and he was the ideal youth: a straight A student in grade school, an altar boy, a kid who'd never talk back to his parents, teachers, or big brother. But something snapped.

Jack was fourteen, a freshman at St. Leo High School, and somehow he didn't fit. At five feet five inches and 115 pounds, he was too small to play on the football team. That hurt. Playing football at St. Leo, as at most Catholic schools, was the badge of manhood. Every Irish kid wanted to star and go on to Notre Dame. But there were even worse problems at home. His father was an alcoholic, and his mother spent virtually all her time caring for him. There was little time for Jack and his problems. Jack Sandner's emotional fabric began to fray.

He quickly lost interest in school and began hanging around the streets. His brother disliked him for it. To show what a maverick he was, Jack, with a friend, went out and got something none of the other kids in the neighborhood had: a tattoo on his left arm dedicated to Mom and Dad (it's still there, and it's safe to say that no other exchange official ever had one either). He was like Tony Manero in *Saturday Night Fever* as he began dancing through life, rock-and-rolling to every jukebox and every record player he came across in his odyssey down the grungy sidewalks of the South Side. He had a good teacher, his mother. Jack danced to local fame when he entered and won the 1956 Harvest Moon Festival, a popular and highly promoted annual event sponsored by the *Chicago Sun-Times* with such celebrity judges as Jerry Lewis, Jayne Mansfield, and Zsa Zsa Gabor. He was the youngest winner and was featured in a page 1 photograph in the *Sun-Times*. The brothers at St. Leo sneered at Jack's accomplishment because church officials were cool to this type of dancing with its Elvis Presley gyrations. Jack's victory was short and sweet. He was convinced the brothers didn't like him anymore. If only they had been a little more patient with him, Jack thought years later, things might have worked out. At fifteen, in his sophomore year, Jack Sandner and St. Leo parted company.

From then it was one school after another. Jack enrolled at Chicago Vocational High School, where he took auto shop courses. Racial tension made the school a nightmare for him, but he managed to hang on for a year. The following year he entered South Shore High School, a respectable school by most standards. The fit was still uncomfortable, and after only two days and a fight with the hall guards, Jack walked out, disheveled, disgruntled, and disoriented. He had had it. He didn't need school. At sixteen John Francis Sandner dropped out to become a pump jockey at a gas station on Clark Street with a career goal that didn't extend beyond either his imagination or his neighborhood. He hoped someday to tend a blast furnace at the nearby Republic Steel plant. Life was simple that way. A fast car, a bottle of wine, a pack of cigarettes, and a few friends were all he needed. And maybe a fight or two.

Jack began boxing in the Golden Gloves. He was seventeen now, and boxing was about the only thing that gave him some sense of worth. Well, almost. Even in boxing, though, he lacked the one thing he had lost when he turned fourteen: discipline. He paid for it one evening. On the way to a Golden Gloves fight he smoked several cigarettes and drank a pint of wine. Jack was numb by the time he entered the ring. Predictably he lost the fight. "I had my ass handed to me," Sandner said. "I was so humiliated that I swore to my self that I'd never smoke or drink again." (The next drink he had was a glass of wine nearly seven years later to settle a spastic colon.) That particular fight, however, dramatically changed the course of Jack's life, both physically and mentally. Among the spectators that night was former world middleweight-champion Tony Zale, who approached Jack after the fight and asked, "Son, would you like to learn how to box?" Still fuzzy-headed, Jack nodded. "First, you must stop smoking," Zale implored. "Meet me at the CYO [Catholic Youth Organization] at Eleven-forty West Jackson."

Jack began a serious amateur boxing career with Zale as his trainer and mentor. A strong natural counterpuncher, swift on his feet with a jab-quick ability to size up his opponent's weakness, Sandner was a winner in the ring. He had a champ's killer instinct. Boxing became an anodyne for him. He seemed to be more relaxed, and the punk kid image began to fade. With his ability, Jack's friends and admirers told him, he should try for a boxing scholarship to college. Everyone agreed Jack had the talent to win one. But he didn't have the credentials. He would have to finish high school.

Sandner loved boxing and seriously considered a professional career. For him, as for the Jack Dempseys, the Tony Zales, and so many other fighters, the boxing ring was a way out: out of obscurity; out of poverty; out of an old life. But so was an education. Convinced he'd be a lot better off developing his brains as well as his muscles, Jack enrolled in the Central YMCA High School in downtown Chicago and hit both the punching bag and books. As it turned out, he was adept at both. In eighteen months he made up three years and was graduated first in his class. He proved his friends right. All along he won his fights—and a chance to box at the University of Arizona, where he was on a work study program.

Set to start college in the fall of 1961, Jack felt like an indomitable lion ready for anything, except the unexpected. As luck would have it, tragedy struck college boxing in 1960. A boxer was killed in the NCAA finals, and the incident subsequently led to a ban on college boxing. The university honored Jack's acceptance with one condition: He become a wrestler. He had worked too hard to say no.

Jack wrestled and studied, and although he waited tables in fraternity and sorority houses for meals, he was chronically broke. Homesick, and without money for transportation, Jack hitchhiked back to Chicago over the Christmas recess. Along one stretch of highway the sparsely clad Sandner shivered in six-degree temperatures one dawn morning and ended up with frostbite and a bad case of exposure. Most of his vacation he spent in a hospital room, recuperating and thinking about his life. Jack left Arizona after one semester and transferred to the University of Southern Illinois, where he felt comfortable. A psychology major, he was active in student government and wrestled for four years on one of the nation's top-rated collegiate teams. In his senior year he decided to apply to Notre Dame Law School. It was the thought of going to Notre Dame that grabbed Jack more than the thought of studying law. The school was the big leagues to Sandner, and he became single-minded about going there. His law SATs and college grades were good, but Notre Dame didn't accept him.

That didn't stop Sandner, a man who didn't like to retreat and who was used to meeting people face-to-face. He was positive Notre Dame would accept him if he could talk to the dean. He drove nonstop from Carbondale, Illinois, to South Bend, Indiana, to meet with the dean of Notre Dame's law school. Jack was prepared for the fight of his life.

He finessed with a lot of verbal footwork, talking about the ups and downs of his life, about his comeback, and about how much Notre Dame meant to him. There was no doubt that Sandner was quick, logical, and convincing. The dean listened patiently, interjecting comments and observations throughout the two-hour conversation. In the end Sandner won. He was accepted by the law school. His ability to verbalize ideas with convincing ease made him a star in law school and later proved equally useful at the exchange.

After the first semester at Notre Dame, Sandner won a scholarship. But it fell short of covering his expenses, so on weekends he'd work in Chicago at the Sutherland Hotel in a dance act called Salt and Pepper named after his partners, a white girl and a black girl. When the dean found out about the weekend job, he wanted to kick Jack out of school, not so much for the type of work Jack was doing but for the time it was taking away from studies. Scholarship students weren't permitted to work more than ten and a half hours a week, and Jack was putting in nearly thirty. Jack "begged" the dean not to kick him out. The dean agreed not to, but Sandner had to give up Salt and Pepper. After that, Jack found himself scrambling to stay afloat, working in the University lunchroom for meals and moving into a seminary. As it turned out, in the Moreau Seminary he could live better than the dean himself. It had a library, two handball courts, and spacious rooms; Jack's was on the fourth floor overlooking a lake. And the price was certainly right—$1 a day. He called it the Moreau Hilton.

During the summers—unbeknownst to the dean—Jack went west to deal blackjack in Las Vegas, a job Chicago friends had lined up. One summer he worked at the Fremont Hotel, and the next summer at the Stardust. It was his first such experience with gamblers and gambling, a firsthand look at the types of people who came en masse to the mythic shrine of risk-taking delirium. They had come to Vegas by day flights, night flights, cars, trucks, buses, motorcycles, and bicycles. A few ended up winning; more than a few, losing. Some had to beg management for Greyhound tickets back home. He could figure the odds all right, but not the people. Why did they gamble? Why couldn't the winners walk away before they turned losers? He did learn something about risk takers and, in the process, about himself: that they were headstrong independent individuals with one cause—themselves. Eventually he would meet pitfuls of them.

Jack's law school days were golden. Given the choice of either law review or moot court, he chose the latter. He throve on moot court competition, and he conned the dean into giving him a set of keys to the law library the third year so he could study there nights. Putting in long hours, he completed what he called a Brandeis-type brief of more than 100 pages. It all came together his senior year, and Jack ended up winning moot court and graduating from Notre Dame's law school with honors in 1968. Two years later, on Valentines' Day, he married Carol, a nurse's aide in a South Bend hospital and the eldest of twelve children.

He wanted to be a trial lawyer in Chicago. There would be no sitting in the alcove of a big law firm for five years, handling the dregs of senior partners' cases. He craved the independence, the hustle of finding cases, and the courtroom histrionics, which suited his competitive nature. And the old gang provided an active clientele. They were the ones who had tempted him, when he came home during college vacations, to steal cars for a $400 cut. Now he was defending them. (At least a half dozen of those boyhood chums, according to Sandner, ended up in the trunks of cars killed gangland-style.) There was a certain euphoria that came with each winning verdict, the same feeling he was to experience later, when he scored in the market.

It was Jack Sandner walking down the streets again, this time more like a Melvin Belli on a legal odyssey trying to drum up business. It was inevitable that he would meet commodity traders along the way. Some of the meetings were amicable. Others, well, Jack knocked them off their feet. One such incident took place at a Merc party he was invited to in 1969. A couple of the boys didn't take to Jack and began harassing him. They may have had too much to drink, or maybe they just didn't like outsiders. Whatever the reason, two traders backed Jack toward an elevator bank and began pushing. He begged off, but they wouldn't let up. He let go, slapping one in the face with an open hand and punching the other in the mouth. It was over in fewer than ten seconds. One trader lay on the floor minus a couple of teeth; the other was too stunned to move. Jack excused himself and left the party, prepared never to see the likes of commodity traders again.

Sandner became friends with Maury Kravitz, then a practicing attorney, and Jack tried a couple of cases for his firm. He also met Everette B. Harris, president of the Merc. That meeting in 1971 changed the direction of Sandner's career. At the time he was handling a personal injury case for Harris's wife, who had been involved in a car crash. Harris was always on the lookout for potential new trader talent, and he liked the way Sandner handled the case and himself. He gave the young attorney a tip: Buy a Merc membership for "only" $80,000 and do some trading on your lunch hours. Harris, in his best ol'-boy booster speech, told Jack that the markets were about to explode. Indeed, they were. Jack was willing to take the part-time chance. He borrowed $80,000 from a bank and began spending his lunch hours in the pits, trading first live cattle, then eggs, and eventually pork bellies. After a year he was a full-time trader and a part-time lawyer, just as Maury Kravitz and Leo Melamed and so many other lawyers had become.

Sandner started off on a fast track trading pork bellies. Over a three-week period he had a string of wins and no losses. He was a counterpuncher type of trader, patient for little scalping victories rather than for half-million-dollar plays, using a mixture of charts and fundamental analysis and plenty of intuition. He was sailing along on a nonstop ticket to trading glory, doing everything right—until he made a mistake. He took a loss on one trade, just one trade, that wiped out the previous three weeks' worth of wins—and then some. He had lost his entire trading bankroll. The day of the loss he stood glumly near the pit, his face contorted in disappointment. Harris walked over and nudged him.

"I don't know what you did wrong," Harris said in a fatherly and consoling tone. "But your greed exceeded your fear and respect of the market."

It wasn't a particularly profound comment, and Harris had said it to scores of traders over the years, but it made Sandner realize early that if he fought the markets, he'd get clobbered. Jack Sandner, the street fighter, boxer, wrestler, party brawler, had to learn not to fight for the first time in his life. It didn't mean taking a passive role, but it did mean knowing when to back away, retreat to a neutral corner, and wait for the next round. He learned to wait and became good at it.

Sandner also became a competent trader, using discipline to work the pork belly and cattle pits. In 1976 he joined the commodities firm of Rufenacht, Bromagen & Hertz, one of the biggest commercial livestock operations in the country with thirty branch offices. Meanwhile, he was gaining a reputation as a cool head when it came to unraveling exchange affairs, which he had become involved in. Whenever there was a crisis in a committee and everyone was riled up, Sandner had a way of entering the fracas to simmer things down. He was a fairly polished arbitrator, proving it in 1977, when he deftly reorganized members' space and telephone allotments on the exchange floor without shattering any of the members' notoriously fragile egos. Such efforts paid off not long after, when a group of fellow traders asked Sandner to run for exchange director. Jack agreed, and within fifteen minutes a nominating petition had gathered 100 signatures. Sandner was elected an exchange director by a rare write-in vote. The next year his fellow directors elected him vice-chairman, and in January 1980 by unanimous vote he became chairman of the exchange. At thirty-eight he was one of the youngest chairmen in Merc history, and no one could quite figure out the meteoric rise, though he had always had the solid backing of Leo Melamed. Sandner figured it was his legal background that attracted support at a time when a number of legal issues were swirling around the pits. Although he was still a novice when it came to Washington political infighting, he had managed to sharpen his claws in exchange politics. By now he was president of RB&H and a millionaire. He could still remember those angry adolescent years when his father would fling a newspaper at him, demanding he find a job, those years, he said, that could have led him into a life of robbing banks.

Sandner, the new Merc chairman, reflected the spirit and image of the Merc itself—a hustling, scrappy, frenetic, young, and wealthy upstart. But two months after his election he was sweating over the real prospect that he could become a tremendous embarrassment to the exchange. The situation had to do with the position he had taken in the cattle market.

Sandner wasn't a flashy trader or a big gun but a scalper with superb timing in the pits. Fundamentalists, he believed, sometimes got wiped out, and technicians usually lived to trade another day. That was why he used both price charts and supply-demand factors to come up with trading strategies. The combination of technical and fundamental analysis had always worked for him. But there were also times when he based his decisions solely on intelligence—those juicy tidbits of inside information—gleaned from the eyes and ears of "friends" in the field.

One such piece of information came from a Texas cattleman in a telephone call to Sandner on March 26, 1980: The Food and Drug Administration (FDA) was about to quarantine large herds of cattle throughout the country that were being fed diethylstilbestrol (DES), an estrogenlike hormone used for fattening. Earlier the FDA had banned DES claiming it was a cancer-producing agent that affected women who ate the beef. The cattleman told

Sandner that nearly "everyone" had continued to use the hormone despite the ban. It took Sandner only a few seconds to mull the report over in his mind and to do a few quick calculations on the effects the quarantine would have on the nation's cattle herds. Not all breeders and ranchers used DES, but enough did. Sandner estimated that at least a quarter of a million cattle would be taken off the market by the ban, creating a severe shortage of cattle and sharply higher prices. He went long, taking his biggest position ever. He bought 450 contracts in April and June live cattle futures, representing some 18 million pounds of beef on the hoof. Then he sat back and waited for the news to reach the pits.

It seemed like a sure winning play, even if it meant taking the public's side by going long. If the public was long, the pros were usually short. But Sandner wasn't betting on ifs because this time he knew something the others didn't. Little did he know, however, that the nation's commodity and financial markets were about to collapse in a spasm of runaway jitters for one afternoon.

It came with the plunge in silver prices as desperate investors worldwide scrambled to unload their holdings. In 1973 the Hunt brothers of Texas had gone into the silver market Texas-style, buying vast hoards of the cheap metal. By 1980 they had all but cornered the world's silver market. But the silver mountain built by the Texan billionaires, along with some mysterious Arabs, blew its top with a volcanic force that sent shock waves through every commodity pit across the country. When silver prices broke, so did practically everything else. The silver bust caused severely depressed prices in gold, copper, and other commodities—including cattle—and threatened to topple major brokerage houses and banks, which had helped finance the speculative boom. House and Senate leaders called for hearings into the debacle that underlined the nation's fragile web of innerconnected financial institutions.

No one—not the shrewdest silver traders, not the Commodity Futures Trading Commission (CFTC), not even the officials of the exchanges where silver futures were traded—had thought it would happen. How could any single group influence the silver market in view of its size and its huge international trading volume in cash markets? Where the Hunts were concerned—that is, in light of their soybean antics three years earlier—the experts should have realized anything was possible as long as all it took was money.

The Hunts collect commodities such as oil, sugar, coal, soybeans, silver the way housewives clip cents-off coupons. And they do it with the economic appetite of a $5 billion family fortune. In 1977 the CFTC sued the Hunts on charges that they had illegally tried to corner nearly a third of the soybean market with the threat of disrupting the market. That threat sent the price of soybeans jumping from $6 a bushel, when the Hunts initially bought 3 million bushels, to $10 a bushel over a three-month period. The Hunts and their children ended up buying soybean contracts which totaled nearly 24 million bushels, eight times the legal limit. The holdings represented 37 percent of the nation's 65-million-bushel soybean crop. After a three-year legal battle (the Hunt family lawyers chalked up 7,200 man-hours at a cost of more than $1 million) the Hunts settled out of court in July 1981 by paying a fine of a half million dollars and agreeing to stay out of soybean futures for two years.

This time it was silver instead of soybeans. Neither the Chicago Board of Trade nor the New York Commodity Exchange (COMEX), where most of the silver futures are traded, had placed position limits on the number of silver contracts a trader could own. But word began to filter through trading circles that the Hunts were holding an enormous number of silver contracts and were about to squeeze the silver supply by demanding delivery on their long positions. The prospect of a squeeze was real. In October 1979 the COMEX depositories held some 60 million ounces of silver, enough to settle 12,000 contracts. The Hunts and their interests held a long position of 12,281 contracts. Just at that time the Board of Trade got nervous and imposed position limits. That move, in turn, shifted the action to the COMEX. By January, with the price of silver at more than $35, COMEX officials finally took action, limiting the number of contracts a speculator could hold to 500; the idea was to get the longs to close out their positions rather than to take delivery. But despite the action taken by the COMEX, the price of silver, which the Hunts had first begun buying at around $3 an ounce, stood at $45 an ounce and looked as if it were going higher. Fearing a problem in the March contracts, the COMEX board declared an "emergency situation" and limited trading to the liquidation of existing positions. In effect, the big traders were being forced to sell off their long positions. For the first time in more than a year the power had shifted to the shorts. On January 22, the day following the emergency rule, silver skidded from $44 to $34 an ounce. It continued its jagged descent until it hit a low of $10.20 on March 27, the day the Hunt's billion-dollar silver bubble burst.

Though the Hunts and Jack Sandner had never met, their fates were to cross that day, each influencing the other. On March 27, during the first hour of trading, Sandner added to his position in the cattle market, increasing his holdings to 450 contracts. For a trader with a scalper's temperament, Sandner was peculiarily calm and comfortable with a position. It was more than a feeling of comfort, though; he felt confident, almost smug.

There was little time to oversee the position in those first couple of trading hours. Sandner had to leave the pit to attend a hastily called meeting over a pressing matter which ironically involved the Hunts and their position in the feeder cattle market. In the wake of the crashing silver market the Hunts were being pressed from all sides to come up with huge sums of cash to cover margin calls. They could not—or did not want to—meet their margin calls in cattle. Nearly all the commodities, including cattle, were being rattled by the silver crisis. There was little debate at the meeting chairmanned by Sandner. The exchange is a no-debt system, the Hunts would have to liquidate their position. The selling would depress the cattle market, Sandner realized, but then it would surely bounce back quickly once the news about DES was out. He was wrong.

The Hunt matter settled, Sandner dashed to the pit, anxious to reassess his position in light of the shaky markets and the impending sell-off in cattle by the Hunts. He was too late. Hit by the silver shocks, the cattle pit had turned into an apocalyptic fresco of white-faced and red-faced traders in a tizzy. Even before he reached the pit, his eyes darted to the electronic trading board, and suddenly he turned mawkish. He glowered at the board in disbelief. Cattle were lock limit down. In between the time he had left the pit and returned, he had lost $280,000. And there was no way for him to get out. There were no buyers. The shorts had the upper hand and were squeezing the situation for all it was worth.

There was no trading the rest of that day, or the next, or the one after that, and after that. For four straight days the market opened—and stayed—lock limit down. Sandner's losses were mounting at the rate of $300,000 a day, the sum of the daily margin call. Down by $1.2 million, he had some staying power left, but not much.

He had seen it happen to other traders before. They had been caught in lock limit positions for days on end, until either the situation eased up or they went belly up, losing everything, including their memberships. He envisioned the worst. How could it have happened to him? How could he have let it happen to him? It wasn't just another trader going down the tubes, he thought; it was Jack Sandner, new chairman of the Chicago Mercantile Exchange. He could see the headlines on the financial pages: MERC CHAIRMAN WIPED OUT. Neither Sandner nor the Merc needed that kind of publicity now or ever.

Outwardly he remained cool. Too cool, his friends thought. They began to worry about him. One old pal, Maury Kravitz, whom Jack had hired as head of RB&H's monetary division in 1978, seemed more upset than Sandner. He was so nervous that he called Sandner's wife one evening to express his concern.

"I'm worried about him," Kravitz said.

"What do you mean?" Carol Sandner replied as if she were giving up on a riddle.

"He's acting normal. No one loses that much and acts normal. No one."

To Carol, Kravitz sounded as if he were indeed talking in riddles. The call came as a complete suprise to her. She knew nothing about Jack's situation and the losses. Jack preferred it that way. He seldom told her what went on in the pits. A bad trade was over and done with, history as it were, and all the tea and sympathy couldn't resolve it. As he put it, "I didn't need a family catharsis at home." A lot of traders have that attitude. Their wives know where they work, but few know how they work. Maybe they didn't want to know. The thought of one's future tied to a soybean or a pork belly could be unsettling. Or maybe there was no way to explain the anxieties of trading or why working the pits was more personally satisfying than working the courtrooms, no way casually to chat about the trade secrets and the perils of risk taking. How could you come home and say to your wife, "How was your day? How are the kids? Oh, by the way, I dropped a half million today."

Nevertheless, when Sandner got home that Thursday night, he

told Carol the whole story, after she asked him if there was anything he wanted to talk about. She listened patiently, touched by a sense of helplessness. "As soon as the market trades," Jack said, "I'm going to get out. We'll count up what we have. It might be embarrassing as far as the chairmanship goes."

He remained calm, speaking in soft, even tones. There was something inside Jack, a mechanism he called it, that somehow permitted him to cope. What he hadn't told Carol about were those few moments in his office one evening when, in the grip of anguish, he asked himself if he could jump. Not him. There had been at least a half dozen suicides over the decade by both Board of Trade and Merc traders who couldn't handle the losses. Those who chose suicide, he believed, saw themselves as worthless. With or without money, Jack could never see himself that way. He had never quit in the ring, or at college, or at anything he had set his mind on. Yet now he felt helpless. Here was Jack Sandner, the boxer, lawyer, and confidant of so many other troubled traders he had counseled, ironically unable to defend himself.

33

Jack's Last Stand

Time was running out. Jack Sandner didn't know if he could take another four days of lock limit losses—financially or emotionally. Mentally he prepared himself for the worst. He told Carol that if he went broke, he could always go back to practicing law or pumping gas. It was too late to figure out what had gone wrong and why the market wouldn't respond the way it was supposed to. It wouldn't have made any difference. And while he knew that nothing in the futures markets went straight up or straight down forever, another day *was* forever. It wasn't only the loss of money; there was a chance that could be made up. It was the blow to his stature as chairman, which was beyond dollar value. The prestige of the Merc chairmanship was hanging in the balance, at least in Jack's mind. The chairmanship meant a great deal to him: "It was a new type of high, more than making money, an instantaneous surge that becomes addictive like a trial lawyer winning a case, or a boxer getting the decision. I wanted to do well for the exchange and myself. Anyone who tells you he's taking on the chairmanship out of altruism, well, that's bullshit. I needed the recognition."

Jack flirted with all sorts of ideas during those four days. If only the market could loosen up on Friday, he thought, so he wouldn't have to hold his position over the weekend. A weekend was too long to sit with a financial time bomb. It created uncertainty, and that drove traders mad. It brought on sleepless nights and stirred the coals of doubt into a blaze of insecurity. Once a trader had become insecure in the pit, he was vulnerable to losing. Thursday evening Carol had slipped a folded piece of paper into Jack's coat pocket, asking him to read it when he got to the office the next morning. It was a restless night.

Tomorrow came. It was a crisp Friday morning as Jack entered his Mercedes for the ritual forty-mile trip from his Victorian three-story house in Lake Forest to the western brink of downtown Chicago, the skyline of which was still a silhouette against the dawn. The forty-five-minute drive took him down Edens Expressway along the perimeter of the affluent northern suburbs to the Kennedy Expressway, which cut through a part of the city's gray industrial belt. At Washington Street he turned off and headed east across the overpass, and he could see the string of cars below beginning to nudge each other in rush-hour adagio. He went right on Des Plaines Street past the Northwestern Station and the few derelicts who were stirring on the sidewalk, passed the Union Station to the parking lot on the corner of Adams. He walked the half block to the exchange in a slow, mechanical cadence, oblivious to his surroundings. He was in his office by 7:00 A.M., two hours before cattle trading began.

The office, where he often spent sixteen hours a day on business and exchange matters, was his retreat; a warm and restive place with thick off-white carpeting that flowed to an antique L-shaped desk with telephone and quotron machines at hand. In front of one dark brown-colored wall stood an ornate grandfather clock the rich chimes and hourly gongs of which filled the room. The opposite wall held bookshelves containing a set of encyclopedias, the *Great Books* series, *The History of Art*, a book of *Masterplots*, assorted lawbooks, and a host of novels, *Fools Die, August 1914, The First Casualty* among them. On yet another wall hung Jack's neatly framed legal accolades, which included the first-place award in the Notre Dame moot court. Then there was the escape hatch, the little, narrow room behind the office. It contained a minigym complete with an exercise bicycle, a set of weights, a custom-made gymnast's practice board for hand stand pushups, and, of course, a punching bag, along with an ample supply of vitamins that Jack constantly popped.

In the fleeting solitude of the morning Sandner carefully unfolded the piece of paper Carol had given him the night before. She called it a prayer. Jack wasn't a deeply religious person, but he was touched by the words as he read them aloud:

> One night I dreamed I was walking along the beach with the Lord. Many scenes from my life flashed across the sky. In each scene I noticed footprints in the sand. Sometimes there were two sets of footprints; other times there was only one.

> This bothered me because I know that during the low periods of my life, when I was suffering from anguish, sorrow, or defeat, I could see only one set of footprints, so I said to the Lord, "You promised me, Lord, that if I followed you, you would walk with me always. But I have noticed that during the most trying periods of my life there has been only one set of footprints in the sand. Why, when I have needed you most, have you not been there for me?"

> The Lord replied, "The times when you have seen only one set of footprints, my child, is when I carried you."

Jack removed the jacket of his three-piece suit and slipped into the RB&H black and gold braid-trimmed trading jacket with its patch declaring "Free Markets for Free Men." He carefully placed the prayer in his pocket and headed for the pit.

It was eight thirty, thirty-five minutes before the opening, when Jack reached the exchange floor. Tim Brennan, a friend and fellow RB&H cattle trader who knew every beat of the market, approached him.

"The market's going to trade today," Brennan said.

"Yeah, I know," Jack said.

"Do you want me to get you out?"

Sandner appreciated the gesture. He well knew, as did every veteran trader, that it was tough, sometimes impossible, to get yourself out of a big losing position. There was a tendency to hesitate or to go too fast. You were fighting not only the market but your nerves as well. It was too big a battle for most to win alone. Paul Rosen had tried—and failed miserably—before he had been blown out of his soybean position financially and psychologically. Whenever a friend asked if he could get you out of the market, he was also saying, "Don't go through all that misery yourself." Jack thought about Brennan's offer for a few moments before he answered.

"No. I want to get out myself," he calmly replied. "I want to pick the time."

"You gonna do it on the opening? There will be enough numbers. You can probably get out of the whole thing on the opening."

"I want to see how the market opens."

"Jack," Brennan said challengingly, "you sound like you're freezing. You sound like you're rationalizing. Why don't you just give me an opening order and I'll get you out, or give it to Jerry Pam and let him get you out?"

"Tim, I've been through an awful lot of ups and downs in my life. Believe me, I'm not freezing."

"When you're freezing," Brennan pleaded, "you never know."

"If that's the case, then I can't argue with you," Jack said. "But you have to have an order from me unless you get me declared incompetent in court, and you haven't done that. If I really feel I'm freezing, I think I'll know it, and I'll give you the order. Now let's go feel our way around the pit."

Just minutes before the market opened, there was an unusual undercurrent of noise in the pit, an indication the traders had a whiff of something about to happen. Everyone realized the market was going to open and trade. The market opened fifty points lower than the previous close. Sandner did nothing. He had hesitated, making no effort to sell out of his position. Instead, he swallowed hard and stepped out of the pit. Immediately Brennan came up to him and asked, "What do you think?"

"Tim, if I were trading without a position, I'd be buying the market right now."

Brennan gaped at him as if he were trying to figure out the rantings of a madman. "You can't buy any more cars," Brennan reminded Jack.

"Right, I know," Jack assured him, "but I just want to let the market trade."

Jack could sense Brennan's frustration. "Look at it," Brennan demanded, "the market's thick enough now to get you out of your position without killing the thing. Why don't you let me get you out?"

Sandner replied with a curt no.

"You're freezing," Brennan charged, his voice rising in anger.

"I'm not freezing," Sandner shot back.

A sellout at that point would have cost Sandner $1.2 million. But he couldn't sell. Something inside him wouldn't allow it. He felt compelled to wait for a few minutes. It was more than a hunch, he told himself. This time he was right. The market began to loosen up, moving higher by some twenty points. It was hardly a runaway rally, but it inspired hope. Still, with no buying to sustain the momentum, the market quickly stalled. Within seconds it had faltered and moved ten points lower.

At that point Brennan ran up to Jack again and asked, "What would you do if you were scalping the market?" He knew the answer, but he wanted Jack to say it, to admit that there was only one move left.

"If the price got lower than the opening range, I would blow out of my scalped position," Sandner said dejectedly.

"Why don't you give me a stop at fifty-eight forty-five?" Brennan asked.

For the first time since the opening Sandner was having doubts. The market was just too weak to rally. Yet it had fallen so far so fast that it was due for some kind of correction, even if it was half of what it had lost. The market was now trading at 58.50 and had fallen $7 from where Jack had bought, a break he called "horrendous." He had never seen the market take such a plunge in so brief a period.

Like a trusty lieutenant, Brennan stood close to Sandner to await instructions. Finally, Sandner turned to him and said, "Tim, I'll tell you what. Not forty-five. Make it thirty-seven to forty-two. Then blow out the position."

They were talking several feet outside the pit, careful to make sure no one heard them. News of a 400-contract sell order could be seismic. Sandner had fixed a selling range at 58.42 to 58.37 for a good reason: to avoid a crush of panic selling. A favorite trick of the pit locals was to low tick prices. For instance, if the price moved near the low of the day, a local would sell another contract in order to nudge the price to a new low. The new low would usually be the first link in a chain reaction of selling which drove the price quickly downward. It's a bully tactic that generally works. The market stood at 58.60, just ten points from the low of the day, when Jack handed the sell orders to Brennan. "If you want to give half of it to Jerry Pam, then do it," Jack said as he stepped farther away from the pit. Now his fate was in the hands of Tim Brennan.

No sooner had Brennan walked back into the pit when the market began to move downward to within three points of the 58.50 low. It was over, Jack thought. The brooding look on his sweaty face said it all.

Then, for no apparent reason (was there a rumor? Did someone know something?), in the time of a teardrop the market turned without hesitation—and shot straight up limit. Miraculously the market had rallied 200 points in a matter of seconds. Brennan looked at Sandner and came dashing out of the pit with a glow.

"God," he shouted, "this is unbelievable."

On that market burst Sandner had made back $280,000. And now he was down only $1 million.

Immediately Jack's senses came alive, and his mind began racing, assessing the possibilities like a chess master contemplating a dozen moves ahead. Word about DES must have got out, he figured. If so, DES in the cattle would have been bullish in the front month of April but bearish the second month (June) and on back (August, October, December, January, February).

Sandner reasoned that DES would wash out of the cattle after about six weeks and that once these cattle were back on the market, there would be an oversupply, leading to lower prices. On the basis of that scenario he set a trading strategy: He would cover the market's up or down with a spread by selling short the second month (June) against his long position in the first month (April). But before he could spread trade, he would have to wait for a price break in the June contract, which was also limit up at the time. But he wasn't in a hurry now that time was with him. The April contract had been lock limit up for three days, and Jack had recouped $840,000.

In a matter of days Sandner's trading psyche had pushed the limit of flexibility from scalper to position trader to spread trader. It was a question of survival, an attempt to regain some control over his trading life. At least now he was calling the shots, and his nightmare was turning into a pleasant dream.

By Wednesday Jack had a newfound confidence as he looked around the cattle pit a couple of minutes before the opening. The mood at first was somber. But that wasn't unusual for the cattle pit, which lacked the humor—and array of characters—of the pork belly pit. The traders began to stir. And soon amid the noisy animation of the other cattle traders Jack could see and hear confusion and indecision.

"What are you doin'?" one local asked another.

"You want to buy 'em limit up?"

"I don't know. I don't think so."

"What do you think?"

"Maybe enough's enough."

No one, of course, had disclosed his orders for the June contract, but Sandner's observations tipped him off that there were a lot of buyers around. He knew from experience that when a market looked as if it were going to open limit up, traders who had stuff to buy became edgy and unsure prior to the opening. They were like cattle trapped in stalls during a fire, bucking to get out. Some pros will tell you that 60 to 70 percent of all trading is accounted for by emotionalism. That's why some of the big speculators choose to stay away from the floor, to sit upstairs in their shag-carpeted offices or in the dens of their homes, plugged into the action through television screens wired to exchange computers. Not Sandner. He needed to be in the thick of it, feeling the emotional rush, mixing it up with the boys in the pit. How else could you grab the edge? The proof was in the way he handled himself that morning when he attempted to short-sell 400 June contracts to pull off his spread.

Just ten seconds before the opening, one of the pit brokers, waving his hand through the air, said, "Okay, it's limit bid, but ..." Immediately Jack told himself, "This is the day." He knew that he wouldn't be the only one selling at limit up and that the chances of shorting all 400 contracts were slim. There would be a lot of others selling short at the same price, and they would attract buyers, too. But if he offered a lower price than anyone else, he could get off his contracts before the next tick. They would have to buy from him.

The bell rang. Before anyone could offer a sale at 65.10,

Sandner fired off a scream at the top of his voice, "Four hundred at oh-five, four hundred at oh-five, four hundred at oh-five," while moving his fingers in a gesticulated financial shorthand. He sold the market at 65.05—145 points from the previous day's close—and a mere 5 points from where everyone was expecting the market to open at. It happened so fast that some of the other traders with sell orders were momentarily stunned. He sold all 400 contracts and at the same time sparked a selling binge in the June contract, which broke some 200 points that day. As it turned out, the market never reached 65.10. The high for the day was 65.05, where Jack had sold the market. Later a few traders who realized what had happened congratulated Sandner on the trade. "Man, what a play," one said in awe, "what a play."

Meanwhile, the April contract remained lock limit up for the day while the June contract moved lower. On paper, Sandner was whole now. He had won everything back—all $1.2 million—plus some. But it was still a paper victory, and until he got out of his position, anything could happen. He had the chance now to get out, and he wasn't about to make a pig of himself. He could have squeezed some more points out of the play, but if the market suddenly went against him, he knew he couldn't handle it psychologically. For the first time since the market had caved in on him, Sandner felt like a whole person.

Ready to get out of everything, he began barking orders like a field general positioning his troops for an attack. He had Brennan standing in the April section of the pit. "If I motion to you, sell my April out," he instructed. Then he began buying his June contracts fifty at a time to get out of his short position. He'd wait for an offer, then buy rather than bid the market. He didn't want it to rally against him. With each trade he could feel the sweat on his forehead and the sweat underneath his jacket soaking his armpits as if he were in the ring. The June contract was weak, and the buying hardly budged prices. It also indicated to him that perhaps the April contract was ready to come off limit. He gave Tim the signal to sell. Once again Jack had called it right. The Aprils moved off limit, and Brennan sold.

It was a bonanza, the most money Sandner had ever made in a day. He had made $610,000 that day in only two hours of trading. Coupled with the three limit-up days in the Aprils, he ended up making the $1.2 million back and another $100,000. Incredibly he had escaped disaster with a respectable profit. He didn't wait for the 12:45 P.M. close. He stopped just long enough in his office to remove his trading jacket, and he left the exchange without telling anyone where he was going.

He was soaking wet, the eight days of horrible nightmares behind him as he scurried along the sidewalk toward Madison Street in the heart of the Loop. He arrived at his destination within fifteen minutes: St. Peter's Church. He entered, knelt, and prayed, careful not to thank God for the material things in life.

Then he broke down and cried.

PART III

Pathologies
of the Pit

Nothing succeeds like excess.

—OSCAR WILDE

34

Why Isn't
$1 Million Enough?

Jack Sandner hobbled toward me on crutches. The pits? I thought. Before I could ask, Sandner volunteered: "I tore my Achilles tendon skiing. I'm a real jock," he said, breaking into a warm, boyish grin that lit up his face.

Nearly three years had passed since the near fiasco. Jack had taken the years well. He was physically fit and trim, and the long hours he had put in as trader, president of a major commodities firm, and Merc chairman hardly showed outwardly. He had successfully served three consecutive years—the maximum allowed—as Merc chairman during the most tumultuous period in exchange history. With Leo Melamed's backing but against fierce trader opposition he brought about a controversial 25 percent increase in the number of seats, from 1,300 to more than 1,600. The increase in membership, some feared, would dilute the value of their seats and cut into profits. As it turned out, no one was shortchanged. There was enough profit to go around with the explosive S&P contract riding a bull stock market. Sandner had also made scores of trips to Washington in a successful lobbying effort for favorable tax treatment for commodities. And he pushed equally hard, and with success, at winning approval of that S&P 500 Index contract and one in Eurodollars, too.

It had been a busy time all right. Sandner's name had hardly been a well-known one in Washington when he became chairman. But the initial obscurity had since faded. The thick picture album on the table in front of his desk was a testament to that: There was Jack in photographs with President Ronald Reagan, with Senator Robert Dole, with Speaker Thomas ("Tip") O'Neill, with Senator Jesse Helms, with Treasury Secretary Donald Regan, with economist Milton Friedman, among scores of others. The album was a who's who of politicians, business leaders, and academicians, with Jack Sandner standing alongside either in his black trading jacket on the exchange floor or in black tie at some social function. Sandner had stepped momentarily out of the pits into the arena of power, where he seemed to be equally adept.

Actually he had never left the pits. He continued to trade, but cautiously, moving into financial futures, including a brief try at the S&Ps. These markets were far more volatile than the cattle market, and when the situation went against him, he was quicker to get out. "The more secure you get, the less aggressive," he said. In the cattle market he had regained his trading touch. For instance, in the summer of 1981 he had one of the biggest winning plays of his career, riding the cattle market all the way down during a severe plunge. Again he had used solid reasoning to take a position. While supplies that summer were abundant, demand was at its lowest ebb since 1948 because of high prices and recession. As a result, Sandner began selling two weeks before the slide, making big profits for himself and RB&H clients.

Oddly enough, of all his trading exploits it was the near disaster in the cattle market a few years earlier that haunted him like some catchy tune he couldn't get out of his head. He even kept a complete set of the buy and sell transactions from those wild days neatly piled in his desk drawer as if they were to be deciphered like a Rorschach test to reveal something about his trading psyche, or a trading blueprint to be used someday in a casebook study, or a valid reminder of just how ruthless the pits could be. And whenever an old friend or an aspiring trader would come to him for advice about getting into the commodities game, he would bluntly say, "I don't know if the pain and anguish are worth it. . . ."

Sandner had made millions over the years, but he didn't seem to be the big free spender like some of the others who had won in the pits. That wasn't to say he didn't indulge himself and his family with the creature comforts. There was the half-million-dollar antique-filled three-story Victorian house in the ritzy North Shore suburb of Lake Forest, and the antique jewelry and Wedgwood collections, and the $48,000 Mercedes with the telephone for staying in touch with the world of commodities and exchange business wherever he was, and the four-wheel-drive jeep with the snowplow as the hedge against the harsh Chicago winters which might keep a trader from reaching the exchange floor, and the summer house on the St. Joseph River near South Bend and his beloved Notre Dame, and the five children, and three dogs, and seven cats.

"I see myself as a survivor," he said one evening in his office during a chat about the makings of a commodity trader. "I've been emotionally down enough to know how to cope. People who seem to do well in this business are those who are able to deal with adversity and come out on top. Maybe you get it out on the street. Maybe the people who surface on the exchange are the ones who know how to deal with survival. That's not to say an M.B.A. can't do as well. But nobody goes straight up. I've been down to a point where a lesser person would have been out the window."

Sandner's dinner was usually a salad, and he seldom ate meat. He had entered a sort of puttering stage as he cut back on personal trading. He contributed articles to various law journals, took night courses in the art of juggling, pasta making, and electrical handiwork. And in the early-morning hours, sometime between midnight and three, he'd work on his novel called *Cure*, a thriller about how a cancer wonder drug is suppressed. Jack had even begun talking about how people should change careers every seven or eight years. That kind of talk usually creeps into the conversations of traders sooner or later.

How much was enough? It was a question I had asked more than 150 traders, and no one could give a definite answer. But there was a point traders reached where the victories seemed to be more important than the spoils. A young millionaire trader once summed it up in an interview with *Futures* magazine in the following exchange:

> *Futures:* What are your long-term goals? Ten years from now how much would you like to have made?
> *Trader:* I want to make two hundred million dollars.

Futures: Trading commodities?

Trader: From commodities.

Futures: And if you made two hundred million, would you quit?

Trader: No, I wouldn't.

Futures: Because the game would still be there?

Trader: The game is what keeps anybody in it. It's not the money, it's the game played in order to get the money.

It was the same answer I had heard repeatedly in scores of interviews with winners who could have walked away from the pits with their millions but chose to stay. They are like the breed of joggers who run seven days a week, rain or shine, refusing to cut back or stop for fear their bodies will fall apart. Most of these traders are so into the commodities game that they actually resent weekends as an intrusion. They can hardly wait for Monday mornings, when they get another chance at playing. Why else would they stash quotron machines in their homes and vacation retreats like rare vintage wines in a wine cellar? For them the quotron is a portable life-support system, which keeps them just a finger's touch away from the pulse of the market, whether they're in Palm Springs or the Colorado Rockies.

It's always been that way. Up until the early 1950s trading on the Chicago Board of Trade took place six days a week. And there was a strong trader contingent pushing for a seven-day trading week. Even when the five-day week was adopted, some traders continued to wheel and deal under the table, trading five and ten carlots on Sunday afternoons in the privacy of their homes and even in the exchange rest rooms long after the closing bell.

There is no question about it: Commodity traders love their work. And when they play the game long enough, luck for even the best of traders, as Leo Melamed had told me, evens out. It certainly did for Jack Sandner.

Some four months after my visit with Sandner, the odds caught up with him. An investment in a feeder cattle operation had gone awry. When all the pluses and minuses were figured, Sandner ended up losing $1.7 million. He was numb for a while. The loss would have been more devastating had it been in the pits.

35

Leaving Before They Get the Rolls

Losses of $1 million or $2 million are nothing to sneeze at. But they pale against those taken by a few of the Gatsbys in recent years. Consider one of the Merc's supertraders, a fellow by the name of Joel Greenberg, who had made tens of millions of dollars in the egg, pork belly, and cattle pits and in assorted investments in various beef- and pork-packing companies. He could have walked away from the pits forever while he was still in his thirties to live a life of leisure. Instead, in 1981, at age forty-three, he carried his legendary trading exploits into the interest-sensitive treasury bill pit, where he was clobbered with staggering losses estimated at between $30 million and $45 million. Only his accountant and the IRS know the precise numbers. Of course, Greenberg would never say, for like most of the successful traders, he had managed to shy away from publicity throughout his career. The fact that he could sustain such a loss is remarkable.

Nevertheless, trying to figure out why Greenberg continued to play the game, and for such huge stakes and subsequently such enormous losses, made for weird speculation. But absurdity has never been a stranger to the pits and its traders.

Greenberg had always been the heaviest of hitters, with a pit reputation as a terror. "When he goes into the pit," a rival once said, "everyone's afraid to bid against him." Greenberg's presence in the pit evoked a sort of awe (and gasp); a stand-back "Let's wait and see what Joel does" air prevailed. He was an intimidator, and few opponents could figure him out. Traders play personalities as much as they play the market. That means knowing when somebody is bluffing and when somebody has a good hand. No one could ever tell by just observing Greenberg. He worked the pits like a seasoned politician, who does his homework, times his decisions well, and cuts his losses quickly. He never traded on hope, because depending on emotions was the surest way of getting his tail whacked off by the others.

Joel Greenberg had grown up in a predominantly Jewish middle-class section of Chicago called Hollywood Park, where he attended Von Steuben High School. After a four-year stint in the navy, he was graduated from the University of Illinois with a marketing degree in 1963. Greenberg was always quick to see opportunity—and quicker to pounce on it. He sold RCA computers until 1969, when he became a broker for Heinhold Commodities, Inc., one of the nation's largest brokerage firms. He had begun trading cotton and eggs four years earlier and bought his Merc membership in 1967. By 1971 Greenberg had already established his reputation as one of Heinhold's up-and-comers with a string of wins and a hardy speculative appetite for big plays. He shouted the praises of the pits to his friends, urging them to take up membership in the house of the Merc. He became the godfather to a number of traders. "Our entire cul-de-sac became Merc members," said a trader and former Greenberg neighbor who answered the call.

His trading prowess brought him power and clout on the floor as Greenberg was elected the Merc's second vice-chairman in 1978. His winnings brought him other deals. He began playing bigger numbers in 1974, when he started buying shares on the open market in Philadelphia-based Bluebird, Inc., the country's largest pig-processing company. Over the years he quietly and painstakingly assembled 2.75 million shares of Bluebird, or 57 percent of the company. The investment was worth some $41 million. By 1979 his holdings in public companies alone amounted to nearly $50 million. He also conceived (for a 22 percent interest) a new Chicago company, Midwest Quality Beef, the seventy-five-year-old chairman and chief financial backer of which was Charles Lubin, the founder of Kitchen of Sara Lee.

Over the years Greenberg had culled certain trading strategies which he used for himself and his customers. A strict fundamental-ist, he never used charts—or stop orders. "If I think that I'm wrong, I don't need stops to get me out of the market. I just go," he once told a group of Heinhold brokers, adding, "The key is light commitment into the market." That meant, by Greenberg's definition, committing no more than 25 percent of a trader's total equity to the market. Nor did he believe in the use of straddles, or spreads, because, he said, they locked in a loss. He spread-traded only when he was seriously considering taking delivery on the commodity. And once the market had begun to move his way—and the margin money doubled—he would usually pyramid on a descending scale. If, for example, he had started out buying five contracts and the price had moved up high enough, he would have added another three contracts to his position. At the next pyramid price point he'd add two contracts. Finally, when the market reached a point where it looked as if there were no more chance to double the money, it was time to take profits and look for a change in fundamentals. "Where a lot of people get fouled up on pyra-miding," he reminded his colleagues, "is that to them, pyramiding means if you have five cars, you add five more. The pitfall here is that if the market moves against you, it's going against you dou-ble."

It all sounded clear and rational. No one doubted that Green-berg knew what he was talking about when it came to trading. He had the personal net worth to prove it. But for all those years his business had been pigs and cows. Why suddenly T-bills?

"He thought he understood money and interest rates" was the way one of his associates put it. And like everything Greenberg went into, he did it in a big way. Nobody realized just how big until the rumors of his losses began to filter up from the trading floor.

Through his outside business dealings and borrowing from banks to finance his investments, Greenberg did indeed know something about interest rates. But what he may not have under-stood was the treasury bill pit and its players. It was a time of vola-tile interest rates, and speculators were betting on which way the money markets would move, while hedgers tried to reduce their interest rate risk. Both the Merc's treasury bill pit and the Board of Trade's treasury bond pit were the realm of the younger Gatsbys, and it was hard to find a face over thrity-five in these packed arenas. The trading was shifting away from grains and livestock. After all, wasn't money a more universally used commodity than, say, soybeans or pork bellies? Moreover, the exchanges had opened their doors to a flock of novice traders by offering far less expensive partial memberships exclusively for trading financial futures. In addition, both exchanges had eased their rules to allow members to lease seats more easily.

No matter who the players were, sophisticated or not, it was still a big guessing game with the federal government calling the shots. T-bond and T-bill yields moved by the Federal Reserve wrench, which tightened and loosened the nation's basic money supply, known as M1, and the other two Ms. (M1 is the total amount of currency held by the public plus private checking deposits, M2 includes the M1 supply along with such things as saving deposits, including those in the money market deposit accounts, and M3 covers all these as well as large certificates of deposit.)

Greenberg apparently had guessed wrong. Here's where the disagreement begins among traders who thought they knew him. Some say with his ego at stake, he wouldn't admit he was wrong. Others believe he just ran out of trading steam and simply froze. Previously Greenberg had bounced back in other markets, but for one reason or another, he couldn't do it in the T-bill pit.

What happened to Joel Greenberg isn't unique. It has happened to others, if not on so grand a scale. Traders who have made it big in one pit can become emotionally blitzed in another. They can forget that each pit has its own character, forget how they were schooled by the lean years, forget about the pain of loss, and, worst of all, forget about the meaning of money. With almost an amused detachment, a number of traders admit to being short on pecuniary perspective. Merc trader Barry Lind, a short, frenetic 127-pound Woody Allen lookalike, summed it up for me: "You tend to lose some respect for money." Lind made his millions around the same golden years Greenberg was making his. From time to time a few traders have had to remind themselves that they were playing for *real* dollars. They've gone to their banks to withdraw neat stacks of tens, twenties, fifties, hundreds to touch and feel *real* money, to remember that this is what the game's all about. Perhaps Greenberg should have played this game of monetary show and tell. Not long after he had taken his loss, a fellow trader asked him about it. "The money didn't have any meaning to me," he said Greenberg told him.

Shortly after that comment Greenberg returned to the familiar territory of the cattle pit and, reportedly, to his winning ways. He may have slowed down, but he didn't stop. In 1983 rumors were again circulating about Greenberg. This time traders were whispering about the million-dollar winning play he had made in the cattle market.

There are traders who know when to call it quits and are happy to leave the pits with their shirts on. Take one Board of Trade member who threw in the towel following a string of bitter losses. As his last gesture he posted a farewell letter on the exchange bulletin board for all his colleagues to see:

Dear Friends:

This time has arrived that in order to continue as a member, I would have to sell my Rolls-Royce and become a floor broker. Well, you fellows are not getting my car, and I will not work for any of you either.

I have had twelve marvelous years. Some of you have noticed the little gray hairs that are sprouting. Well, I've seen them, too. I have grown up here and feel like I'm leaving home. I am sort of scared but, on the other hand, quite excited. I know where my next stop is, for I have found something that is important to me and I must do.

I love the Board of Trade—the last great frontier. Leaving hurts. It's been fun. You guys treated me like a star.

Finally, to all of you who have given me advice on how I should shave, dress, and trade, and also to those who have worried about my health and social life, and even to the ones who have aided in spiritual growth—"get fucked."

Good luck, and buy the lows and sell the highs

After a couple of years the trader who had penned that letter was back in the pits to try again. What keeps traders from leaving and others coming back for another shot? The key is risk appetite. All commodity traders—winners and losers alike—are hungry for risk. It's only the risk-to-reward ratio that varies. And it's also the reason why the trading floor is essentially a young man's and woman's world. By the late thirties and early forties most people have too many financial commitments to take chances. So the traders are like thousands of budding entrepreneurs with vision, however limited, along with a portfolio of self-confidence and need: the need to be in charge, to have some feeling of control over their own destinies. There is a certain audacity about them, a dedicated selfishness, a willingness to sweat things out and to cope with the pits even though they assault the eye and numb the brain.

There is a crucial difference between the average commodity trader and the venture capitalist. Traders play not with risk capital but rather with savings, loans, funds for education, equity in houses—money they can't afford to lose. That's why most traders play hard and will do anything to win and why, as a group, they take more chances than most others. Besides the contagion of wealth that sweeps the pits (and the flu because of the proximity of the traders) risk also becomes infectious. Social psychologists have a name for this behavior: risky shift. It's only a theory, but in the pits it seems to hold, that in groups people tend to take more risks than they do individually.

At times, traders have even gone underground to continue their risk-taking ways. It began on the Chicago Board of Trade with a dentist and trader named Doc Crawford. The year was 1934, when so-called privileges were traded. A privilege was an option to buy or sell wheat, corn, or rye. But these were very short-term options and were traded just overnight. They were bought at the close of one day and expired the next morning at the opening. A privilege roughly cost one-quarter cent a bushel for 5,000 bushels, and was widely used by commercial interests for overnight protection rather than for buying or selling the more costly futures contract. Often traders treated privileges like so many chips in a table-stakes poker game. Doc Crawford, it seemed, had given up on filling teeth and instead filled his pockets with huge numbers of privileges. Over one evening he had amassed so many, in fact, that he caused a sharp run-up in the price of wheat and corn.

Normally such tactics may not have drawn any fire. But the doc's timing couldn't have been worse. Most people didn't take well to falsely inflated prices in the Depression. The market collapsed a few days later, and it was only a matter of time before the government banned the trading of privileges.

That didn't stop everyone, especially those who earned their livings trading privileges. The ban drove the trading of privileges underground into a sub rosa market, where it flourished until the early 1950s in defiance of government regulations. Not everyone participated, but there were just enough to make the game interesting. It was strictly a cash exchange, and of course, no records were kept. The covert market encouraged some traders willingly to lose a little money in the futures market as legitimate tax deductions in order to gain cash under the table.

To this day exchange officials won't acknowledge the underground market ever existed. Nevertheless, old-timers still remember the days of the privilege markets. Recalled sixty-five-year-old veteran trader Ben Raskin: "Every morning a couple of clerks would scoot across the floor like syndicate bagmen collecting for the numbers game. A lot of money changed hands. I saw it with my own eyes."

Trading in options on futures was legally revived in October 1982 in the hope that a wave of new speculators would be brought into the market. Under a three-year pilot program, approved by the Commodity Futures Trading Commission, three exchanges opened trading in options. Options were offered by the Chicago Board of Trade on its treasury bond futures, by the Commodity Exchange in New York on gold futures, and by the Coffee, Sugar and Cocoa Exchange in New York on its three main commodities.

If the pits do anything, they unleash the riverboat gambler that lurks in practically everyone. Publically, most traders quibble with the comparison of high-risk speculators to high-rolling gamblers. But it's easy to find traders who can identify with Fyodor Dostoyevsky's compulsive gambler. With a single coin left in his pocket for food he returns to the gaming table for that one last chance—with the empty promise that he will stop gambling tomorrow. There are traders who have made that same promise.

"I stopped the bookies when I got married," said one dejected Gatsby who had made $2 million only to lose $3 million trading cattle. It had happened to him twice. And each time he went belly up he'd return to the pit as an order filler to make a living, pay off his debt, and build up another trading stake. He ended up going to a psychoanalyst to understand why he was so vulnerable and why he lost big whenever he was ahead. "He [the psychoanalyst] didn't have the answers," he said lamentingly, "other than to conclude I had no goals. But the pits are like betting on a sporting event; I don't care what anybody says. It's a matter of semantics; it's all gambling."

36

Ya Wanna Bet?

Dan Rice, a legendary grain trader of the 1930s and 1940s, used to run a roulette wheel in his brokerage office, located right under the corn pit on the third floor of the Board of Trade Building. After trading hours a coterie of traders would gather around the wheel, some of them with hopes of winning back their trading losses for the day. If it wasn't roulette, it would be a hot and high-stake game of klaviash, a Hungarian rummy game, which was a Rice favorite. And then there would be all-night poker games. One morning Rice walked into his office, bleary-eyed, unshaved, hair askew. He had arrived at seven sharp, straight from an all-night game of seven-card stud.

"Did you win?" asked one of his clerks innocently.

Rice glared at him for a few moments and then dug into his pockets, producing handfuls of bills and heaving them into the air like so much confetti to create a storm of singles, fives, tens, twenties, fifty-dollar bills blanketing the floors, the desks, anything they could cling to. The clerk dropped to his knees, scooping up fistfuls of money and counting as fast as he could. He counted up $52,000. "That's what I won," snapped Rice, who proceeded to freshen up for a day of hard trading.

Times haven't changed; only the players have. You can still find traders huddled in an office in any of the exchange buildings engaged in a game of $20-a-throw coin pitching or a hot poker game with more action than the pits can offer on a particular day—all within sight of a video screen flashing the latest futures prices. The pots can be worth thousands. More than a few traders have been known to take positions in the market at the opening, then hustle to friendly games of poker until a few minutes before the close. After the close they're back at the games for a few more hours. One popular during-hours game among the crowd at the Board of Trade's sister exchange, the Chicago Board Options Exchange, is lowball poker, a game in which the low hand wins. Five-thousand-dollar pots aren't uncommon, and some traders are still able to offset poor trading days at the poker table. And those marathon games with traders running straight from the tables to the pits still go on Dan Rice style.

Even the runners—many of whom worship the pit traders in mock fashion—have their own poker games. On a slow trading day they'll stand around for hours engrossed in liar's poker, a game played by matching the serial numbers of one dollar bill against another as if the numbers were a poker hand.

Then there are the outright bets, bets that at times thrust the entire exchange populace into a gambling euphoria. Take, for example, the weekly butter pool at the Mercantile Exchange. Since the butter market is so small and stable, butter trades only on Fridays—if any traders show up to trade it. It's a commodity appendix, a vestige left from the days when the Merc throve as the butter-and-egg exchange.

There is no butter pit. It's a cash market, and the bids and offers are scribbled on a forlorn blackboard off to one side of the trading floor. A long trading day in butter lasts fifteen minutes. Much of the time the market opens and closes within two minutes. But that's more than enough time for traders to turn butter into cream for the Gatsbys. How? By creating the butter pool, a sort of weekly sweepstakes tied to the closing of the butter market. Shortly before the market opens at 10:00 A.M., the wagers fly. Brokers, phone clerks, runners put $5 each into a pool and pick a time between 10:00 A.M. and 10:15 A.M. The one who comes closest to the time the market closes wins the pool, usually at least a $500 purse. Even in this little intramural game, traders use brinksmanship in order to win. One broker wanted to win so badly he continued to bid butter prices higher just to keep the market going long enough to close at the time slot he had picked. He won the pool, lost on the butter trade, but still came out ahead for the minute and a half of action. The very commodity that helped establish the Merc back in 1910, a trading staple for many years thereafter, is now a toy of the traders.

Traders will wager on everything, it seems. Take the time of the Great Arm Wrestle. A phone clerk for Heinhold Commodities had put out the challenge that he could beat anyone at the Merc in an arm wrestling match. He had good reason for such confidence: He was a man mountain, a towering six-foot-five-inch farm lad with a pair of granite shoulders and a black belt in karate to boot. He found a taker from the rival brokerage house of Woodstock, Inc., and the bets were on. Harry the Hat, one of Heinhold's super pit brokers, himself bet $1,000 on the man mountain. There's no way of telling how many more thousands were riding on the sweaty palms of two hands, but some guess it was upwards of $70,000. One afternoon, following the close of pork belly trading, hundreds of traders rushed to the east wall of the trading floor, where they encircled the two gladiators locked in hand-to-hand combat. As predicted by the odds makers, the man mountain won. The battle represented more than just brawny clerk against brawny clerk. The real stake in the Great Arm Wrestle was the pride of the brokerage houses they represented.

Nothing, however, beat the Great Ball Toss at the Board of Trade. This time it was a matter of personal (rather than organizational) honor. The man of the hour was soybean trader Bobby Douglas, a former hard-throwing quarterback for the Chicago Bears until the mid-1970s. No one remembers exactly how the conversation began, but it ended in a betcha-I-can, betcha-you-can't wager between Douglas and a fellow trader. The challenge was straightforward: Could Bobby Douglas throw a softball 385 feet from home plate into the left-field seats at Comiskey Park? It would take a mighty arm to do it. At first someone bet $20. That small wager provoked another trader to chip in $50 for anybody who cared to match it. One bet led to another, and before long the challenge turned into serious business, with a pool of some 200 anxious bettors who had wagered an estimated $180,000. The Great Ball Toss had taken on the earmarks of a hot futures contract: There was plenty of open interest and plenty of liquidity to make the game financially exciting and profitable. Only one problem remained. How was Bobby Douglas going to get into the ball park?

At times like this commodity traders show their real muscle. The mere fact that the feat at hand required getting inside a major-league ball park was hardly a deterrent. One of the traders, who also happened to own part interest in the Chicago White Sox, fixed it. Arrangements were made to get into the park on a day when the team was on the road.

What began as more or less a private wager had turned into an unofficial exchange event, a sort of gala like one of those "challenge of the stars" TV sports specials. In the spirit of a true athletic event, the traders even chartered buses to shuttle them to the park. If a man was ever like a Casey at the Bat, it was Bobby Douglas that day.

He had five tries to do it. The Mighty Bobby stepped up to the plate for the Great Ball Toss. He was an imposing athletic figure at six-feet three-inches and 220 pounds, possibly a bit softer than in his playing days, but the same weight and with the same determination. With all the might he could muster, he heaved the ball into the sky in a perfect parabola from the plate to the fence, the throngs urging him on. The ball fell a couple of feet short. He tried again: short again. On the fifth and last try he concentrated hard as if he were in Soldier Field on a Sunday afternoon with the home crowd screaming for a victory against the Green Bay Packers and the Bears in the last two minutes going for the winning touchdown. Athletes do that; they reach for that exalted state, moving into a sort of self-hypnotic zone, locking their minds in on the opportunity ahead. In that sense athletes and commodity traders have something in common. They both become so involved in the game that they are able to block out the ear-piercing noise of the crowd, using rituals, superstitions, hypnosis, meditation, their bodies, their minds—anything—to win. But the fifth try came up short. Douglas lost the bet.

Feeling deep inside he could still do it, however, he gave it two more tries. On the seventh toss he unleashed a corker, straining every fiber in his arm. The ball sailed into the left-field stands. It was a personal victory for Douglas but an irrelevant one for his backers.

Sometimes that zeal to win on a gamble shows itself in the oddest ways. Take the time a couple of traders and their wives were on a cruise in the Caribbean. The traders became so embroiled in a hot game of bingo they did what any red-blooded pit fighter would do: cornered the market. That's right, they cornered the bingo card market aboard ship, buying up more than 100 bingo cards (at $1 each) to assure themselves a victory. That's how some commodity traders are. What drives them to such extremes? Perhaps it's their conditioning from the daily rigors of the pit. It could be that winning is addictive.

Traders have described that winning feeling in the pit the way a horseplayer at a meeting of Gamblers Anonymous once put it: "The feeling of winning is unbelievably intoxicating to me. I get the greatest thrill out of thinking that I've outsmarted everyone else. I do want to go back to the track. There is not an hour I don't think about it."

That statement echoes the comment of a gold trader who had his ups and downs over the years. "What's more beautiful than to buy twenty-five contracts of gold and sell out five minutes later and make twelve thousand dollars," he told me. "When you're right, you're godlike. You get adulation from your peers, like a matador walking into a bullring. It's exhilarating. You don't want the weekends to come."

Call it cockiness, conceit, overconfidence, or plain greed that drives the Gatsbys. Unfortunately the same compulsion can turn a winner into a loser.

37

Up, Up, and Away

Timothy Anderson had promise. Everyone said so. At twenty-six he was an affable young man making a name for himself as one of the up-and-comers at the Chicago Board of Trade. He had earned a reputation as a trading whiz in treasury bonds for the Donaldson, Lufkin & Jenrette Securities Corp. before he decided to strike out on his own in late 1982 as an independent order filler at the Board of Trade. You could make more money that way, provided the order deck was big enough and the action volatile enough—as it was in the bond pit, overflowing with some 400 frantic traders.

Order fillers are the mechanics of the pits. Pit locals liken them to plumbers or carpenters, craftsmen who have mastered their trade with a certain skill and proficiency. Their job is to get the best possible prices for their customers with the fewest mistakes. While they aren't risking their own money, order fillers are responsible for those costly outtrades that at times can eat up more than their commissions. Depending on the size of their decks, however, order fillers can control the flow of the trading action and can usually choose the traders with whom they will work. That is why traders are nice to order fillers, treating them like prime athletes who are wooed, courted, and pampered.

Harry ("the Hat") Lowrance over at the Merc was a glowing example of the kind of money an ambitious order filler could make. Harry worked the live cattle pit, earning a mere $2 on average per order he executed. Mere? On an average day he did 1,400 orders, grossing $2,800 per day. That's an average of $56,000 a month, or $670,000 for an average year. By the time Harry was thirty-two in 1981 he was a multimillionaire, and as one observer put it, that made the Hat "all but a god to the new breed of traders." The income was more than enough for Harry, the tall, skinny, mustachioed bachelor, who was once a poor kid from the South Side of Chicago. Every morning a long, burgundy, chauffeur-driven limousine with (of course) the license plate "HAT," brought Harry to the exchange. And every afternoon the limo would be waiting for Harry to whisk him to his mansion in the suburb of Evanston on the north shore of Lake Michigan, to his glass sauna overlooking the lake, to his living room with the beveled glass mirrors and walls of blue quilted wool adorned with gold and silver leaf, to his soda fountain, luxuries Harry might never have dreamed of if he hadn't ventured into the pits.

Tim Anderson wasn't in Harry the Hat's class—not yet. But he was probably aspiring to be. "He was a nice guy," recalled one of Anderson's fellow traders, "just beginning to make money." It wasn't enough to buy lakeshore mansions, but apparently it was enough to afford expensive habits. On January 14, 1983, Timothy Anderson's promising career ended with his death. According to the Cook County medical examiner, he had died from "acute cocaine toxicity."

Anderson's death was a waste, his exchange friends said. Beyond that observation, no one cared to comment. It wasn't the first time drugs had taken their toll on trading talent. Nor would it be the last.

The use of cocaine by Timothy Anderson was an unpleasant reminder that drugs are as much a part of a Gatsby's life-style as a Mercedes 450SL. That's not to say every trader uses drugs—or owns a Mercedes-Benz car. But it's no secret just how widespread the use of drugs has become among the trader set—both off and on the floor. Like athletes, entertainers, and other achievers, they are part of an achievement-oriented culture tied to a jet-age pharmacology that subscribes to a pill for every ill. Why shouldn't they pop pills? Traders track the highs and lows in the pits with their blood pressure. When the market recoils, there's no way to remain calm in the pit. Arteries constrict; blood pressure shoots up; the glands squirt their nerve-stimulating chemicals, which wend their way through the body like some corrosive force eating away at the membranes. Doctors call it stress. Traders relieve it any way they can. It's not surprising that the biggest single selling item in the candy-tobacco-sundries shop on the main floor of the Board of Trade Building is Rolaids. Or that Leo Melamed over at the Merc has a big gum ball machine in his office that dispenses Di-Gel tablets to cut the acids from those volcanoes of tension that constantly erupt in the pits of a trader's stomach. Or that in some of the back offices of brokers and clearinghouses you can find enough uppers and downers to start a neighborhood pharmacy. Or that traders take five-minute "toot breaks" to get half an hour of trading energy, drive, and confidence.

For obvious reasons, exchange officials play down drug use, pointing their fingers at a few traders, a few brokers, a few clerk types as possible abusers. Just isolated cases, they say. Certainly federal drug agents didn't see it that way one cold February afternoon in 1979, when they swooped down on the floor of the Chicago Board Options Exchange (CBOE) minutes after the bell sounded at 3:10 P.M. to end the day's trading. As more than 1,000 people were leaving the floor, agents of the Drug Enforcement Administration (DEA) had positioned themselves at the two exit doors and arrested 12 traders, brokers, and financial professionals who were suspected cocaine dealers. The arrests followed a year-long stakeout code-named Operation Candy (*candy* is a word used in the drug trade to describe cocaine), during which undercover DEA agents bought fifty-three ounces of cocaine valued at $100,000 in two dozen transactions on the floor of the exchange. Once the shock of the raid had dissipated in the financial community, traders dismissed the arrests as a cheap shot, a ploy to get some fast publicity for the DEA at the expense of a handful of nickel-dimers. And CBOE officials issued a statement deploring the manner in which the DEA had handled the arrests, noting that they involved "a very few people out of hundreds on the trading floor." The DEA agents insisted that cocaine use was so commonplace at times that some business deals were fouled up, forgotten, or misplaced by workers apparently under the influence of the drug.

The bust was turned into a television extravaganza. The cam-

228

eras of local TV stations were on the scene, filming the arrests for the 6:00 P.M. and 10:00 P.M. newscasts. What escaped the camera lens, however, was a scramble among some traders to dump pills in wastebaskets and flush bags of coke down toilets. Here's how one of those traders remembered it: "I had a two-gram bottle of coke in my pocket. There had been a lot of rumors that a bust was coming, and when someone spotted agents, word got out. I threw my coke down the john, bottle and all. There were probably more than a hundred little bottles of coke and countless pills and joints thrown away. How do I know? Because after the bust you could see the clerks running around scavenging the wastebaskets. One guy I knew had five thousand ludes [methaqualone, a sedative pill brand-named Quāāludes] in a bathrobe-size box in his office and was dishing out fistfuls to anyone who wanted them. It was sheer panic all around. But things got back to normal a couple of weeks later."

Of the fourteen persons arrested (two had been arrested outside the exchange), only two were convicted. One received a one-year term in federal prison, and the other got three years' probation. A handpicked team of four DEA agents with working knowledge of financial dealings was credited with cracking the case. As part of his undercover garb, one DEA agent who made cocaine buys wore a set of gold chains, a gold watch, and gold rings to fit into the group, he explained. "Coke is a status drug, and you're cool if you use it," he told me. "The older guys were happy we busted the young traders, who felt they were protected by the walls of the exchange."

The white tornado hit the commodity culture hard for good reason. There are few professions—or trust funds—that can support a $200- or $300-a-day coke habit. Commodities trading is one. Cocaine made its way from the sniffs of high society to become the drug of choice for traders in the early 1970s. (It's only fitting that commodities traders sniff their good times from one of the biggest commodities in the world. Cocaine in the United States alone is a $30-billion-a-year business, which puts it in the top ten of the *Fortune* 500, just below the Ford Motor Company. The leverage certainly is better than that of a futures contract: A kilo—2.2 pounds—of 90 percent pure cocaine that costs $4,000 in Bogotá, Colombia, is worth $500,000 by the time it hits the streets of

North America. In 1983 the cost of cocaine at $2,200 an ounce was five times the price of gold. In view of the demand for coke, if it were a legal drug, it could easily become a futures contract on some exchange somewhere.)

More than one trader has thrown a party at which he offered his guests bowls of the white powder, sitting on tables along with trays of rolled joints. At a drug abuse center in a Chicago suburb the stream of traders and brokers during 1983 enabled the medical director to put together a profile of professional traders with cocaine problems: Nearly all were male, married, between the ages of thirty and forty-five, and very energetic, imaginative, intelligent, ambitious, competitive, and self-confident. Alcohol, marijuana, amphetamines, barbituarates, and a number of other illicit drugs were also popular crutches. Coke made you high; a sedative brought you down or took the edge off that yearning for another snort.

The traders became the carriage trade for pill pushers and their so-called stress clinics, which popped up on the scene in the late 1970s and early 1980s. Young commodity and options traders, along with stockbrokers, lawyers, insurance salesmen, and manufacturers' reps, among a host of other professional types, flocked to them. A popular storefront clinic was located at Franklin and Illinois streets on the rim of Chicago's downtown Loop within an easy twenty-minute walk of the commodity exchanges. Some had a nickname for this particular clinic: Quaalude Heaven.

From the looks of the spacious, standing room only reception area, it appeared as if the clinic had either discovered the cure for cancer or was giving something away for nothing. Neither was the case. It was strictly a pay-as-you-go situation. The clinic was geared to fast service. Two receptionists in the waiting room kept the production line moving. The doctor handled distribution.

The entire process took a half hour. First, the patient took a fifteen-minute stress test, a questionnaire which required either "yes" or "no" answers. Have you lost a parent? Have you lost a mate? Have you been divorced? Do you have any health problems? Are you separated? It made no difference what the answers were because everyone who came to the clinic got what he came for: a prescription for forty-five Quaaludes. That's what the doctor ordered for every patient whether it was needed or not. The cost of those pills and the doctor's sympathy was $125. Each subsequent visit cost $60, and the patient got another thirty Quaaludes To keep the pipeline filled, some brokers sent their clerks to the clinic for treatment. "It was like finding a gold mine," said one options trader, who sighed as he recalled those days. "There must have been close to a hundred guys from the floor who went to that clinic. We'd watch each other's positions when we'd have an appointment."

By 1982 the authorities had caught up with the clinic and the quack doctor who ran it, and the "gold mine" was shut down. That, of course, didn't mean the end of narcotic delights. Traders usually have the financial muscle to buy what they covet.

38

The High Side of Whoopee

The new Gatsbys reside in a sort of parallel world that mimics the forms of upper-class reality but operates by its own set of laws. They are a bawdy, irreverent bunch, but unlike the haughty, youthful entrepreneurs of, say, the high-technology businesses that have emerged in recent years, the Gatsbys aren't leading the United States into any kind of technological future. They aren't out to build the world through industrial sweat. They don't plow capital back into machines to multiply production, as Adam Smith would have had it. They don't deal with factories, production lines, inventories, pro formas, employees, stockholders. They are the ultimate consumers, graduates cum laude of economist Stanley Jevons's so-called hedonist school, those who use economics "to maximize happiness by purchasing pleasure, as it were, at the lowest cost of pain." Money, not power, is their ultimate aphrodisiac.

"Money talks; shit walks" was the way Sonny, a thirty-year-old Merc trader put it to me. "It makes life easy," he continued. "I don't make reservations at restaurants, not when all I have to do is slip a fifty-dollar bill in a man's hand. Or take traffic tickets. Haven't had one in years. Whenever a cop stops me for speeding, I lay a fifty on the seat next to me, and all I get is a warning. Money is expedient, an incredible convenience. There is less of a hassle with it. I'll pay twenty or thirty dollars over the price of a first-row seat at a show if I want to see it badly enough. I'll easily spend thirty thousand dollars a year on extras like that. I'll pick up a three-hundred-dollar bar tab. Everything is trivial. All it is is a tick in the market. I relate spending to the market."

Traders may understand the wisdom of the dictum that less is more, but most ignore it. More is more. The attitude is tied into the speed at which a Gatsby can make money unlike that of any of his youthful counterparts in other professions. Even doctors and lawyers must plod through their careers at some point, spending lean years in school and then building a practice, patient by patient, case by case. But a trader with less than a high school education can earn $100,000 and more within the first six months in the pit and then go on to make $1 million. If he has the trading knack, he may begin raking it in all too fast, without building up a psychological base to handle it or even to understand it.

Odds are Thorstein Veblen would have been intrigued by the Gatsbys, who seem to fit like old gloves into *The Theory of the Leisure Class*. He could very well have been observing them when he wrote back in 1899: "The quasi-peaceable gentlemen of leisure, then, not only consumes of the staff of life beyond the minimum required for sustenance and physical efficiency, but his consumption also undergoes a specialization as he regards the quality of the goods consumed. He consumes freely and of the best in food, drink, narcotics, shelter, services, ornaments, apparel, weapons and accoutrements, amusements, amulets, and idols or divinities. . . ." Veblen, who himself had practiced a leisure life of sorts, spending years just sitting around and reading, concluded: "Since the consumption of these more excellent goods is an evidence of wealth, it becomes honorific; and conversely, the failure to consume in due quantity and quality becomes a mark of inferiority and demerit."

So it goes with the new Gatsbys, an honorific breed, cavalier in their material mannerisms. They consume like people who regret the missed opportunities of life and then by some magic are given another chance. The Gatsbys have become legendary in Chicago, not so much for their exploits in the pits as for their spending habits.

For a week in February 1985, the public gawked with envy at the Rolls-Royce on display during the annual Chicago Automobile

Show. The price tag: $185,000. The one bidder: commodity trader Alan Freeman, who was no stranger to Rolls-Royces. He already owned a Corniche convertible valued at $150,000. Freeman's bid prompted one local gossip columnist to observe, "Commodities brokers are today's last of the big spenders."

A favorite pastime among the middle-class would-haves is commodity trader watching, a game played much the same way children try to spot out-of-town license plates. You judge a Gatsby by his opulence and the car he drives. In fact, you can actually tell some traders by their license plates, displayed like the badges they wear on their trading jackets. Here is a sampling of a few plates seen on the streets of Chicago: "Grain," "I Trade," "Corn," "B-and-S" (buy-and-sell), "Uptick," "Beans," "T-Bills," "Cattle." As for their cars, if there's a youthful face behind the wheel of a Rolls-Royce, a Mercedes, an Excalibur, the first impulse is to say, "That's a commodity trader." The hunch is usually right, if you judge from the parking lots near the exchanges, which are filled with every exotic car imaginable. And the cars are usually equipped with telephones. It's the next stage in the evolution of possessions, a status milestone.

Another clue can be personal accouterments. Many traders wear gold chains around their necks like amulets, and on their wrists are the warrior bracelets of victory from those pit battles: gold Rolex watches. If a Gatsby is married, his wife will have a Rolex, too. Gold seems to be a favorite. That became clear during an interview with a young trader who had recently been divorced. "Look what I had the kids buy their mother for Valentine's Day," he said proudly, producing a gold-chain necklace with the gold initial *C* for Catherine, his former wife's name. With a proud Santa Claus chuckle he opened a drawer and beckoned me over. There were four more necklaces exactly the same except for the gold initials. "This one's for Pam; these for Margo, Amy, and Diane," he said. "Makes a nice gift, doesn't it?" I agreed. He was so enamored of gold that he bought a part interest in an East Coast metals smelting and processing operation which specialized in gold and silver recycling. Gatsbys have gold-plated their houses and mailbox keys, and some even wear $10,000 gold replicas of their trading cards around their necks. One had his toilet seat festooned with Krugerrands under Plexiglas.

234

A former trader I came across had cultivated such a yen for precious metals that he began collecting and dealing in gold, rare coins, and currencies. In 1978 he plunked down $400,000 for a Brasher Doubloon, worth an estimated $750,000 three years later. He considered it the best trade of his life.

For every winning trade there is, of course, a losing one. For instance, the third marriage of a Merc millionaire ended in divorce six months after the vows. The prenuptial agreement called for a $50,000 cash settlement. "It was a bad trade," said the trader of his shattered short-term marriage. At that rate he figured out he could afford another fifty wives before he would have to liquidate assets.

When it comes to pleasing their bodies and palates, the Gatsbys know no boundaries. They spend weekends in Vegas, California's $275-a-day LaCosta Spa, Acapulco, the Caribbean, London, and Paris, squeezed in between the Friday afternoon market close and the Monday morning opening. With cultlike devotion one group of traders has combed the Midwest for the best barbecue ribs. Not content with the fare at Chicago rib houses, they've dispatched runners to St. Louis, Kansas City, and Detroit to bring back lunchtime carryouts.

While the runners at the Board of Trade were on the Great Rib Hunt, the runners over at the Merc were busy scouring Chicago's Italian neighborhood in search of the ideal beef sandwiches. One of the Gatsbys' favorite steak houses is Morton's on the Near North Side of Chicago, which serves a prime marbled twenty-ounce steak for about $18 and where traders think nothing of shelling out $1,000 for a bottle of wine to go with the steak. No wonder proprietor Arnie Morton calls his restaurant "a saloon for the rich."

For sweat suit socializing the traders even had their own inner-city playground, a $20 million glass-and-steel five-story-high edifice otherwise known as the East Bank Club, once described by *Time* magazine as "a secular cathedral built to the glory of the body." The East Bank Club (fondly called EBC by its members) wasn't built with commodity money, but it was built with the youthful commodity traders in mind. It's only a couple of minutes by car from the exchanges. And a large portion of its 5,000 upper-middle-class and mostly single members are traders who gladly pay the $750 initial fee to join what many of them refer to as the

Biggest Meat Market. The coed aerobics classes are mating grounds for the singles (and some marrieds, too), especially for those gold diggers who are determined to end up with wealthy bachelor commodities traders.

Some prefer to maintain their very own personal playgrounds, outfitting their houses with everything from exercise equipment and ballet bars to locker rooms and pool tables and turning their dens into penny arcades filled with video games and pinball machines. One trader, who fancied himself a football jock, had two goalposts erected on his property for fall Sunday morning games with fellow traders. Another installed twenty-foot- and fifteen-foot putting greens of synthetic grass. Still another built a twenty-by-thirty-foot gymnasium with a twenty-foot-high ceiling, a maple floor marked with court lines, and two basketball backboards. All the gym lacked was a set of bleachers and some Andy Frain ushers. Others have their tennis courts and their in-house weight rooms, saunas, whirlpools, hot tubs, and indoor swimming pools.

Wherever the Gatsbys live, it's in comfort. Many are partial to the northern suburbs of Chicago, strung along the shore of Lake Michigan amid oak- and maple-covered ravines. These areas with such names as Kenilworth, Winnetka, Glencoe, Highland Park, and Lake Forest are a blend of old-fashioned luxury and new wealth. For every social luminary, there is a Johnny-come-lately, and for every walnut-paneled library there is a media room with Ultrasuede walls. It's an area where the new rich don't hide their Jaguars and Rolls-Royces in musty garages. When one collector wanted a garage for his seven vintage roadsters, he had a thirty-five- by forty-foot terrazzo-floored pavilion built of steel and glass to display the vehicles in a museumlike setting. The cars also served as a backdrop for parties held in the pavilion, which was reached from a twenty-eight-foot-wide steel bridge spanning a ravine.

If anything, the new Gatsbys were good for the real estate market during the best and worst of economic times. Many of them seemed immune to the 1980 recession and 21 percent interest rates because they bought everything with cash, including their houses. They settled into the old mansions once the exclusive domain of Chicago merchant and industrial barons. They were mansions like the one built for Maxine Spitz as a wedding present in 1926 by her father, one of the owners of the Hart, Schaffner & Marx clothing company. It was a gracious thirteen-room brick English-styled manor house with 130 windows, a hand-carved staircase, a wine cellar, a small pantry where the servants had kept and polished the silver tableware, and even an elevator that led to a second-floor bedroom. The mansion also came with a $750,000 price tag, a bargain the real estate salesman assured. While there was no standing room only crowd of buyers for such a property, there was a market, however thin. The Gatsbys made sure of that.

One childless couple spent $450,000 on an eleven-bedroom house. Why? "We figured we'd use them for our antique collection," the trader said, adding, "Having a lot of money isn't a problem. Knowing what to do with it causes problems."

This same trader, dressed in patched blue jeans and a torn flannel shirt, once casually walked into a Cadillac dealership in 1980 to buy a new Eldorado for cash. Only hours after he had returned home he was feeling guilty—not because he had bought the car but because he had bought the car for himself. That very day he bought his wife a Volkswagen Rabbit diesel. Now the couple owned a Cadillac, Volkswagen, Porsche, Austin-Healy and a four-wheel-drive International Scout, enough to start their own dealership.

The new Gatsbys hire architects to sculpt rooms with soffits and platforms, to create undulating curves that are emphasized with perimeter lighting and the latest electronic wonders and gadgets. One trader, who was a film buff, had his den's high-powered sound system controlled from a circular booth outfitted with a Plexiglas viewing window along with a set of commercial theater seats anchored into several carpeted tiers. Another had the interior walls of the family room built exactly like a log cabin, partly for the amusement of his children and partly out of fond memories for the time he played with Lincoln Logs when he was a kid.

There's no end to their lust for eye-popping exotica. Some, however, prefer *camp* to *class*, like the Gatsby who has a twenty-foot sculpture of King Kong clinging to the outside of his mansion and peering through a second-story window. When a bachelor trader wanted a unique kitchen for his condominium, his interior designer gave him one with yellow, blue, and pink neon lights set beneath an onyx-covered glass floor. This culinary disco matched his bedroom with its mirrored bed shaped like a tiered wedding cake.

There also are the new mansions of a new era of wealth. To find them, drive through a section called High Ridge, off Ridge Road in a far north suburb of Highland Park. A decade ago High Ridge was mostly farmland. Today outsiders call it High Risk in deference to the commodity traders who live in the secluded enclave of streets that lead to cul-de-sacs where million-dollar houses with their multistories and multicar garages stand on large wooded lots as monuments to the more successful traders. The head of a pig is sported by the mailbox of one such house, the proud owner of which obviously made his fortune trading pork bellies on the Merc. Parked in the driveways are every exotic automobile imaginable. You won't find just a BMW, but a BMW 7331, the one that goes for $35,000. And the Mercedes 380SEL. And the Jaguars. And the $100,000 Rolls-Royce black convertible.

The new Gatsbys are born-again spenders. Sometimes they spend for the sheer thrill of it, like the $100 tip one handed a cabdriver, as he put it, "to see what it was like." Sometimes it's for sheer expediency. One trader, for instance, had a tennis match at the East Bank Club after the market close. That morning he had left the house hurriedly, forgetting his racket and gear. He dashed over to Morrie Mages sports store, a few blocks from the club, and outfitted himself from head to toe with everything from sweatband to tennis shoes, including a new racket. The bill was more than $200. The absentminded trader repeated the exercise twice the same month.

Sometimes they spend to conquer those little walls of indecision. Take the trader who didn't know whether he wanted a Danish or a doughnut when the morning coffee cart came around. So, using trader's instinct, he cornered the market by buying all the doughnuts and Danishes for $60.

Like novice film actors who rise to become superstars, the traders are eager to share their wealth with family and friends. It isn't uncommon for one to buy a new car or even a house for his parents or a BMW for a brother or sister.

Even when a Gatsby falls on hard trading times, he may never let on. Some, in fact, take on the airs of the landed gentry of old

238

England whose fashionable duty it was to rack up debts. That's why some merchants familiar with a Gatsby's life-style prefer dealing in cash and no carry. The interior designer of the onyx-covered neon-lit kitchen floor explained it this way. "You've got to sign the contract the day they call," he said assuredly, "because the next day they may not have the money." Why else would Rubovits cigar store in the lobby of the Board of Trade Building have diversified into gold jewelry? That's right, cheroots and karats. On a good trading day a Gatsby is apt to walk in and celebrate with a $5 cigar and a $500 gold chain. Anything can become an impulse item, including a new Cadillac or Mercedes.

At parties the Gatsbys favor the high side of whoopee. Not all of them are party types. Yet a good number trade hard and play hard. Nor, unlike the Great Gatsby himself, do they prefer to stand in the shadows of their parties like some mysterious Bacchus. Instead, they are likely to be at the centers of their dazzling affairs. A few use their parties as "coming-out" affairs to show who they are and what they have.

For sheer extravagance few could match commodity baron Ray Friedman's sixty-fifth birthday party in 1978. The three-day affair for four hundred of his "closest friends" had all the scope and color of a Cecil B. De Mille production down to the videotape filming of events. It opened to rave reviews at the time with the *Des Moines Register* noting it was perhaps one of the biggest birthday parties of its kind ever held in Iowa. Friedman, who made his fortune as a cattle broker, put up some two hundred out-of-towners (including one from England) at the Hilton Inn in Souix City, where he lived on his five-acre estate adjacent to the Souix City Country Club in the so-called silk stocking district.

A registration table set up in the Hilton lobby provided guests with a wish list of activities: tennis at the Racquet Club, boat rides on the Missouri River, limousines chauffeuring guests downtown for shopping, or to the nearby racetrack in South Dakota, or to wherever else they desired. The dinner dance was held in a 120-by-60-foot tent to the right of the guest house near the two tennis courts and across the footbridge that spanned the pond to Friedman's sprawling home. The tent was complete with a stage and dance floor. To commemorate the commodity that afforded Friedman such luxury was a King Kong-size plastic cow and a table embellished with an hors d'oeuvre sculpted in the shape of a cow.

The Sioux City social wags (and guests) began speculating on the cost of the birthday bash, throwing out numbers as if they were playing a lottery. Some guessed $100,000; others estimated three times that amount.

What difference did it make? Of the cost, Friedman told an inquisitive reporter from the *Des Moines Register*, ". . . personally, I don't give a darn. As long as you can afford it, more power to yourself."

Once a Gatsby and his wife found themselves in a frenzy over a party they were throwing for a hundred or so guests. The problem: The party was to take place in a new wing of the house still under construction. The solution: a quick-fix face-lift. The couple spent $50,000 on a few dry walls, shortcut carpentry, and such, putting the room together like a stage set. After the party the entire room was dismantled and rebuilt in accordance to the original plan.

At one party guests were greeted at the door with "His" and "Hers" bathrobes monogrammed with their names. After undressing and slipping on a robe, each retired to the room of his or her choice for a massage by either a masseuse or masseur. Others went straight to the showers with their fountains of nozzles that sprayed you everywhere from every direction and the chrome levers that, at a touch, could turn a shower stall into a dense cloud of mist or a tropical rain forest. Some preferred to immerse themselves into the swirls and eddies of sunken ebony tubs with their whirlpools, then enter the sauna before their rubdowns.

And there were mounds of food, trays of caviar, pâtés, miniature quiches, oysters in the half shell, salmon mousses, pasta primavera, and assorted dips, chips, and Armenian crackers. Two ramrod-tall chefs stood behind a hot table, preparing orders for crepes filled with shrimps, crabs, blueberries, or strawberries, while a third chef ground fresh beef into steak tartar and broiled miniature fillets for sandwiches. On another table were tub-size silver bowls filled with fresh crab legs. A bartender served up beer from kegs and offered every spirit for every course, including white and pink champagne in crystal goblets and coffees from Irish to Turkish.

For guests with a different appetite, an upstairs room offered a

far different buffet. On tables were sugar bowls filled with miniature dunes of white cocaine and small platters of Mexican-grown
hallucinogenic mushrooms known as psilocybin. The pungent
smell of marijuana drifted from another room, along with the wails
of a lead singer from a blaring five-piece reggae rock band.

The parties, of course, varied with the respective tastes of their
hosts. There was the casual Sunday afternoon affair for 50 or so
friends in the sky box of Soldier Field to watch the Chicago Bears,
with lunch catered by the Hilton Hotel. And the lawn party for
300 guests. And the party where all the servants were mimes who
waited on the guests and entertained them. And the party where
all the servants were professional actors who insulted the guests.
And the party where everyone boarded a chartered bus and was
driven to a movie theater to see the *Rocky Horror Picture Show.*
And the birthday party for a trader's one-year-old son with black
tie optional. And the birthday party of a trader's wife, who gathered up a dozen of her close friends and whisked them off on a
chartered flight to New York for a daylong shop-lunch-theater
matinee fete. And the party at which the host treated his guests as
if they were Masters and Johnson's specimens by providing videotape equipment for those who cared to film themselves while
making love (they could take the tapes home with them). And the
party where everyone was taught to paint in oils by a noted local
artist. And the party to celebrate the glory of the Super Bowl.

One such Super Bowl party was appropriately held at the East
Bank Club, given by a female trader, who was single, wealthy, and
a *bon vivant* of sorts. Like a party out of *The Great Gatsby,* it had
a guest list built on a chain of acquaintances. There were other
traders, society types, businessmen, journalists, and even a U.S.
senator from California. Yet few knew the hostess personally. In
any case the Super Bowl had a special nostalgia for her. The first
bet she had ever made at the Merc was on the 1974 Super Bowl,
when she was a newcomer. A trader casually asked if she wanted
to bet a nickel on the game. She accepted and won. When she
went to collect her nickel the following Monday morning after the
Super Bowl, she was astounded. The trader with whom she had
bet handed her a check for $5,000. In the pit culture where deals
were made in financial shorthand, a nickel wasn't what it seemed
to be.

39

Odds and Ends

The new Gatsbys, in one respect, aren't that different from their counterparts of the 1920s who spent and shimmied through the jazz age to forget the troubles of the World War I years. Today's Gatsbys, though not plagued by memories of war, seem to want to forget their troubles, too, and to concentrate on living high. That's why they spend and speculate on more than just soybeans, pork bellies, and interest rates. They diversify for different reasons: to make more money, to shelter taxes, to win prestige, to indulge fantasies, or simply to break away from the pits to try something new. It boils down to spreading risk and parlaying winnings.

Their investments add up to a shoe box of odds and ends that include real estate, professional sports teams, movie ventures, oil wells, racehorses, restaurants, Broadway shows, bars, jazz joints, blues clubs, discos, among hundreds of ventures. One group of traders decided to open a Mexican restaurant just because they liked Mexican food. Another told me the reason he put up $300,000 for a 20 percent interest in a blues club was to impress friends and dates when he took them there. Regardless of what they get into, most never stray far from the pits, which afforded them the new opportunities. At the new Mercantile Exchange Building they stayed within a floor of the pits: There a score of traders formed a syndicate and opened an Italian restaurant on the first floor called "Mama Mia Pasta."

The Board of Trade's Gene Cashman left the pits for years to spend his millions on racehorses and oil wells. He lived in Houston but clung to his Chicago roots and exchange membership. He returned to Chicago and the Board of Trade in 1983 partly, his associates said, out of a desire to get back on a winning track. The O'Connor brothers, Edmund J. and William F., took to a different game: the tricky, high-stake business of risk arbitrage, the art of buying shares in companies being taken over in hopes of turning a quick profit. Cashman and the O'Connors were among the crop of rich people who sprang up from the heady days of $12-a-bushel soybeans. They acquired insatiable appetites for the big plays, which were the key to their rapid wealth. They became known as limit players because of the maximum trading positions—allowed by the exchange rules—they took. These types of players are still around, bigger and brasher than ever. They see one man's pork bellies as another man's bacon.

"One man's volatility is another man's profit" was the way Richard Dennis put it in 1983. At thirty-four, Dennis had become a legend, lionized by the young trader set at the Board of Trade. Whenever they heard the name Dennis, they'd practically stand at attention and salute in awe. Dennis had made more than $100 million in the fourteen years he had been trading, and his buying power in both dollars and number of contracts rivaled the biggest and most sophisticated of institutional investors. He had long given up playing the market strictly on hunch to become a technician, basing his strategy on pricing patterns. Instead of stalking the pits as he had done in the old days, he now sat behind a battery of television screens and a $150,000 computer that spit out the price history of all sorts of commodities. From his office nineteen stories above the trading floor of the Board of Trade he could help drive down or push markets up. On a typical day he would sell $200 million worth of treasury bonds. Or he'd buy 3 million bushels of soybeans—the limit—valued at about $25 million, or sell 20,000 ounces of gold valued at $8 million. There, of course, were losing trades, too, sometimes as much as $5 million. But most of the profits were made on just 5 percent of the trades.

Physically Dennis had changed over the years, but his adroit trading sense remained intact. He was a good thirty pounds heavier than when he had first come to the pits. And despite his wealth, he managed to sidestep the high-stepping image of other Gatsbys. This Prince of the Pit lived more like deposed royalty, driving around in a beat-up 1977 Mercedes and wearing polyester pants. Yet he was every bit as much the capitalist as the others. It was wealth that allowed him to mix raw capitalism with his populist views, to keep his liberal heart pumping for causes. His politics set him apart from most other traders. In 1982, with an endowment of $3 million, Dennis created the Roosevelt Center for American Policy Studies, a liberal think tank based in Washington, D.C. Economic proposals, Dennis believed, should be judged by their ultimate impact on the bottom 50 percent of the population. He donated big sums to liberal Democrats from presidential to mayoral candidates. Liberals are a rare breed at commodity exchanges, which view themselves as the last bastion of free enterprise.

There was no doubt that Richard Dennis's strengths had served him well. Whereas most traders would have burned themselves out just from the pressures of trading huge volumes, Dennis was every bit as good and in control as when he had become a trading phenomenon at twenty-two. By 1981 his firm, C&D Commodities, founded in 1975 with partner Lawrence Carroll, had grown into one of the nation's largest independent commodity concerns. Trading by C&D probably influenced prices not by the size of orders it placed but by the fact that other traders followed in its footsteps. Explained one trader: "The minute the broker for C&D walks into the pit and puts up his hands, they all start to go ahead of him." And the snowball begins rolling.

Nobody could "go ahead" of the O'Connors because they did their big hitting beyond the pits in another arena. After making tens of millions of dollars in soybeans and then stock options (the O'Connors were among the movers and shakers who started the Chicago Board Options Exchange, a spin-off of the Board of Trade), the silver-haired brothers, known in the pits for their green trading jackets, turned to playing with corporations. Among their arbitrage holdings in 1982 were an $86 million stake in the MGIC Investment Corporation, which earned them $6.8 million when MGIC was taken over by the Baldwin-United Corporation. There was a $10 million holding in Host International before it was taken over by the Marriott Corporation and a $19 million investment in the Cannon Mills Company, the shares of which were tendered to the Pacific Holding Corporation. The O'Connors' biggest holdings were estimated at 1 million shares of Conoco Inc., worth about $98 million at the time it was merged into E.I. du Pont de Nemours and Company, and between an estimated 1 million and 1.5 million shares of Cities Service, worth between $40 and $60 a share when the Gulf Oil Company called off its takeover bid. Gulf's withdrawal may have cost the O'Connors more than $10 million, according to other arbitragers, as the price of Cities Service stock plunged to $33 a share. But the O'Connors were reportedly big shareholders again when the Occidental Petroleum Corporation announced its intention to acquire Cities Service, pushing the stock back up.

There are few traders with the awesome financial muscle of the O'Connors, able to export their brash Chicago La Salle Street style to New York's Wall Street. Rather than collect shares of companies, others go in for the more mundane collectables such as paintings, books, antiques. But, they do it with a certain panache. In the living room of one Gatsby hangs a $1 million Jasper Johns American flag. Another Gatsby makes the rounds of the Chicago galleries in the afternoons after trading hours, carefully searching for new talent and building a modern art collection worth millions. Trader and bibliophile Lawrence Gutter amassed a rare book collection in his converted attic library of some 9,000 volumes of Chicago-related literature, ranging from Theodore Dreiser's first novel, *Sister Carrie*, to a 1911 illustrated brochure from the Everleigh Club, Chicago's most elegant brothel where many a commodity trader spent evenings unwinding. Gutter had become the dean of private Chicagoana collectors. In 1982 he sold the collection valued at $600,000 to the University of Illinois for its rare book library. But he kept the nucleus of a new collection, about 3,000 volumes of nineteenth- and twentieth-century first-edition fiction.

Commodity trader Jim Stuart turned his dream into reality without going off to some TV fantasy island. He had only to take the plane from Chicago to Scottsdale, Arizona, where, for $2,500, he spent a week of spring training at the All-Star Baseball School for Men 35 and Older. The school is run by former members of the 1969 Chicago Cubs, catcher Randy Huntley, third baseman Ron

Santo, and second baseman Glenn Beckert, himself a trader at the Chicago Board of Trade. Stuart, who played shortstop in high school and then at Grinnell College in Iowa, had always dreamed of playing in the pros, and this was the nearest to glory he could come.

Pork belly trader James Kaulentis had a dream, too. He wanted to manage a world heavyweight boxing champion. The boxer was twenty-one-year-old James "Quick" Tillis, a former runner at the Merc. Tillis had arrived in Chicago in the late 1970s from Oklahoma with $30 in his pocket and a false promise from a guy who said he'd give him some chances to fight. Tillis, instead, had to settle for a low-paying job as a Merc runner. And for a while his biggest fight was convincing anyone who would listen that he was a serious boxer and someday would be a contender for the heavyweight championship.

Kaulentis, a boxing fan with a soft spot for athletes from the days when they used to drop around his father's restaurant and lounge at Schiller and Clark streets in the 1950s, paused long enough to give Tillis $200. Then Kaulentis passed the hat around and formed Quick Associates. His brother, Dean, also a trader, put up $5,000, and Harry "the Hat" Lowrance chipped in another $5,000. In no time Kaulentis had five partners and a $50,000 bankroll to stake Tillis and his dream.

Kaulentis figured that Tillis would fight every five or six weeks and the backers would go to see him, treating it as a sort of boys' night out. But Tillis began winning and winning big as he beat better opponents and fought matches on cable television. Eventually the group hired Angelo Dundee, who had trained Muhammad Ali. By 1980 Tillis's 20–0 record put him among the top ten professional heavyweights. Quick Associates had grown to fifteen partners and the stake to $200,000. The group had even passed up an $800,000 purse for a fight with a lesser opponent in order to get a chance at the fight with Mike Weaver for the championship of the World Boxing Association. The decision contradicted simple pit strategy: Take quick profits.

But there was another part of the dream for thirty-six-year-old Kaulentis aside from a chance at winning big. There was a chance for glory, too. In the back of his mind he hoped to do what then fifty-two-year-old trader Lee Stern had done. Stern, who made his fortune trading soybeans, wheat, and corn in the pits at the Chicago Board of Trade, was the owner of the Chicago Sting soccer team and part owner of the Chicago White Sox. In 1981 the Sting won the North American Soccer League championship, bringing Chicago its first professional sports championship in eighteen years. It won again in 1984. Granted, soccer didn't have the magic of professional baseball, or football, or basketball for that matter, but for the champion-starved Second City it hardly made a difference.

Stern and his team became instant heroes. Mayor Jane Byrne led the festivities, which included a parade up La Salle Street, flanked by thousands of wildly cheering denizens, and a victory rally at the Daley Center Plaza, where the mayor presented medals of honor to Stern and his Sting players. Afterward the team's star forward, Karl-Heinz Granitza, said, "The parade was beautiful. It was my dream, to ride through the streets like that."

It was Lee Stern's dream, too. Stern's was the classic Gatsby rise, from poor runner to millionaire trader. The son of a traveling salesman who sold shirts and ties and a mother who was a millinery buyer, Stern grew up on Chicago's North Side. The family could afford neither a car nor vacations, and as a youngster Stern had to hustle free passes to Chicago Cub games. He graduated from high school in 1945. The next year he was with the occupation troops in Germany. There he worked as a correspondent for the military-run *Stars and Stripes*, covering first sports and then the war crime trials in Nuremberg. Back in the States nearly two years later, Stern enrolled at Chicago's Roosevelt University with his mind set on becoming a newspaper reporter.

That was before the day he came across a curious job listing for a runner at the Board of Trade which paid $100 a month. Stern got the job. In the mornings he was a runner, in the afternoons, a student. And like all runners, he could see the possibilities and excitement of commodity trading.

So, in November 1949, Stern's mother sold her war bonds—25 percent of her net assets—and gave Lee the $2,250 he needed to buy a Board of Trade membership. If things didn't go right, he promised her, he could always sell the seat back. He remained in school but not for long. One morning after a $12 loss in the market, he found himself brooding and unable to concentrate in class. It was too demanding, he realized, to be a full-time student and trader. He dropped out of college to become an order filler in the soybean pit, working under the wing of Merrill Lynch's head soybean trader.

Stern was able to withstand the market's changing moods, and in 1966 he was financially secure enough to form Lee B. Stern and Company Ltd., a family business that today includes his wife, three sons, and a daughter, all of whom are members of the Board of Trade.

Stern bought the Sting in 1975 after earlier deciding against buying the New Orleans Saints football team. It was more fun to own a team in his own city, he believed. Ownership of the Sting became an expensive proposition, but one Stern could apparently afford. For the first four years it cost him nearly $1 million a season in losses. All along, he insisted that he was not a promoter and that money was not the object. Rather, he said, he was "a pioneer" fortunate to be in a business where he could become one.

"I'm not a gambler, I'm not in a crapshoot," he had told a *Chicago Tribune* sportswriter. "You've never seen a gambler with money in the bank and without frayed cuffs. I'm a speculator. Here's the difference. In gambling, you create the risk. In speculating, you assume the risk."

Lee Stern sounded like a trader I once met who described himself and his colleagues as people caught somewhere between being men and boys. "I'm in soccer for the excitement of owning a team," Stern explained. "There's a little boy in all of us that enjoys that excitement. Anyone who stands up on a pedestal and says he owns a team for the good of the city, all that, that's bull. There's that little bit of boy, that little bit of ego, too. I like going into a restaurant and being recognized. I was recognized before, but I still had to wait for a table. I like getting the table. I guess a $10 tip would do the same thing, but this is a kick. Sure there's a little boy in all of us."

That "little boy" was certainly in Jimmy Kaulentis when he had visions of managing a world heavyweight champion. Unfortunately Kaulentis's dream came to an abrupt end when Tillis lost the fight with Weaver, a fight described by a sportswriter as "a mean little monument to the lure of the almighty buck. . . ." Obviously the sportswriter didn't know anything about commodity trading, that in the pits where dreams die fast, some come true. And when opportunity arrives, you let profits run.

40

My Analyst Tells Me So

Every afternoon at two Stuart left his office in the Board of Trade Building. He settled into his steel blue Cadillac, unloosened his tie, and telephoned his wife the moment he pulled out of the garage. The message was brief: "I'm on my way." The forty-minute trip was methodical: Adams Street west to Franklin, Franklin north to Randolph, then west to the Edens Expressway, and home to a suburb called Winnetka. The drive was a welcome respite. For the first time in nearly five tumultuous hours he could actually hear himself think. The "pits of madness," as he called them, were behind him.

He kept glancing at this watch. Years of conditioning had turned him into a clock watcher. No capitalist has the relationship with time that commodity traders do. The inexorable passage of one second to the next and one tick to the next worked magic on traders. The plots and surprises crammed into a few seconds of trading created instantaneous drama—Shakespeare in the pits. But this time, Stuart felt, time was working against him.

Slowly his mind reached back to the trades of the day. There was no way to keep them out of his head. Then suddenly he would blurt out to himself, "Oh, God. What the fuck have I done?" He was a loser on those days. Losing days, in fact, were turning up more and more. Today he had dropped $50,000, maybe $60,000. What difference did it make? He was asking himself questions he could no longer answer.

As he approached the Willow Road exit, something inside urged him to let go, to floor the gas pedal, and never look back. But he couldn't. In another ten minutes he'd be home, and he needed that.

Stuart pulled into a circular driveway in front of a sprawling stone and redwood ranch house flanked by tawny oaks with a giant weeping willow in the front yard. It was the kind of house he and his wife had fantasized about in the early years of their marriage when he was a special education gym teacher for retarded children. The kids called him Mr. Balls because they couldn't remember his name but knew he was the one who showed up with a soccer ball, a basketball, a volleyball. That had been more than fifteen years earlier.

Stuart walked into the foyer and greeted his wife with a quick nod and an "I'm beat." He slipped out of his loafers, threw his jacket down at the foot of the bed, and sank into the comfort of the custom-made mattress. Thrusting his face deep into the down pillows, he pulled the covers over his head. He began to sob.

Stuart was losing, and he didn't know why. A trader at the Merc who became a millionaire on the gold surge in the late 1970s, he had hit dry spells before. But he had always been able to shake the losses off and come back with confidence. Now he was feeling inadequate, weak, and inferior. There was emotional pain and physical distress. He knew he had an ulcer but was afraid to find out. Why else would soda pop burn like hell before it'd settle in his stomach? But it wasn't his gut that worried him. It was his head.

The pattern was the same whether he was trading T-bills, bellies, or gold. He'd swagger into a pit, chest out, cocky as ever, and begin scalping in big numbers, taunting and prodding traders around him. He'd lose in big numbers, too, up $50,000 one day, down $80,000 the next. Always he took losses with an icy aloofness as though they didn't matter. After a rough day in the pits some traders would commiserate with each other over a game of cards or backgammon in brokerage house lounges. Or they headed for the Sign of the Trader or the Iron Horse, where they could grab quick bites and drown their woes in a couple of scotches straight up. These were dark, noisy places with television screens flickering the latest commodity prices and traders' eyes glued to them with the intensity of patrons at neighborhood taverns caught up in a World Series game. Not Stuart. He headed straight for the privacy of his bedroom to deal with his anxieties.

Why did he trade so recklessly? A year and nearly 150 visits to a psychoanalyst later, he thought he had an answer. "I wanted to be thought of as being a big shot," Stuart explained. "I wanted people to think I was an A student by how much I made and the size of the trades. In high school and college I was a C student, and my peers never took me seriously. Grades were important in the suburb I grew up in, and it was only the smarter students who were considered winners. I guess I overcompensated by becoming the class jokester and never taking anything seriously, including my losses in the pits. Or I never let on that they bothered me. Most of the time I was merely trading for attention."

There are a lot of Stuarts in the pits who make vain attempts to handle tension and losses with drugs, alcohol, ulcers, and even suicide. One trader I met recalled how he came unglued while driving his car after a tough trading day. Suddenly he became disoriented as his eyes fixed on the steering wheel. Whose hands were on the wheel? he wondered. Those white fingers gripping the wheel—whose were they? Of course, they were his hands. But his brain couldn't make the connection. In a panic he pulled off Lake Shore Drive and parked on a side street, where he sat for more than an hour until, he said, "I was able to get a hold on reality." Some hold. Two weeks later he left the exchange, a burned-out, shell-shocked veteran who needed rest and therapy before he returned to the pit wars.

Among the myriad statistics the exchanges maintain, there are none on burnout rate, or how many traders belly up, or the longevity of a trader's life. Even if such box scores were kept, it probably wouldn't deter anyone from trying to become a trader. There are all sorts of figures bandied around on the number of traders who drop out for one reason or another. I've heard some exchange officials say six out of ten traders don't make it. Others say the number is higher. That may be so, in view of the volatile markets and all the new contracts introduced in recent years. As far as the Chicago Board of Trade was concerned, there weren't enough traders to fill its commodity options pits in the winter of 1984. So the exchange went about recruiting traders with the verve of a

251

marine enlistment center. It was the first time a commodity exchange had actually tried recruiting prospective traders off the street. On a Tuesday night in late February the Board of Trade held its first recruitment meeting to prattle about the glories and agonies of commodity trading. There was even a mock trading session in which prospective recruits were encouraged to step right up into a pit and face off against a *real* trader and scream like a *real* trader to get the feel of *real* trading. What they should have allowed the recruits to do was talk to *real* losers.

There are two kinds of losers: those who lose and leave the exchange to do something else and those who fall into a slump and try to hang on. For those who try to correct their losing courses, the situation can be painfully soul-searching. I realized just how painful when I spoke to Alex, a bond trader on a losing streak.

We met at a place called Juke Box Saturday Night, a fifties-style club on Lincoln Avenue, the walls of which were plastered with memorabilia of the Silent Generation. When I arrived, Alex was sitting at the bar like a still, brooding character in an Edward Hopper painting. His chin propped up by one hand, the other stirring a martini with four olives, Alex began to unload.

"This is insidious," he groused. "I haven't had a winning day in six months. I can't win. I was up eight hundred dollars for the day and ended up losing thirty-five hundred. I'm doing it on only ten cars. It's crazy. You know what I mean?"

I nodded ruefully and just listened.

"I'm scared. I'm so fucking scared," Alex continued. "I think about what I'd be doing if I had to stop trading, and I can't think of anything. I can't do anything when I'm like this. I can't relax. I feel guilty about having a good time. It's tough on my family."

Alex downed the martini in a gulp, closing his eyes and pursing his lips as if to swallow a dose of castor oil, and in a sweeping motion he raised the glass to catch the bartender's eye. By now Alex was half-trader and half-drunk.

"Another of the same," he said. "It's my fourth, and I don't even feel it."

"You want some air?" I asked.

"I don't need it yet," he said. "You know," he murmured, "when I first started trading, I set my goal at a hundred dollars a day. That's all I wanted to make, just a hundred bucks a day. Then it was two hundred. Then three hundred. Then five hundred. And now that's not enough.

"I know what I'm doing is wrong, but I can't help myself. Last year I went to a shrink for six months, and it worked for a while. I got back to my winning ways. But this year I've done zip. I need a shrink who understands traders, not one who wants to know how I interacted with my parents when I was a kid. You can make money in this market. It's moving enough to make money."

I spoke to Alex a half dozen times over a year, and each time he was depressed, drinking heavily, and popping pills. Even the patch-up therapy couldn't plug the leak in his shattered confidence that eroded further each time he walked into the bond pit. All the guile and arrogance he had while he was winning had dissipated, and the orotund voice that once boomed from his belly had become a muffle. No longer could he play the commodities game with vigor and skill. Clearly he had lost the edge, in and out of the pit. He had gone from a trader maven, the kind others asked opinions of, to a self-doubting Thomas.

"I'll tell you how bad it is," Alex said, slurring his words. "If I'm in the pit and the guy next to me tells me to get out of my position, I do it. Two years ago I'd tell him to fuck off. But now I listen to anybody who has an opinion. I don't trust my own. . . ."

There is no place on earth where a person can ascend and descend the socioeconomic scale as quickly as on the floor of a commodities exchange. And like all pit fighters, Alex knew it. He was living with an unremitting threat to his security, identity, habits. Now he was slipping uncontrollably like a fast, fast market heading for limit down. He needed to pause, to get away and clear his head. But he couldn't afford to do that. He was confused and bewildered, and there was no longer any reliable way for him to calculate the options in his life. Nothing added up. As far as he was concerned, there were only two kinds of people at the exchange: those who had a lot of money and those who had to make a living. He had moved from the former group to the latter and was now, in his words, "a blue-collar worker" who knew only how to trade pit conditions. He was a scalper and refused to listen to what the experts had to say about the markets because, he insisted, "You can't be too cerebral." Instincts always first, then brains. At least one East Coast retail commodity house refuses to hire anyone with more than an undergraduate degree. The conventional wisdom at this particular firm holds that traders lose their trading guts if they use their brains too much.

More than a few traders have gone for broke by trading hundreds of contracts with a win-on-one-roll attempt. That type of desperation trading is jokingly known as the Costa Rican Hedge. If the trader loses, he walks away from his losses and hops the next train for Costa Rica, never to be seen or heard from again. Or he may go straight to Chicago's O'Hare International Airport to pull off the "O'Hare Spread: Sell Chicago; buy Mexico." One trader at the Merc who bellied up didn't go as far as Mexico or Costa Rica, he got off in Kansas.

This trader happened to be a lawyer from a prestigious Chicago firm who was bitten by the trading bug. On a bright spring morning he walked into the cattle pit with high hopes. For reasons known only to himself, he promptly bought several hundred contracts. The market promptly turned downward. And he promptly panicked. Rather than take his losses, he decided to dollar average—that is, to continue buying more contracts as the price moved lower with the hope that the market would turn around and rally. To a scalper that trading strategy is Russian roulette. When the market closed limit down that day, the lawyer-trader had lost $700,000. The next thing anyone knew was that he left the exchange and his losses behind—and vanished. A couple of weeks later he turned up at Menninger Clinic in Topeka, Kansas, where he spent the next six months undergoing psychiatric treatment. His Merc membership was sold at auction to pay for part of the loss. The clearinghouse he traded through had to eat the balance.

Outtrades, too, have pushed traders to the brink. It happened to a crack Swiss franc broker at the Merc. He lost $400,000 in nine minutes because he mistakenly bought 300 contracts instead of selling them. That night he locked himself in the den, refusing to talk to his wife, who had no idea what had happened. The distraught wife phoned an exchange official with her concern. For the next three hours the official pleaded with the broker like a cop trying to coax someone down from a window ledge. At least a half dozen traders in recent years have committed suicide because of big losses. The balconies which overlook the fifteen-story atrium at the Board of Trade are jokingly called by some traders the debit rails, but so far no one has taken a dive off one of them out of desperation. There probably would have been more suicides if some of the big traders at the exchanges hadn't helped out the big losers. There have been instances when a group of traders in a pit have rallied to the aid of a loser, giving him a tick here, a tick there, until he was even.

Burnout also takes its toll, and traders cope with it in different ways. After losing everything, including his wife in a bitter divorce, one trader left the markets behind to do penitence like some lost soul. He ended up doing volunteer work, coaching the baseball team at a Catholic school in Chicago. "I bumped heads and burned my brains out," he said, talking about his career as a grain trader and his use of drugs. A high school dropout who had driven a truck before he came to the Board of Trade, he was considered a brilliant trader by many of the locals. That was before things went bad. "I remember those days," he recalled. "I'd sweat, and the salt would drop into my eyes and burn like hell. I remember taking one trade away from another guy and he spit in my eyes. My timing was off. Timing was everything."

He couldn't stay away from the pits. A friend staked him to a membership on the smaller MidAmerica, the orphan of the Chicago exchanges where beginners get their starts. In return for the seat he had only to split profits with the friend. Here was the ex-veteran among the novices, a snarled and withered Goliath fighting a pit of Davids. It wasn't long before he lost his equilibrium. He wanted to trade limit positions, but his friend became nervous and kept him on a short financial tether. His style was cramped, and he didn't want anybody telling him what to do. Worst of all, he still couldn't win. He left the MidAmerica after six months and drifted with bittersweet memories of his glory days at the Board of Trade, days when there was no high like having things go right.

Another trader had blown his mind with a combination of Quaaludes and cocaine. The abuse was showing up in the pits: a loss of memory; missed trades; outtrades; the inability to concentrate. He no longer felt the tempo, and he was scared. He had socked away more than $1 million in certificates of deposits and was financially secure. But in the pits he was insecure, and that made all the difference in the world. A trivia nut who had prided himself on his retentive ability, now he had a difficult time recalling his own Social Security number. He decided to go cold turkey in the confines of his house. Isolation was the answer: to drop out of the market temporarily, to escape the din that never left his ears. He turned to television, the quiz shows in particular. Day after day he'd stare at the tube, trying to answer the questions. Some shows he taped and replayed. Slowly he knew he was recuperating because as the days passed, he answered more and more of the questions. The strange cure had apparently worked. Six weeks later he was back in the pits, bulling ahead at full steam.

41

It's Just a Game

The wonder is that more traders don't go off the deep end. There is a relentless, self-imposed pressure to perform in the pits. If the market is fast, every trader wants his fair share of the action. If the market is slow, there is the guilt of not making money or making too little. It's a hustler's mentality because it's a hustler's game. You hustle the guy next to you, the guy in front of you, the guy across the pit, the commercials, the public, anyone who uses the pits for whatever economic means he finds justifiable. Ask most traders, and they'll confidently tell you they know who they are, where they're going, and how they intend to get there. What they can't seem to calculate, especially those who carry the pandemonium of their pit lives into their personal lives, is the emotional cost involved. That's why a losing streak can cave a trader in like a house of cards. And that's why pit life sometimes looks like a scene from *Lord of the Flies* with grown men running around, lashing out at one another, screaming (and crying) like kids in puberty.

It's bound to take its toll on relationships. Some wives, like those of many men on fast tracks to success, have a difficult time adapting and get lost in the shuffle. Some of the traders themselves have a hard time coping. They become caught in the velvet trap of high living and hard drugs, prodigal capitalists gone wrong. They are fueled by small-boy daydreams of riches, and the pace in the pits fires their inner urgency to prove themselves and to find themselves. While the rich own swimming pools, a few of the Gatsbys have their own ponds. At least one vacations with both his wife and his mistress at the same time. He even bought his mistress an exchange seat as if to buy her a membership in some exclusive country club. Commodity girl friends are the recipients of cars, condominiums, and any number of luxuries. Even in the pits hedonistic pleasure can be as close as an elevator ride. Prostitutes have been stashed in back clearinghouse offices for traders' pit breaks.

Thrice-married forty-five-year-old millionaire trader Barry Lind explained it this way: "There's a loss of values. All of a sudden at the dinner dances [for exchange members] you would see a lot of the men elevated in their tastes and styles. They were dressed better. They weren't wearing white socks, but their wives were wearing polka-dot dresses. The women hadn't moved and the men passed their wives by. A lot of divorces ensued. You don't think the same way."

For some wives the pain of divorce can be considerably eased even if they don't know the difference between a Ginnie Mae and Sally Ann. Trader Joseph Siegel's wife seemed to have done all right without ever having stepped into a trading pit. The $5 million in cash, property, and securities Siegel agreed to pay her in 1984 was the biggest divorce settlement in Illinois history, according to Mrs. Siegel's attorney. The couple had no children.

All the prospective wealth on the floors of the exchanges has drawn flocks of young women as clerks into what essentially is a man's world. Instead of running, some waltz around the pits like Miss America pageant beauties, and they go after the silver spoon guys, those who got their seats from their fathers. Some eye a trader's badge as a tip-off to whether he rents or owns his seat. Moving across an exchange floor is like a stroll down Rome's Via Veneto for many a female runner, ogled and pinched along the way by faceless admirers. Eighty-seven-year-old Julius Frankel, a salty multimillionaire wheat trader who used to come to the Board of Trade every day until shortly before he died in 1982, would pass out $5 bills to female runners in return for kisses. Dressed in a black suit, a black hat, and a floral print tie, Frankel sat on a chair like some rabbinic sage. He would trade wheat through brokers, never going into the pit. I once asked him why he maintained his exchange membership. He replied, "Does a plumber ever work without his plunger?"

Certain women become known as typical commodity wives, mates with spending appetites as big as their husbands'. You hear about them buying clothes at exclusive stores with names like Ultimo, or traipsing off to health spas for the rich and famous, or shelling out $250 to spend a half hour with Jane Fonda in an aerobics workout, or returning to college to find themselves, or starting new business ventures with hopes of getting out of the shadows of their husbands' wealth. What you hear most about is not how much they spend but the manner in which they spend. One such wife walked into a crafts and objets d'art boutique near her North Shore home. While she was browsing, her eye caught a handmade basket from West Africa. When she saw the $180 price tag, she began shaking her head. Anxious to make the sale, the shopowner scurried over, prepared to compromise on the price. But that wasn't the problem. The commodity wife didn't think the price was too high, she thought it was too low. "If this were more expensive," she said with a sniff, "I'd buy it."

Carolyn had been like that at one time. The pert, attractive thirty-year-old woman had been married to a hotshot options trader at the Chicago Board Options Exchange. When her husband, Sam, went belly up, so did their marriage.

The couple had migrated from California in the late 1970s, looking for their Sutter's mill in Chicago. Sam was of the breed known as a market maker, one of some 500 options traders who trade mainly for their own accounts. They are like the locals of the commodity pits (they trade at so-called posts) with one exception. While they, too, are led by the "invisible hand" of free competition to provide liquid markets, the market maker must always be a willing buyer or seller no matter how big the order. Sam dealt in call options in mainly the stock of International Business Machines (IBM). Similar to a futures contract, calls are options, or rights, to buy 100 shares of a given stock, but at a pre-fixed price called the striking price during a certain period. In return for that right, the call buyer pays the seller a fee, or premium, which is a small cost of the actual shares.

The options are parasitic—that is, they have no life separate from the underlying stock. Instead, they rise and fall in lock step with the stock price during most of their nine months or less of existence. If a trader guessed right, his profits were magnified many times over. One time, for example, IBM stock traded at $232 a share with the option trading at $5.25 a share. Three weeks later, on a 9 percent rise in the stock to $254 a share, the option soared nearly 300 percent in value to $20.50 a share. On the other hand, if the market goes against them, a post can end up looking like the last act of *Hamlet* with bodies of market makers strewn everywhere. Sam played that act a number of times. Each time he did Carolyn died a little, too.

Now she sat on a floral pink couch, nursing a cold brought on, she was sure, by the emotional upheaval in her life. She reminded me of a dethroned princess surrounded by the vestiges of a former life: the few pieces of furniture and a $5,000 stereo set she had salvaged in the divorce settlement. Her eyes and nose were red and puffy, and she was wrapped in a terry-cloth robe, clutching a crumpled wad of Kleenex. I had been referred to her by a mutual friend who said Carolyn was anxious to talk. I listened as she recounted the saga of a five-year marriage, the tone of which was set by the vagaries of the market. On winning days, spirits soared. On losing days, there was hell to pay in Sam's moodiness. Eventually he became evasive, secretive, and deceitful, a good example of a bad, unconvincing actor. She bacame frustrated, confused, and depressed without any influence on Sam. The experts say people suffer guilt over a failed marriage. But in this case Carolyn's guilt seemed to be compounded because she was unable to save her husband.

Sam was the complete angler, a sweet talker with a mathematical bent who was forever playing the angles like a personal injury lawyer who sees a pot of gold at the end of every whiplash. For Sam, as for so many others, trading became a way of life, a game that outweighed reality. And like the others, Sam would tell you that the money was just the means of keeping score.

"Every other word out of his mouth was 'you wanna bet,'" Carolyn said in between sniffs and sobs. "That's how he goes through life, betting. He loved to figure the odds in craps, blackjack, and poker. Even in high school he'd skip classes to play poker with the guys. During his college years most mornings he'd be at a brokerage house by seven, buying calls, and then off to classes. At one time he was down some fifty thousand dollars, but he always made up his losses at Vegas. We'd go there nearly every weekend to gamble. Even there he had a deal. He had a kickback scheme with several dealers until he got caught. He got off the hook, and the dealers were fired. He loved to gamble.

"But gambling never controlled him. The only thing that controlled him was cocaine. He spent a thousand dollars a week on coke. He felt he couldn't be as intimidating a trader without coke. . . . We had moved here from California because Chicago was the ultimate place for a market maker. He loved the markets, loved what he was doing. He couldn't wait for Mondays. And in the beginning we'd talk about the business. But he began to drift, slowly shutting me out. And he'd spend hours figuring out how much he won and lost.

"He could never relax. No matter where we went on vacation, he'd spend part of the day trading and the other part thinking about what positions he would take the next day. We'd go on a skiing trip to Sun Valley, and he'd spend the first four hours of each day trading at a brokerage house he'd found. He traded from Mexico, Tahiti, Samoa, anyplace in the world we'd be vacationing, anyplace with a phone. I wanted to be supportive. But he'd lose everything on vacations, hundreds of thousands of dollars. And every time before we'd leave on a trip, he'd swear to me that he was even, that he didn't have a position because he didn't want it weighing on his mind.

"He always told me the game was more important. The whole thing is a game. 'I can live without the money,' he'd tell me. Maybe it was a game. But he could never seem to get enough. There would be all-night poker games in our house with twenty-thousand-dollar pots, and everyone would get up on coke and head straight for the exchange to trade.

"I seldom met any of the wives of the other traders. They were invisible like me. I once went to a party and was introduced as his wife, and the first thing that came out of another trader's mouth was 'God! Sam is married?' The wives accepted their husbands' life-styles. Why not? They were content as long as their checking accounts were full."

So was Carolyn. They had bought a Victorian brownstone on Chicago's Near North Side in the exclusive Lincoln Park area of million-dollar mansions and row houses once occupied by the city's 1920s snobbiest. Sam put $50,000 into Carolyn's checking account to furnish and decorate their home. There was a Mercedes for her, a Ferrari for him. And the gifts he showered on her: a ruby ring, a mink coat, a $30,000 white fox coat, and, of course, a gold Rolex watch to match his. They had traveled a long way in a short time on the financial road to success, a long way from the time she was a bank teller and he was a carefree student at the University of California in Los Angeles. She wanted to stop. In Sam's head there were miles to go.

"The money he made was incredible," Carolyn continued, patting her eyes with the Kleenex. "In a matter of two months he went from eight thousand to five hundred thousand dollars. He'd brag about the incredible roll he was on. And then he would lose everything and go back for another stake. At first it was the banks. They would do anything for a market maker on the rise. He once borrowed a hundred sixty thousand dollars on his name alone. But he even got too big for the banks. He told a vice-president that he lost more money in two minutes of trading than the banker made in a year. That pissed the banker off, and he called Sam's loan. Then sometimes he'd borrow the money from friends. There was even one time when he took a second mortgage out on his mother's home. When he finally lost everything, that didn't stop him. He found a backer to give him a seat in return for profits. He ended up working for twenty-five hundred a week and eighteen percent of the profits. But that didn't last."

By now she had given up fighting the tears, and there was an incredulous tone in her voice. "He lost everything," she whispered as if to make sure no one else was listening. "He lost the house and more than a million dollars. He had been a millionaire and broke at least eleven times in four years. The cars were lost, too. They were pledged on loans to a drug dealer who had been supplying the coke. I couldn't take it any longer. I wanted out. . . ."

About six weeks after that conversation with Carolyn, Sam was hospitalized with a severe case of hepatitis and mononucleosis. By then Carolyn had begun supporting herself as a paralegal secretary in a downtown law firm.

Why marry someone who makes and loses money the way a manic-depressive changes moods? The mistress of one trader, who has observed scores of commodity wives over the years, explained it this way: "It's their fantasy come true. They seldom understand the business, and they spend as if the money will pour in forever. When they can't go to Palm Springs on vacations or on a fall Paris shopping spree because there is no more money, they can't face their friends. They leave. They become married to a life-style as opposed to a man."

PART IV

Pasts and Futures

The future is not what it used to be.

—Paul Valéry

42

Welcome to the Club

He is keeper of the commodity futures gate.

He sits at the guard's podium just outside the Board of Trade's cavernous trading floor, his blue eyes darting back and forth from face to face as he greets traders by their first names. He knows who belongs, who doesn't. He's cat-quick to stop anyone who doesn't look right to him or doesn't have an official badge.

The ruddy-complexioned gentleman with a monk's fringe of white hair and the singsong "hiya" is Edward E. ("Eddie") Mansfield. By 1984 he had spent sixty of his seventy-seven years working for the Board of Trade. The exchange's main trading room and the employees' lunchroom are named after him, and in 1982 the Board of Trade paid a tribute to the veteran trading floor guard by bestowing on him the title of Grand Marshal of the Chicago Board of Trade. Mansfield told a crowd of some 350 friends and traders gathered in the Sign of the Trader: "When I took this job, I made the best trade of my life—to use the words of our business. . . ."

Old Eddie's eyes had seen some of the biggest plungers in trading history. "Arthur Cutten? Oh, yeah, he was a big man when I first came here in 1924," he recalled one day as we casually chatted at the podium. "Dan Rice? Sure, he was a good friend of Ike Weinberg's. . . ."

When it comes to contemporary history, though, there seems to be a gap. He knows most of the traders who trade the agricultural commodities. But in the section of the exchange where financial futures are traded—primarily the domain of the younger traders, where the pits are obstacle courses without stoplights—there are too many new faces to master. "I don't know many of them over there," Eddie said apologetically, nodding his head toward the entrance to the old exchange floor that now serves the financial futures traders.

Mansfield is one of the few people around who can talk about the old days with nostalgia and authority—if he chooses. But he has become an animal of the exchange, suspicious of outsiders, reluctant to talk about family business. "The exchange is like his family," explained corn trader Louis Weinberg, whose father, Ike, first met Mansfield shortly after Eddie had started at the board as a messenger.

It's not that Eddie Mansfield has anything to hide or that he's snobbish. But it's a streak of loyalty toward the hand that has fed him most of his life, uneasiness over the possibility he may say something that would cast the exchange in a negative public light. So he is protective, perhaps overly. But so are most at the exchanges. A few years ago, for instance, the Chicago Mercantile Exchange refused to allow the movie comedy *Trading Places* to be filmed at the exchange without prior script approval. Why? Because, Merc officials said, they were afraid the traders would be shown simply as gamblers (not to mention buffoons). Eventually filming was done at the Commodity Exchange (COMEX) in New York, with the climactic short-selling scene taking place in the orange juice trading ring instead of the Merc's pork belly pit, as called for in the original script. A decade before that a cover story in *Forbes* magazine showed a hand holding a .38 revolver to the temple of a head. Titled "Russian Roulette," the story was about the futures markets and mainly the Chicago exchanges.

There aren't many occupations portrayed as zany, cutthroat, ill-mannered, loud, raucous, explosive, self-destructive. You'd think that after coping with that image for so long, exchange officials would be thicker-skinned. But what with the waves of new investors and scores of new exotic contracts along with record trading volume in recent years, the industry has become hypersensitive. Of course, the off-exchange shenanigans haven't done much to bolster image. There have been a rash of scams among gold bullion dealers and shady commodities boiler-room operators across the country that have bilked customers out of hundreds of millions of dollars. There are swarms of these unscrupulous operators, a number of them moving from state to state, changing their names but never their pitch. In one stretch of Florida, where they've set up shop repeatedly, federal authorities call the area Maggot Mile. They exist because greed is their magnet.

The exchanges, as a result, have built up a tight-lipped fraternalism over the years. It begins with a trader's orientation. At the Merc, for example, novice traders are told by the exchange that before they talk to the press, they must clear it through public relations. The directive was handed down in the wake of a comment by a trader to a television newsman that an exchange membership was "a license to steal." The member was severely reprimanded by the exchange officials and for a time was ostracized by other traders. No one would trade with him because he had broken the law of silence, a strange law for such a loud place.

Understandably exchange officials become testy over publicity that puts the exchanges in questionable light. They spend millions of promotional dollars every year to pump new blood into the markets. In April 1983, for example, the Merc launched a major television ad campaign with Herbert Stein, former chairman of the president's Council of Economic Advisers, and Monte Gordon, an economist with the Dreyfus Corporation, explaining the role of the Merc to prospective investors. The commercials aired for thirteen weeks in Chicago, New York, Los Angeles, San Francisco, Philadelphia, Miami, Dallas, and Houston as if they were a feature film opening nationwide. The exchanges spend millions more through political action committees, backing Washington politicians who vote favorably on legislation affecting the futures industry. Routinely the Merc and Board of Trade jointly bring senators and representatives to the exchanges for a day of show and tell. If the politician says a few words during lunch, he makes a quick $1,000. Otherwise, it's a $500 honorarium plus air fare. With such costly efforts no wonder exchange officials shudder every time there's a story about insider trading, market manipulation, the weakness of federal regulators to oversee the exchanges effectively. The exchanges themselves, they insist, are perfectly capable of self-regulation.

So, to outsiders, the exchanges proffer a dour visage rather than a smiling face. Commodity trading, after all, is a serious business and a big one. That's why the two major Chicago exchanges were willing to spend more than $300 million for the construction of new trading facilities, betting, in effect, that they will be handling double the 1983 trading volume by 1985.

All this is not to say that traders cannot laugh at themselves. But they prefer to do so among themselves. There are, in fact, more jokes and gags in a pit than at a Friars Club roast. Nothing highbrow or subtle, mostly Abbott and Costello slapstick. Take the time that some fifty or so traders at the Merc's S&P pit donned Groucho Marx types of mustaches, eyebrows, and glasses in mocking fun of a trader who happened to resemble Groucho, minus the wit.

If an aspiring trader has the price of admission (In mid-November 1984 a Merc seat cost $170,000 and $237,000 for a Board of Trade membership) and a few character references from members in good standing, he or she may join the club with an ownership stake. Or he or she may join as a nonequity associate member for as little as $500 a month, the cost to lease a Merc seat, which allows the person to trade futures in stock indexes, stock index options, lumber, gold, and energy. It was a lot cheaper back in the good old days of 1865, when a membership at the Board of Trade was $5 and traders could buy and sell with empty pockets because there were no margins. There were no pits either. Traders met in a long, narrow room on the second floor of a South Water Street building, huddling in a group, buying and selling from each other without hand signals, just the usual shouts. There was plenty of pushing and shoving, too. Sometimes in a euphoric outburst the traders threw samples of wheat, corn, and flour into the air to cascade over their heads in a torrent of jubiliation. It was all in the spirit of fraternal camaraderie.

Not even the great Chicago fire of 1871 could destroy the trading spirit. The fire burned down the Board of Trade Building, taking with it all the records. But while the city was still smoldering, the board was back in business, improvising to accommodate its members. For a while the Board of Trade looked more like a Wild West show than the grain trading capital of America. A ninety- by ninety-foot wigwam was set up at Washington and

Market streets as the temporary exchange. There were no pits and one common trading area. The new hours were from 9:00 A.M. to 5:00 P.M., with no smoking between 11:00 A.M. and 1:30 P.M., the most active trading hours. The following year the annual dues were cut from $20 to $10 to ease the financial burden many traders found themselves under.

The deep-rooted character of the exchanges has hardly changed over the years. They are still clubs owned by their members who follow rules and codes of conduct, written and unwritten. Up until the 1960s it was strictly a men's club with the very qualities observed by sociologist Lionel Tiger in *Men in Groups*. Men's clubs, wrote Tiger, "are projections of unconscious materials and processes, involving isolation from women, a bonded group, commitment, and fellowship."

So it was with the exchanges, bastions of fellowship until 1966, when a young woman named Sandra Stephens, working for R. J. O'Brien & Associates, Inc., was allowed on the floor of the Merc as a clerk. The nod, however, wasn't given until the board of directors engaged in heated debate over a dress code. It was the era of the Beatles, hair, madras, and miniskirts, and the board didn't want the traders' minds to wander. So the barrier for women was lowered along with their skirts—two to three inches below their knees. But it would take another seven years before the first female entered the inner sanctum of the pits as a trader. She was a twenty-eight-year-old five-foot-six-inch brown-eyed blonde named Mariam Schmitt, who was a broker for L. D. Schreiber & Company in the cattle and pork belly pits. The same year the first woman to own her membership and trade strictly for herself was Carol Norton, whose husband, Burton, was also a trader and a master bridge player to boot. The first black woman on any Chicago Exchange was Valery Turner, who bought a seat on the Merc's International Monetary Market in 1974. Turner had worked her way up from Leo Melamed's legal secretary to chief operating officer of his brokerage firm. She still remains the only black female member at either exchange. In 1968 the membership rules at the Board of Trade were rewritten to allow Carol Jane Ovitz to trade. (Then a member under thirty-five years old was rare, whereas today one out of every three applicants is between the ages of twenty-one and thirty-five.) Up until 1925 at the Board of Trade manliness alone could not guarantee a seat. Besides being male, a member had to be a resident citizen of Chicago. No outsiders, thank you.

The Board of Trade did allow women to tread on the trading floor as early as the 1890s when a succession of Apple Annies began hawking their Jonathans for a nickle each. Invariably Annie would be an old, crinkle-skinned Italian woman dressed in funeral black. To the best of anyone's memory, the last Apple Annie disappeared sometime in the 1930s, undoubtedly the victim of oversupply in the Depression years when there was an apple seller on nearly every corner.

But the telltale clue to a woman's status at the Board of Trade was the toilet situation. As recently as 1981 there were no women's restrooms on the trading floor level. Women had to use the scant third and fifth floor facilities—when they were available. "There would be long, long lines," recalled Patricia Bules, who was a phone clerk for one of the major wire houses. "If you were in a hurry you'd have to pay $5 to get a spot at the front of the line." One time it cost Pat $10. And when she returned to the unattended phone about five minutes later, she was almost fired. In a raging outburst her boss ordered her never to abandon the phone again even if it meant peeing in her pants. "The entire secret to this business is communication," he yelled.

The pits still mostly belong to the men. Out of some 5,000 members at both exchanges, there are an estimated 400 females, but not all of them go into the pits.

The exchanges, for the most part, still coddle their members. Some, in fact, have compared the exchange atmosphere to the clubbiness of a professional sports franchise. But such comparison misses the point. In *North Dallas Forty*, a 1979 bittersweet film about the harsh realities of professional football, the hero Phil Eliot—a wide receiver who plays in pain for a living—sums up a player's plight: It's the millionaire corporate tycoon team owner and the steely-eyed coach who are the *real* team. The players, the battered hero sadly concludes, are merely the equipment. On the commodity exchanges the opposite is true. The pit players are the real team. They own the exchanges. The players reign supreme, and everything else is equipment.

"It's a complete Copernican system with the trader in the

middle of it," said Owen Gregory, the tousle-haired Board of Trade archivist and finance professor at the University of Illinois Chicago campus. Indeed, everything is done for the traders in the pit; their financial, legal, logistical support is packaged down to the lighting, heating, and communications. It's a self-contained trading universe with "everything in orbit around the trader," said Gregory, who has been working on a Board of Trade history.

In the 1850s the board even used to feed the traders. In the early years the directors offered free lunches of cheese, crackers, and ale to traders as perquisites, hoping to build membership. It brought the trading crowd in, all right, and nearly every other freeloader. The board countered by hiring a bouncer to throw out the crashers. A year later the bouncer himself got the heave-ho after he had accidentally tossed out several members along with the hungry strangers. By the beginning of the Civil War trading had become an all-day sucker for the traders who no longer needed the lure of a free lunch. They traded at the board in the morning, on the street in the afternoon, and in the saloon of the Tremont House in the evening. When the serious drinkers became disturbed by the bellowing traders, they chased them over to the Sherman House, which had a much bigger saloon. The Civil War was under way, and speculators took advantage.

Wheat for the stomachs of the Union Army and oats for its horses meant a booming business for futures traders. The board even sponsored three Union regiments known as the Board of Trade Regiments as well as raised $220,000 for medical supplies toward the war effort. It seemed the board was always raising money for some cause. In 1871 it gave $5,000 to help France fight the Franco-Prussian War. A year later it raised $49,000 among its members for a gift to the city of Boston, which was also swept by a ravaging fire.

By 1885 the futures business was so good that the board built a new half-million-dollar building on the site of the current one. For a time it was Chicago's biggest building. It was so big that officials boasted they could put Marshall Field's department store on the trading floor and it wouldn't touch the sides or the top. Such braggadocio meant little to Field, Chicago's great merchant prince, who once audaciously walked onto the floor of the exchange in search of deadbeats who owed him a princely sum for merchandise purchased at his store. To the best of anyone's knowledge Field never speculated in commodities. He probably didn't have time. He was too busy amassing an estate worth between $100 and $175 million by 1906, when he died at age seventy-one. But Joseph Leiter, the son of Field's former partner, Levi Leiter, was a legendary plunger in wheat who ended up a legendary loser.

43

The Plungers

The year 1868 was known as the year of the corner. A corner worked like this: A trader purchased all, or nearly all, of the grain in storage at Chicago. Then he'd begin buying contracts for huge quantities of grain for future delivery. And when the delivery date rolled around, those who had sold the futures began to sweat. They could buy grain in storage to fulfill the futures contracts only from the man who had also bought the contracts. He could arbitrarily set the price at which the sellers had to settle with him. Thus he became both profiteer and puppeteer with the "shorts" dangling at his greedy whim. His only restraint: his conscience or public opinion. Usually neither was strong enough.

One such unconscionable plunger was Benjamin Peters Hutchinson, or Old Hutch, as he was called at the time he cornered the wheat market in 1888, long after he had passed his prime. A onetime Massachusetts shoe manufacturer, Hutchinson went west after he'd gone broke in the Panic of 1857. He began a new life dealing in wines and whiskeys and amassed a great deal of money during the Civil War. After the war he turned to grain speculating. By 1868 he was known as the Prince of Scalpers with an insatiable appetite for chance and a superstitious streak. He would never leave the exchange floor during trading hours whenever he held an active position. To have done so would have invited the

Bad Luck. When he wasn't perched on the exchange floor of the board, Hutchinson moved about Chicago as a socialite and businessman with a ready eye for opportunity. He was, for instance, one of the principle founders of the First National Bank of Chicago.

In 1888 he struck the mother lode. Because of a crop failure in the Northwest that year, wheat became scarce. As luck would have it, Old Hutch had bought up nearly all the wheat available for September delivery. When September rolled around, much to the shock of the grain trade, Hutchinson owned a mountain of wheat at less than $1 a bushel. Smugly he sat on his chair on the board floor and watched the price run up to $1.28 a bushel. He boasted that he knew what wheat was really worth because he'd read four or five newspapers every morning before the other traders were out of bed. He instructed his brokers to let the shorts have all the wheat they wanted at $1.25 per bushel. The desperate shorts stood in line like a string of hooked fish gasping for air. They got their wheat. But not every short accepted the bondage. A few, in fact, threatened to hire special trains to bring wheat into Chicago from St. Louis, a threat that irked Old Hutch. He retaliated by upping the price to $1.50 a bushel the next day. More shorts settled there. The holdouts were hammered harder. A day later he pushed wheat to $2.

When it was all over, Old Hutch had run a $5 investment, the cost of his board membership, into the then staggering sum of $10 million. Unfortunately, like many traders before and after him, he couldn't leave the game with his winnings to retire in comfort. Obviously he had more than enough money to do so. It wasn't the money that kept him coming back to the board every day. He wanted to do it again, to become king of the grain hill one more time. Old Hutch went broke trying. In the subsequent years he lost heavily. The more he lost, the more he drank. Broke and tired, he moved back east to spend the last few years of his life operating a secondhand notions store in Manhattan under the shadow of the Brooklyn Bridge.

Nine years after Old Hutch had pulled off his corner, it was Joseph Leiter's turn. The two were alike in some ways: Both had a mania for cornering markets, and both were bent on self-destruction. There the similarities end. Hutchinson was a self-made man

276

well up in his years when he attempted his corner. Leiter was a silver-spooned scion in his prime when he tried. Some considered him the Nelson Bunker Hunt of his time. Others saw him as the spoiled rich kid who was spared tramping rural roads with a peddler's pack as his father had before helping to build Marshall Field & Company. In 1897, when Joseph was twenty-nine, his sole desire was to corner the world market in wheat.

Leiter's story is best summed up in a single word in the handwritten ledger of the stately, snooty Chicago Club, historically the exclusive retreat of the city's financial elite, whose members included such names as Field, Pullman, Lincoln, McCormick, Blair, and Sheridan. Beside Joseph Leiter's name in the ledger, now encased in a glass box on the club's second floor, is the word *withdrawn.*

In 1897 crop failures across Europe began pushing corn and wheat prices higher with the prospects of burgeoning demands on American grain supplies. The dramatic advance in prices inspired one anonymous Board of Trade poet to write:

> Last winter farmers burned the corn
> They raised on western hills;
> This winter they will sell the corn
> And burn ten-dollar bills.

Within the first several months of the year wheat prices climbed from 60 cents per bushel to $1 and were expected to move higher. All along, Joe Leiter was buying enormous quantities of wheat for delivery on January 1, 1898. Soon he owned more than 10 million bushels, more wheat than any American had ever owned, more wheat than all the elevators in Chicago could control. It was a classic corner in the Old Hutch tradition. But while young Joe was busy adding up his bushels of wheat, there was one thing he hadn't counted on: old Philip D. Armour.

On the other side of Leiter's corner stood the sixty-five-year-old Armour, the meat-packing patriarch of the Armour fortune who employed 50,000 people in his pork-packing plant, his Armour elevator company, and his Armour Refrigerator Line on the railroads and who was also a member in good standing of the Chicago Club. A feisty, crafty man, Armour knew a thing about corners. In 1881 he had cornered the pork market in Chicago. Earlier, during the Civil War, he reaped $1.5 million speculating in various commodities. In 1897 Armour had millions riding on his hunch that wheat prices would decline. He wasn't about to be caught on the short side of the market to answer to a young Joe Leiter on reckoning day.

Just three weeks before the January 1 delivery date, Armour's grain warehouses stood empty. That's when he swung his millions into action. He dispatched his emissaries into the Northwest and Canada to buy up all the available wheat and ship it to Duluth, Minnesota. He then hired a Great Lakes shipping fleet of some thirty vessels to carry the wheat, along with a fleet of tugs loaded with dynamite to crash through the ice-choked Duluth Harbor into Lake Superior. The boats slowly made their way from Lake Superior to Lake Michigan and on to Chicago, where trains were arriving daily with millions more bushels of wheat. Armour elevators began filling up so fast he had a new one built, engaging hundreds of carpenters and laborers to work three shifts around the clock. Within two weeks Armour had one of the world's largest grain warehouses. And he began dumping the wheat on Leiter.

On December 31 Armour notified Leiter that he was ready with 8 million bushels of wheat. Young Joe was astounded, and a worried Papa Levi went to see Armour. "Papa Levi and I have become great chums," Armour later wrote. "We have had our arms around one another for the past few days and we are a very loving couple."

While Armour was embracing Levi, his invisible hands of a free marketplace were strangling hapless young Joe into submission. Joe had been forced to sell the cash wheat he had collected, breaking the price and ruining himself. The corner collapsed.

It was a costly ride through the pit that gouged $10 million out of the Leiter fortune, forcing Papa Leiter to sell off much of his choice real estate and blue-chip securities in order to settle all accounts. The loss was the equivalent of more than $60 million in today's money. As a painful reminder of Leiter's ordeal, Armour sent his photograph to young Joe simply inscribed "With best regards."

Joseph Leiter's story is the stuff novels are made of (today it would be a TV miniseries). In fact, Joe Leiter was the model for

278

Curtis Jadwin, the protagonist of Frank Norris's *The Pit*, the famous novel about a man who tries, but fails, to corner the wheat market on the Board of Trade. In the end, just as with Joseph Leiter, the wheat cornered Jadwin, not he the wheat.

By 1924, when Eddie Mansfield began working at the Board of Trade as a wide-eyed messenger and the upstart fourteen-year-old Chicago Mercantile Exchange was pushing butter and eggs, Arthur Cutten dominated grain trading. A penny-pinching, puritanical teetotaler, Cutten, at twenty, had arrived in Chicago in 1890 from Guelph, Canada, with about $60, a high-wheeled bicycle, and high hopes of striking it rich. He became a trading legend, the man who owned more grain at one time than Joseph Leiter or probably any other man in history. Not only did the "Great Bull" stun the La Salle Street commodity crowd with his startling string of winning trades, but he did the same on Wall Street when he eventually turned to stocks.

Cutten's first job in Chicago was a clerk for commodity broker A. S. White & Company at a weekly salary of $4. Within five years a determined Cutten had managed to save $1,000 and to buy a Board of Trade membership. At that time a former Illinois farm boy, James A. Patten, was storming through the pits like a prairie tornado. Patten, in fact, was the only person ever to have successfully run corners in wheat, corn, oats, and cotton. The biggest Patten corner came in May 1910, when he kept a score of correspondents across the country constantly reporting crop conditions of wheat in code. Another Patten cadre was stationed in Argentina, doing the same thing. The reports indicated a shortfall in both American and Argentine crops. Patten began buying all the wheat he could. By the end of May he had complete control of the market and began to squeeze the shorts, but not as hard as he might have. That's not to say they didn't pay the price for going against Patten. On May 30 the price of wheat stood at $1.33 a bushel, up from $1 just weeks before. The next day Patten boosted the price just one cent, and the shorts were able to settle there. Certainly Patten could have squeezed more than an extra cent out of the shorts, but it wasn't a matter of money that concerned him at this stage in his trading career. He viewed the additional penny that nudged wheat to $1.34 per bushel as a sort of tag to certify he was right, a confirmation of judgment which did as much for his ego as it did for his pocketbook. Like a gene passed from one generation to the next, that indomitable need to be right exists in every trader today.

Patten couldn't have handpicked a more fearless plunger to carry on the freewheeling trading tradition than Arthur Cutten. He had the knack. Though their trading styles were different, the results were the same. The both could corner markets. Cutten wasn't a fundamentalist like Patten, nor did he ever bother to peruse a chart. And he would never have thought of resorting to an intelligence network of crop reporters sitting in fields watching wheat grow. His trading technique was that of a scalper, not in the way quick profits were sliced off but in the way he could feel the market move. He would test the market by operating through various brokerage houses. He bought through some and sold through others, often simultaneously, in order to confuse the trade about his net position in the market. He had little faith in the ability of brokers to keep secrets, especially when they, too, could profit.

In one 1924 squeeze Cutten forced the price of wheat over $2 a bushel for the first time in history. One of the shorts in that squeeze was the "Great Bear" himself, Jesse Livermore, who lost $3 million, most of it to Cutten. After that Cutten was perceived by many, including the press, as a sort of swami of futures. And whenever anyone would ask Cutten, the "Great Bull," what direction wheat was heading, the answer would always be "higher," whether he was long or short the market. Two-dollar wheat enticed an entire crop of public speculators, from taxi drivers to upper-crust luminaries, to try their hands at this thing called commodity trading. And just as it had in Patten's day, it also aroused the federal authorities to begin seriously looking for ways to restrain plungers like Cutten from cornering markets.

Despite the publicity he was getting, Cutten still managed to trade in a shroud of secrecy. He even went as far as to hide himself in a private office on LaSalle Street with the name Chicago Prorating Company on the door. In the evenings he would retreat to the pastoral seclusion of his 800-acre farm, a forty-minute drive west of the city, where he lived with his wife, 20 work horses, 80 cows, and 500 hogs.

Cutten traded in such big numbers that once the Board of Trade directors persuaded him to sell some of his wheat for the "good of the board." Other traders, seeing him ride the elevator to the directors' room, rushed to the exchange floor and dumped wheat, breaking the price. Cutten later figured the elevator ride cost him $1 million. It was still far short of what the stock market crash of 1929 cost him: $50 million.

44

Little Ike

Another remarkable trader showed up at the board about two years before Eddie Mansfield had arrived. He was an imp of a man named Frank Weinberg, whom everyone called Little Ike, a peripatetic mover able to thread his way in and around the pits, pausing just long enough to blurt out a trade. At five feet three inches he towered over most of the others as a quick-minded scalper, trading wheat, corn, soybeans, rye within ticks of each other. No one, least of all his sons, Sidney and Louis, who were traders, too, could figure out his trading method.

Unlike the Arthur Cuttens, Dan Rices, and other plungers, Little Ike set out to create a dynasty of traders. He saw in his sons the reflection of his own impact, perhaps a measure of himself. Sidney had other thoughts, of becoming an architect, and Louis looked toward canvas rather than corn, desiring to become an artist. But Ike wouldn't have it. Trading was an occupation, he convinced them; art, merely a hobby.

But more significant than that, a membership was a legacy to capitalism, a means of building wealth that could be passed on like a family-owned business or like land or real estate, a ticket to financial perpetuity. Besides, wasn't nepotism the bedrock of the exchanges? It fitted snugly with the clubby atmosphere. Today families continue to multiply around the pits, and family ties help get one's foot in the ever-narrowing exchange door. Even a runner's job these days often hinges on a relative or on long-standing friendships between families, who pass the jobs out as favors that will eventually be returned. The trader dynasties have multiplied as rapidly as the number of new contracts introduced (nearly seventy in the past four years alone), and there are more third-generation traders than ever. The exchanges, in fact, are kennels of trader bloodlines with exchange membership rosters looking more like histories of genealogies. For instance, an analysis of a 1980 Mercantile Exchange membership list revealed a startling fact: More than 35 percent of the 620 members listed were related. That was before membership ranks swelled to 3,000 through a host of associate memberships, many grabbed up by established traders for their families.

While Ike couldn't impart his trading knack to his sons, he could dispense doses of his home-brewed adages. "Lose your opinion, not your money," he'd remind Louis. Or he'd advise Sidney, "The first loss is the easiest." And to both he cautioned: "He who sells what isn't 'his'n' ends up in the state prison."

Dressed in Charlie Chaplin baggy breeches, tie askew, and sneakers, (along with his Road Runner pace), he looked like a wayward hobo who had just hopped off a boxcar that pulled into the stockyards, hightailing it one step ahead of some club-swinging railroad detective. "The way he dressed," recalled Louis, "made bums look good." Ike's fortunes changed like the seasons. In the summer he could be a millionaire; by fall, a pauper. When Sidney, the elder son, told his father he planned to go to college, Ike curtly replied, "I'll see how I do next week." But Ike always managed to come through. The family never felt the shocks of the Great Depression, and Sidney did eventually attend college when he returned from World War II. Then it was back to the pits.

At the close of the markets in the afternoon or whenever there was a lull in trading activity, Ike turned to his avocation: hawking kosher salamis. It was a strictly cash market—and an active one. The other traders were big buyers of Little Ike's salamis, which were delivered each morning by his friend Jack Levin, owner of a company that made Sinai 48 brand salamis. The supply was stored in the board's coatroom. In 1960, when Robert Briscoe, lord mayor of Dublin, Ireland, visited the exchange as part of a cross-country tour, he walked away with two fresh salamis presented by a beaming Ike.

If Ike had had his way, the Board of Trade would have been

open seven days a week. His entire life was the board, and his routine never varied: up every morning at four, a quick breakfast, and a four-mile hike to the exchange from the North Side residential hotel (he didn't believe in ownership) where the family resided. Home in the late afternoon, Ike was asleep by seven every evening. And he demanded the same regimen of his sons. Whenever Louis would go to an opera on a Monday evening, Ike would chide: "How could you do that? You need rest." And Louis would reply, "I don't want to die on the way to the Board of Trade."

Little Ike didn't start out to be a trader. As a youngster growing up in Flat River, Missouri, a small town seventy miles south of St. Louis, where dreams of glory seemed more important than visions of wealth, he wanted to throw fast balls in the major leagues. But his outlook changed when he went off to World War I as a telegraph operator in France. Upon returning, he went to St. Louis to work for the James E. Bennett Company, one of the nation's biggest grain houses at the time. The elder Mr. Bennett, who had taken a liking to Ike and admired his spunk, promised to buy him a membership on the Board of Trade. Four years later he made good on the promise, and Ike began a career that was to span two years short of five decades.

He was a hit from the start, thanks in good part to his military experience. At one end of the exchange stood the ticker tape machine beating out the orders that came in from around the country. Ike's telegrapher ears picked out those orders seconds before anyone could read them, and he would trade ahead, knowing the market was about to move. Eventually, when his fellow traders realized that Little Ike was getting a big jump, irate exchange officials immediately capped the ticker with a glass bubble to cut off the sound and curb Ike's edge. What they couldn't take away from Ike, though, was his speed to react and his uncanny ability to size up others. He was motivated, his sons say, to outsmart people. Ike looked at trading like a parlor game of poker where in the pits there was always somebody bluffing and somebody with a pat hand. The old-timers like Eddie Mansfield still talk about Ike's exploits.

"It was an awful lot of pressure to have a father who was a whiz," said Louis one afternoon. Little Ike had been dead for twelve years, but his ghost seemed to haunt his sons.

On a crisp spring Saturday afternoon, far from the looniness of the exchange crowd, far from the noises of city traffic, I met with Louis and Sidney to talk about Ike. We chatted amid scattered photographs and camera equipment in the den of Louis's airy four-bedroom spit-level Highland Park house, which he had paid for with $40,000 in cash back in 1964. It wasn't the plush digs of a new Gatsby. Rather, it was the home of a trader who had made a steady living over the years, who had married off a daughter with a master's degree, and who had a son at Yale. Another son, Lee, was a trader in the board's bond pit, along with Sidney's son Peter. The third generation was in place.

Louis was the extrovert, the chatty one, the Boy Scout master, the photographer who shot bar mitzvahs and weddings of other board traders. Physically he closely resembled Ike. By contrast, an air of sophistication and formality surrounded Sidney. Anyone would have pegged Louis as the riverboat gambler of the two. But when it came to trading, Louis was the conservative one.

There were times when Ike would lash out at Louis for not being a big enough trader in the corn pit, where he scalped. Sidney, on the other hand, was more like Ike, willing to take the bigger chances for the bigger profits. He became a spread trader, playing one position off against another. "My father never liked me maybe because I was too conservative," Louis said. It was clear that Sidney, sixty at the time, and Louis, fifty-four, felt deep resentment toward Ike, who had pushed them to become traders. Apparently he had pushed too hard. Shortly after Ike's death in 1970 Sidney decided to catch up with his dreams and at age fifty left the exchange and returned to college to become an architect. He took with him an ulcer and a bundle of money. Today he practices architecture, rehabilitating old Chicago buildings, designing new ones. Sidney had made enough as a trader to do anything he wanted, to retire if he had chosen.

The important thing for Ike was that his sons became traders. And whenever they were discouraged they had him to talk to. Yet neither son, it seemed, could break through the emotional barrier between themselves and their father. Ike, on the other hand, wanted a different sort of closeness with his sons: the bond that comes from sharing interests and values. For Little Ike commodity trading was the noblest of vocations and the one, he was sure of, his sons would find fulfilling.

The brothers vowed they wouldn't pressure their sons into becoming traders. Louis's wife, Elaine, summed it up: "My biggest fear was that I was going to live through with Louis and Lee what I lived through with Louis and his father. Fortunately that never came to be. . . ."

When Lee Weinberg was ten years old, Louis reprimanded him for forgetting his mother's birthday. Ashamed and crying, Lee dashed out of the house to the Convenient Food Mart where he promptly picked out a couple of items and plunked down cash. The gift: two twenty-eight-cent ashtrays.

Lee is now a successful bond trader at the Board of Trade. He started in January 1980, following his graduation from the University of Arizona with a degree in business administration. A year later, this time without the prodding of Louis, Lee remembered his mother's birthday. Just as he had when he was ten, he paid cash for the gift. It was a single item—a shiny new Mazda automobile. The car was a way of thanking his mother for enduring his years at college. At one point, he had dropped out for six months to do what he did best: gamble. Every day he went to the race track and for a time he considered becoming a professional gambler. In high school he had been such an adept poker player that classmates would call Louis complaining about Lee's uncanniness at winning. "Don't play with him. He knows the game," Louis replied.

At twenty-two years old, Lee was the youngest trader on the exchange floor. Even after he had become a success, he often spent weekends in Las Vegas playing the games there. Lee was the high roller that Louis could never be. But that suited Louis just fine.

"Lee is where he belongs," Elaine Weinberg said. "But my husband isn't where he belongs."

The summer before college Lee was a runner and had a chance to see the Wild Bunch in action. The parade of trader personalities baffled him. There were the ones with capricious natures, and the ones with petulant faces, and the Neanderthals, those brooding self-doubters who harbored grandiose ideas of breaking the bank. It seemed more like a circus ring than a capitalistic arena. But he wanted to join.

Indeed Lee was like Ike. Aside from his small stature, his facile mind and love of risk made him a big winner from the start. But unlike Ike, he became a big spender. Immediately he bought himself a new BMW and in the spring of 1981 he treated his brother and sister to a vacation in Acapulco and Mexico City. In the first year he paid back the $40,000 he had borrowed to buy his seat.

By no means was Lee's trading a fluke. The markets were as brutal as ever. Within the first eighteen months, some thirty other young traders he had started with had washed out. Just Lee and one other survived. At one point, Lee's rapid-fire success forced Louis to consider his own nature. "Why am I so conservative?" he asked himself. "Maybe I see it all as money and the others don't."

There was no jealousy, however, only a father's pride and whenever Lee's name came up at the exchange Louis's face lit up with one of those "That's my boy" looks. Louis had a right to gloat because he felt responsible for Lee's decision to become a trader. Louis never pushed. Had he, Lee probably would have done something else.

For some sons and daughters of successful traders, it becomes a hard act to follow. Some fathers simply can't let go as was the case with one, who pinned a note to his son's trading jacket with the letters "DOT," a reminder meaning "Don't Overtrade."

45

Pit Brats

No one, regardless of his or her trading skills, welcomes having to live up to a legend. Certainly, Jordan Melamed didn't. The twenty-six-year-old son of Leo Melamed—the millionaire trader, power behind the Mercantile Exchange, and pioneer of the financial futures industry—was a scalper in the Merc's Standard & Poor's stock index pit. Jordan, who had dropped out of Stanford Law School to become a trader (against his father's wishes), was trying to rebound from a trading slump when I met him in the summer of 1984. In the past year he had been driving a flashy $35,000 Porsche. Now he owned an American Motors Eagle, a more affordable vehicle in line with his changed status. After earning fistfuls of dollars in 1982, he hit a trendless market in 1983, and he said, "I didn't know how to handle it.

"There's a fear involved of not being successful, a fear of comparison," Jordan said. "It pushes me harder. I've always performed better under pressure. I have a tremendous drive to conquer this business. It's better to be fearful than not."

Howard Harris was the typical "pit baby" who grew up around an exchange. When he was five years old, his father took him on frequent excursions to the Merc, where he'd playfully stamp trading cards and become lulled by the ticker tape. It was like conditioning a child to appreciate classical music by exposing him to nothing else. Howard knew what feeder cattle and pork bellies were before he could do long division. By the time he was a teenager, he had one goal: to become a commodities trader like his father and grandfather. Starting as a runner and moving up to clerk, Howard began working full time for his father in 1971 after his sophomore year in high school. He compressed the remaining two years of high school into one, completing his studies at night. He continued his self-imposed apprenticeship by working as a telephone man at a number of trading houses, including Heinhold Commodities, Inc., where he worked for the master, Joel Greenberg, the terror of the pits at the time. Howard's job was to write buy and sell orders for the traders in the pits and to keep accurate records of the transactions. It gave him a feel for both trading and timing orders to hit the market.

In 1976, at twenty-one, when most of his friends were still searching for a mission in life, Howard Harris became the youngest member ever at the Chicago Mercantile Exchange. By 1983 he had become one of the biggest traders in feeder cattle and had put himself through Loyola University's evening school, where he majored in finance.

Howard had begun calculating early in life, like his father and grandfather, Harry Harris, who had been president of New York City-based Great Western Egg Producers. Howard used his father's old trading symbol. As he put it, "It's like carrying around a little bit of history." It was also like carrying a coat of arms that could open the door to some exclusive club. "I knew that if I had walked in off the street and had never worked here before, they [the other traders] just wouldn't have been as helpful. It's no accident that about seven of every ten people here are related to someone else—either as a brother, or son, or brother-in-law." Not surprisingly, Howard's partner was his mother, Dorothy, who along with her son owned a total of seven full and associate memberships on the Merc.

Not every trading mantle is handed from father to son painlessly. Sometimes the pressures erupt into tragedy. That occurred a few years ago when the son of a prominent trader at the Board of Trade got himself into a bind. The twenty-eight-year-old had been a broker with his own order deck, making money hand over fist in the treasury bond pit. When he decided to give up the deck and trade for himself, he began losing heavily. Traders who knew him said he had lost upwards of $125,000 one time and gone to his father for a bailout. The millionaire father obliged, cautioning his son to be less reckless in his trading. The son took the money but not the advice. He took a string of hits and was out another $100,000. Again he went to his father to be rescued. This time his father refused. No one knows what words father and son had. Some say the father had given the son an ultimatum that he quit trading in return for settling the debt. Others say the son was involved with a shadowy woman, a fast crowd, and drugs, an intolerable situation for the father to cope with. In any case the son ended up committing suicide, blowing a hole in his head with a revolver. The incident never made the newspapers. Nor does anyone at the board seem to know the details. It remains in the family closet or, like a bad trade, better forgotten.

46

Is There Life
After the Pits?

It took Louis Weinberg twenty-eight years to exorcise the ghost of his father.

One day he came home from work and told his wife he was leasing his exchange seat for six months and taking off.

"Teachers take sabbaticals," he told her. "After twenty-eight years I want to take mine."

For a moment Elaine Weinberg was stunned in silence.

"I'm taking a trip all by myself to nowhere," he said.

"Louis, you must be going somewhere," she said.

"I'm going nowhere," he replied. "I'm going nowhere."

For years he had fantasized about packing his Deardorff camera under his arm, throwing a few pieces of clothing into a duffle bag, and just roaming. He wanted to stop where he wanted to stop and shoot the photographs he wanted to shoot.

On one sunny summer morning he left it all behind: the exchange; the commuting; the irate wife who wouldn't utter a word to him for days.

Louis headed south. He crisscrossed the back roads of southern Illinois, stopping along the way to photograph fields of corn, wheat, and soybeans. He visited relatives in St. Louis and ambled aboard a ferryboat down the Mississippi from Alton to Pere Marquette, the site near where Lewis and Clark launched their historic expedition. He talked to farmers and river town people and waitresses in the rural cafés he ate at.

Partly out of habit and partly to salve his conscience by making sure the markets were quiet, every evening he searched for a newspaper with the closing commodity prices. A slow market reinforced Louis's decision that leasing his seat had been the right thing to do. Like everything else in futures trading, leasing a seat in a market lull was a matter of timing, too.

The odyssey lasted for only a week, but during that period, Louis said, he learned "I'm not so bad by myself. I can survive."

When he returned home, he made peace with his wife. Elaine, a perceptive, witty woman, who was an entrepreneur in her own right with a company she had founded to provide sightseeing tours for the wives of conventioneers, understood Louis better than anyone. She knew the years of frustrations he had lived with and the toll his relationship with Ike had taken. But she also knew she married a grain trader, not a photographer. Louis knew it too. And besides, everyone was entitled to a mid-life crisis no matter the age.

Throughout his trip he was haunted by a conversation he had had years earlier with Milton Friedman. Before Friedman won his Nobel Prize for economics, the two had met at the home of a mutual friend. It was a brief and casual exchange.

"I asked him what he would do if he had made a million dollars," recalled Louis.

"I'd spend it before the government got it," Friedman replied. "I'd buy good food because they can't take that away. I'd buy paintings because they can't take that away. I'd get more education because they can't take that away."

The trip had become part of Louis's education, something no one could take away, not even the government. He remembered something else Friedman had said to him in a cryptic manner: "You are an individualist and that's why you make money. You don't know all the rules you're breaking."

If anything, the comment reminded Louis of just how far he had come from those days shortly after he had been married when he was earning $22.50 a week as a Merrill Lynch clerk.

Louis had no intention of giving up trading as his brother had. He wanted only a respite, time to himself, a chance to chase a fantasy. Over the next few months he painted, photographed, and read a long list of books that had collected dust. And he prepared himself for his return to the pits.

The ease with which Louis was able to rent out his seat was indicative of what was happening at the exchanges, which were becoming more like the congested streets on Chicago's Near North Side: Every time a car pulled away from the curb, there was one anxiously waiting behind to park. So it was with the exchanges. With more numerous and less expensive associate memberships, liberal leasing arrangements, and a flock of new contracts, prospective traders were waiting in line for their chance.

One such prospect was Leon Lurie. At thirty-two he had gotten the Gatsby itch. "I looked at my life and knew where I was going to be in twenty years. You live only once. I needed to take the shot," he said just after applying for a Merc membership.

A graduate of Washington University in St. Louis with an economics degree, Lurie gave up a $50,000-a-year job as vice-president of sales for a company that marketed paper cutters and photographic equipment.

He was going through hard emotional times. "I was tense; I couldn't sleep: I realized I couldn't work for someone else," he said. What's more, he couldn't wait for some executive to step up or step down to make room for him on a corporate ladder. In the pits there were no office politics to contend with. It all seemed so simple and direct: You fought it out for six hours face-to-face with your opponent, then settled up at the end of the day. You knew where you stood financially—and emotionally—and there was solace in knowing you could start fresh the next day

Leon had it figured out for at least the next six months. That was the period he gave himself to see if he could make it or not. The strategy among new pit recruits hadn't changed in decades: Minimize losses, and trade no more than two contracts at a time. That meant more, however, than just a casual trade if he wanted to cover the $2,700 a month he paid to lease the seat.

During one orientation session sponsored by the Merc he was told that once in the pits, he was going to learn things about himself that he didn't know before. There was nothing profound in that particular observation. He had always known that speculation requires self-awareness. No one, though, bothered to alert him to the traders like the twenty-six-year-old medical school dropout who had the disposition of a starving great white shark. "I don't like to talk to anyone," he groused. "I don't want anyone to be my friend." That reflected his good side. As for his trading attitude, he bluntly summed that up with an ominous retort: "You have to be willing to watch the guy next to you die."

Leon wasn't prepared to go that far. On an August morning Leon Lurie walked into the treasury bill pit to do battle. It was the most volatile and busiest contract at the exchange at that particular time.

I showed up on Leon's first day, which predictably turned out to be a humbling one. From the visitors' gallery overlooking the pit I could barely make him out. Standing toward the back of the pit, his balding pate bobbed like a floating cork amid a sea of thrashing traders. How he was heard and who traded with him were beyond my comprehension. But he managed to cry out ten trades, none of which was profitable. Later I asked him what he had been trying to do. "I was trying to exist in the pit," he said. "I wanted to establish a pit presence."

There was little time to think, he said, adding, "No one knows what's going on. Everyone has a theory about what's going to happen in the next five minutes."

At the end of the first month Leon was $80 down, after covering the cost of leasing his seat. He was on target, he assured me, hoping to break even in the first year of trading. But things didn't pick up much from that point. There were good days and bad ones, but not enough great ones. For a time Leon tried a different approach by using a computer program for trading gold that a friend of his at the University of Chicago Business School had developed. Nothing seemed to work. After a year Leon called it quits and left the exchange.

Perhaps the soft-spoken, gentle-natured Lurie was never cut out to be a raucous trader. Yet like so many others, he returned to the pit some months later to try again. This time it was Standard & Poor's stock indexes.

Why do they go back? It's as though there were no life after the pits.

You can see it in the old burned-out traders who linger daily on the fringes of the pits like washed-up prizefighters loitering in musty gyms. Once they've tasted the excitement and been propelled into the frenzy of a dream that eludes so many, where else can they go? What else can they do? The exchanges are an exaggerated, intensified parody of the American Dream, and everything else pales against its lure and wonder.

"It's the ideal and epitome of what everybody wants," mused Leon Lurie.

So the new Gatsbys beat on, pressing against the odds. They are like children pushing their faces against a window at a party, hoping that someone will invite them in. They live on promises and great expectations. There seems to be no distance between them and their images; what you see is what you get. Some outsiders see it as a vulgar vision: a waste of devotion; a waste of resources; a waste of ambition. But for insiders it's the ultimate quest: capturing the fairy princess with a golden net.

In the pits they are combative, direct, decisive, seemingly heedless of the consequences. Their emotions are reduced to reactions, like the muscles of a frog that twitch to an electrical jolt. They live in a world of gestures. And they don't seem to appreciate the future or understand the past. But they've seen the "invisible hand" of Adam Smith's marketplace open to provide rewards beyond belief, then close into a tight fist to deliver a sucker punch. Across the exchange floors they've seen all the minute possibilities coalescing to change their lives forever. A few grow in the pits, but most swell. Yet, in essence, they are like West Virginia coal miners, or Maine lobster fishermen, or Iowa dirt farmers, a breed that runs with a herd yet maintains a streak of independence. The exchange is merely the skeleton and they provide the soul—capitalistic, sweaty, loud, bruised, funny, sad, flabby, taut—perpetually after wealth.

The masters of body language, the knights of bad habits, the worshipers of the dollar, they are the new breed playing an old game.